One Day at a Time

TALES FROM THE SADDLE
ON THE ROAD FROM DORSET TO DUNDEE

Enid Fookes

First Edition November 2013

British Library Cataloguing in Publication Data.
A catalogue record for this book is available from the British Library.

Published by CM2D Publishing
www.facebook.com/enids.book

Cover Design by Adam Gritz, www.itzcreative.com

ISBN 978-0-9927412-0-4

Printed by Remous Limited
Milborne Port, Dorset
www.remous.com

For Donald (1945-1989) and Alan (1949-2008),

my brothers whose lives were too short

Acknowledgements

I want to thank both of my sons for their help and support throughout the challenge of the cycle ride and while writing and getting the book ready for publication. James, for his time spent on editing the original text and his invaluable advice always so willingly given. Andrew for his computing skills without which I could not have produced the book in the required format and for the patience which he showed in guiding me throughout the whole process.

My thanks also go to Mary Galloway, my long-time friend, who has been with me every inch of the way, both on the ride and the writing of the book. I am very grateful to her for the many hours she put into editing and proof-reading my drafts.

I would also like to thank all my family and friends who provided me with accommodation on my cycle ride, put my dirty clothes through their washing machines and sent me on my way with much kindness and words of support.

Finally thanks to Keith, Alan and Shaun at Remous who led me through the process of getting my book in print.

The Road and the Miles to Dundee

(A traditional Scottish folk song, author unknown)

Cauld winter was howlin', o'er moor and o'er mountain
And wild was the surge, of the dark rolling sea
When I met about daybreak, a bonnie young lassie,
Wha asked me the road, and the miles to Dundee

Says I' my young lassie, I canna' weel tell ye,
The road and the distance, I canna' weel gie,
But if you'll permit me, tae gang a wee bittie,
I'll show ye the road, and the miles to Dundee

At once she consented, and gave me her arm,
Ne' er a word did I speir, wha the lassie micht be
She appeared like an angel, in feature and form,
As she walked by my side, on the road to Dundee

At length wi' the Howe, O' Strathmartine behind us
The spires O' the toon, in full view we could see,
She said gentle sir, I can never forget ye
For showing me far, on the road to Dundee

This ring and this purse take to show I am grateful,
And some simple token I trust you'll gie me,
And in times to come I'll remember the laddie,
Wha showed me the road and the miles to Dundee

I took the gowd pin, from the scarf on my bosom,
And said "keep ye this, in remembrance O' me",
Then bravely I kissed, the sweet lips O' the lassie
E'er I parted wi' her, On the road to Dundee

So here's to the lassie, I ne'er can forget her
And ilka young laddie, that's list'ning to me,
O never be sweer, to convoy a young lassie
Though it's only to show her, the road to Dundee

CONTENTS

CYCLE ROUTE FROM DORSET TO DUNDEE

Chapter One

BLAME IT ALL ON THE OLD FORD

'Not far to go now,' I sighed to myself as I heard the distant rumble of traffic, 'I must be near the main road. I only need to get to the other side of it and find the pub then I can stop.'

It had been an awful, awful afternoon; rain and more rain, face bent down against the headwind, spray from passing traffic, and floods to negotiate on the cycle tracks.

I crossed the main road carefully, found my way through the streets of the small town of Sandy in Bedfordshire and left my laden bicycle propped up at the back of The King's Arms. I shuffled into the bar where I instantly became the centre of attention for the only two people present. They gaped in bewilderment, looked me up and down and stared at this sodden and dripping middle-aged be-spectacled woman attired in a plastic yellow cycle cape, helmet and mud-spattered shoes.

'I, erm, have a room booked,' I announced, trying to sound as if I was a normal sane person. The bemused barmaid gave an expressive look to the other person standing beside me at the bar, glanced in a diary kept on the shelf, then tapped a number into her phone but got no reply:

'The landlord isn't answering; he's probably watching the football [*the Euro 2012 football tournament was then being played*]. I don't know what room he's put you in.'

Twenty minutes or so later I was led along a garden path with a row of small chalets on the left. I followed the landlord, who had now appeared, as he avoided a large puddle and went up a step to a wooden chalet; he unlocked the door, and I was shown into a simple room with a shower and toilet compartment. He went round the other side of the bed, which filled most of the room, and switched on a heater: 'You'll soon warm up once you get into some dry clothes. We don't do food but can order a take-away for you. Come back to the bar when you're ready.'

Having asked for a secure place to leave my bike I was shown an unlocked lean-to shed crammed with all sorts of paraphernalia. I manoeuvred my bike around a couple of barrels, a mower and a workbench then padlocked it on to a solid-looking table leg.

After showering and drying myself on a surprisingly large and fluffy towel, I ordered a *Chicken Special Chow Mein*. I ate it alone sitting in the bar, gazing at the empty tables, trying not to think about anything except the food in front of me.

Back in my room, sitting propped up by pillows on the bed, I reflected on my situation. I texted my son: 'It has just been the most dreadful day. It's all too much for me – thinking of giving up.' Seconds later back came the reply: 'No way can you give up, you've only just started!!'

🚲 🚲 🚲 🚲 🚲 🚲 🚲 🚲

I had set off six days earlier to cycle from Dorset to Dundee. Why was I doing it? I would be sixty in less than three months time and wanted to mark the occasion by doing something that would be quite tough but manageable, enjoyable, and also meaningful. A decade earlier on my fiftieth birthday, accompanied by both my sons, I climbed three Munros, Scottish mountains over 3000 feet (914m): *Meall a'Chrasgaidh, Sgurr nan Clach Geala* and *Sgurr nan Each* in the Fannich Hills, south of Ullapool.

My diary entries for that day included:

Very steep and rough going - extremely windy on top. Grand achievement for my 50th birthday! Superb meal later to celebrate - smoked salmon to start, sika deer for main course, finished off with a raspberry pavlova. Great birthday.

Through the intervening years I started to do more cycling. My sons were growing up, doing more of their own thing, and I got back on my bike after many years of it standing unused in the garage. It only had five gears and had been bought second, third, or even fourth-hand, who knows, from a student when we lived in Cambridgeshire. I used to go out for runs on it by myself for half an hour or so while my husband looked after the children – it was only a couple of minutes from our house on to the Fens, which were flat as a pancake as far as the eye could see. I liked the emptiness and the freedom it gave me. From the fields came the humming sound of the lapwings as they tumbled down from the sky, their distinctive *'peewit, peewit'* call piercing the air. Breathing in through my nostrils I smelt the fresh country air and sometimes the tang from a field of peas or sugar beet. The ever present wind blowing across the flat land made up for the lack of hills and I returned home feeling revitalised.

The countryside had always given me that feeling of belonging and was where I felt most at peace. Life's worries were left behind; there was nothing to get between me and the natural world. I was in my element and whenever my mind was too busy or troubled it was to the countryside I went.

I guess it goes back to my earliest childhood, in Dundee. My Dad took any opportunity he could to take the family into the hills and the glens of Angus. I have a memory of leaping up and down heather-covered craggy slopes imagining myself to be a mountain goat.

At nearly sixty years of age I could no longer bound through the heather but my love for wild places was as strong as ever. My first bike, at age ten, was a hand-me-down from a cousin; it had no gears and was a dingy grey colour. It wasn't long before I smartened it up with two shades of blue paint, a new saddle and a shiny bell. Then, freedom! The bike enabled me to find by myself some of these places where I'd only been before by car with my Dad. Now I had a way of going to these secret spots, with the added benefit of solitude – there was no one to break the silence, except the sounds of the crows cawing, the leaves rustling, water lapping in a burn or the new lambs bleating. I treasured it all.

In that way I was my father's daughter, all right, for his passion was with the great outdoors. He was a pioneer scout and scoutmaster in the 1930s, hauling a trek-cart laden with camping gear out past the Trotticks and into the lee of the Sidlaws north of Dundee every weekend possible. My mother and he met on a rambling holiday in the Lake District; after their marriage she moved from London where she'd grown up, to Dundee. They had seven children in ten years, so there were few occasions to get away from the city except for a two week break in the summer, to a rented caravan by the coast.

That all changed when my Dad bought his first car soon after the sixth member of the family was born – that was me. He obtained a very old shooting brake, one of a kind, a Ford Allard with a V8 engine probably built to the personal specifications of a local bigwig – we never saw another one like it; it was an ideal vehicle for the aspiring countryman with space for two adults and seven children, just. The four youngest sat on a platform space behind the rear seat, jostling for best position, age usually the deciding factor. We looked out through the back window, sometimes grazing it a bit too closely with our faces when my father braked suddenly – there were no seatbelts in those days.

A few years later an ancient caravan fabricated from hardboard was acquired and thus began a series of summer touring holidays in the Highlands. The car and caravan were a means to an end for my father, as it enabled him to reach the big outdoors with his family in tow and so launched my fascination for it too, and there it has stayed with me always.

My family with the car and caravan photographed by dad
(I am in front of mum on the far left)

So, what to do to celebrate my sixtieth year on this planet? I liked the idea of a long solo bike ride and played around with several ideas in my head: *Lands End to John O'Groats? Through France to the Mediterranean?* But the thought that appealed most to me was visiting as many friends and family as possible in the UK. This idea developed into what would be a journey from my present home on the south coast in Dorset, to the city where I was born, Dundee, a distance of 500 miles by motorway, but nearer one thousand miles by the route I deliberately chose, to take in as many of my family and friends as I could visit on the way. This plan fulfilled my main aims: it would be tough enough to provide a challenge, made more bearable by staying with friends and family along part of the route; as I was doing it in June/July the expectation of some reasonable weather and long days would all help to make the ride an enjoyable experience; cycling back to my roots would give me time to reflect on the previous sixty years of my life; and I would also raise funds for Cancer Research UK.

The weekend before my departure was spent on last minute preparations, what to pack and what to leave, and putting my house and garden in order for while I was away. The concert for the Queen's Diamond Jubilee held in front of Buckingham Palace was on the television on my final night at home. Andy, my younger son was staying at mine as he had agreed to be there for my final preparations and ride the first few miles with me. I knew I would appreciate his company to help settle my nerves and prevent me thinking too much about the long distance to be covered in the days ahead.

The weather forecast came on after the News and I saw that there was to be rain in the south of England for the next five days. This was the first moment that I had any doubts about my trip. Up until this point I had been busy with all the planning and fundraising, interspersed by occasional training rides taken on glorious days which raised my confidence about the feasibility and rationality of the journey I was about to embark upon. But that night when I saw the unequivocal rain symbol over my route for the foreseeable future I began to have doubts about my sanity.

'I'm not sure I want to do this after all,' I confessed to Andy. I only ever cycled when it was dry; I cycled for pleasure so would no sooner have set out for a ride in the rain than worn a bikini on my bike. Oh yes, I'd been caught in showers before, maybe even a downpour or two, but

I'd always known I would shortly be home and able to get into a warm bath and dry clothes.

'You'll be okay, Mum, you'll cope with a bit of rain.' His unruffled faith in me didn't do much to reassure me, but deep down I knew there was no stopping me now; I was not one for opting out of something I had decided to do.

My bags were packed. Two rear panniers, a small rucsac to sit on the rear rack containing toolkit, spare inner tube and a pump, and a front handlebar bag. After reaching Dundee I was going to my nephew's wedding in Dryburgh Abbey, so perhaps not unsurprisingly the most frequently asked question leading up to my trip was a jocular, 'Are you taking your wedding outfit on the bike with you?' To which the answer was, 'No, I've sent it to my sister's house in Dunbar as I'm staying with them the night before the wedding.'

It was important to me that I didn't carry too much weight on my bicycle as I felt sure my main problem would be lack of fitness and strength. So I took the minimum of clothes and footwear that I felt I could get away with but still look reasonably presentable when I was with friends and family. I went prepared to wash my cycling kit each evening, which mostly worked out fine. I took small amounts of toiletries although I didn't go the extent of sawing off my toothbrush handle, and was grateful when I was given scented shower gel or a soft towel to use.

The bag containing my gadgets was something I thought carefully about – I wanted to write a blog of my journey so my netbook computer and a wi-fi dongle were packed, along with a camera, phone and GPS. In went several rechargeable batteries plus a battery charger, and additional chargers for the computer, camera and phone – oh, for a universal battery charger, preferably pedal-powered. A light set of headphones were added for listening to pre-loaded films on my computer and for calls via the Internet to James, my other son, who lives abroad, and also my binoculars because I am a keen bird and wildlife watcher.

For sustenance while in the saddle I took dextrose sweets and tablets to pop into my water bottle to make energy drinks. I put in some tea bags and coffee for when I stayed in hostels. Other items included maps for my route as far as Cambridge, the rest I posted ahead; a first aid kit, a copy of Colin Thubron's 'To a Mountain in Tibet' to read, a few crosswords and sudoku, penknife and a silk sleeping bag (compact and weighing a minuscule 100g).

Interesting isn't it what each person would choose to take? Everyone is different. My phone and computer were packed with detailed information of my route, accommodation and everything I might need to know as I went along. There was also plenty of entertainment on there if I should need it. It was me who had to transport it to Dundee so everything I took with me was for a reason.

My overnight stops were all arranged, either with friends or family, or pre-booked into hostels, bed and breakfasts or cheap hotels. This forward planning would allow me to enjoy the cycling without worrying about where my bed for the night would be.

I'd set up a fundraising page on my computer for Cancer Research which had already received many donations and thoughtful messages of support for me.

My bike and I had been out for some training rides together, but I knew that the best way to get fit for the hillier sections of the ride in Yorkshire and the Borders was simply the ride I would do every day on the trip.

So everything I could plan was in place and tomorrow would be day one of my journey which, by the end of it, would take me back to where my life began. I hoped for a good night's sleep and prayed that the long-range weather forecast might be wrong.

Chapter Two

CATHEDRAL PUNCTURE

With a few last-minute adjustments to my kit (yes, the long yellow plastic cycle cape would go with me. 'Throw it away if you don't get on with it,' said Andy), the following morning we set off to the good wishes from some of my neighbours who stood on the pavements or waved from windows. The last they saw of me for a while was the simple message printed on the back of my hi-vis vest: *Cycle Dorset to Dundee for Cancer Research.*

Setting off from home in Corfe Mullen, Dorset

It was dry, but ominous dark clouds were already visible. The plan was that after the first five miles, Andy would be replaced by Peter (a colleague) who had volunteered to ride for the next couple of hours with me. Minutes later as the first drops fell; it was on with the waterproof trousers, then a stop for coffee at the local Country Park café. As the rain was steady now, the cape was employed and enshrouded me (and the handlebars) and the waterproof covers went over my pannier bags, not to come off for the next four days.

We had been travelling in an easterly direction and it was a poignant moment for me as we swung north – *The Road to Dundee*. Peter peeled off from my route a few miles later to head home and from then on I was on my own, which would have been fine but I still had butterflies in my stomach from pondering the enormity of what I had taken on.

A bit further on I began to feel peckish so looked for somewhere dryish to stop to eat the food I was carrying for a lunch-break. I turned in behind an empty-looking building and by sitting on the top doorstep managed to prevent the worst of the lashing rain making my sandwiches soggy, but as I was to find out in the coming days and weeks it wasn't possible to stop rainwater finding its way into every nook and cranny of either me or my bike gear. I had planned a beautiful route alongside the western edge of the New Forest and had been looking forward to it, but now with the rain coming down in torrents and the road resembling a river, my gloves sodden, my shoes saturated, I was far from enjoying it. My only thought was to get to Salisbury in the least amount of time to meet my friend, Carol, who was going to escort me the last few miles to her home in a pretty Wiltshire village.

But, I reckoned without 'The Puncture', which was accompanied with a bump, bump coming from the front tyre as I rode past the Cathedral. 'Yikes, find a bike shop,' I muttered to myself, and marched off at a fast pace pushing my bike around the city streets before realising that the extra day's Bank Holiday for the Queen's Jubilee meant I had no chance of finding one open.

Rendezvous and explanations made to Carol, we went looking for a dry place to do the repair. 'Let's look for the nearest covered car-park,' I suggested. I had been fortunate in the past not to have to repair a puncture myself while out on a ride – I had either walked home or had helpful cycling companions to lend a hand, but oddly enough one of the most frequently asked questions before this trip was 'Can you repair a puncture?'

My reply: 'Well, I know what I'm supposed to do, have managed it previously but it hasn't happened very often.'

So now, in Salisbury I started off with a fair amount of confidence, which quickly diminished when neither Carol *nor* I, nor Carol *and* I together could get the tyre off the rim. We resorted to phoning John, Carol's husband, who immediately jumped into his car to come to our rescue; however, we had actually made some further progress before he joined us and together we completed the job.

Graciously declining the offer of a lift Carol & I cycled on to their house, the rain having eased, it was a pleasant enough ride. Passing a field, Carol teased, 'I can't see the camel from here, but I'll show it to you tomorrow.'

Carol and I had first met when we were both lecturers at Salisbury College. A couple of years earlier I had returned from teaching abroad and looked around for another job in Dorset. My sons were just starting secondary school, my husband and I parted company, and it was not for me to do the expected and 'normal' thing which at that time with my qualifications and experience would have been Supply Teaching. I had studied geography and maths to honours degree level at the University of Edinburgh, and qualified as a secondary school teacher at the University of Glasgow. I taught in that city for five years, was at the point of promotion, when I decided a change in career and a new place to live were what I needed. Being an 'East Coaster' I'd found Glasgow on the west and wetter side of the country a damp place and for me there was too much greyness and gloominess.

As part of my degree course I had studied computer science/studies/programming /technology – the name kept changing as this fast-evolving discipline took hold. Thus, armed with some knowledge of computers, I secured the post of trainee programmer with a computer typesetting firm in West London. It wasn't long before they made me project leader and sent me off to newspaper offices which were updating to computerised-typesetting systems; as I was the only Scot in the team I expect it was natural for them to dispatch me to the Daily Record and Sunday Mail in Glasgow as they thought I would speak the same lingo. I found myself the only female (still relatively young) in a newspaper printing room full of older males used to 'hot metal' typesetting who were quite set in their ways and not interested in computers because as far as they were concerned the only outcome for them would be redundancy, as this 'new-fangled' thing would mean the journalists would do their own electronic composition.

My job was to hand over a metal case containing a magnetic tape with the most recent version of our software on it, to install it and debug it on site. The majority of my time was spent holding a telephone to my ear and listening to instructions from one of my managers back in London as he directed me what to do. When that failed I would hand the phone over to one of the chaps next to me who seemed to be the most knowledgeable and let him take over. This seemed to satisfy my bosses as I continued with these visits to Glasgow for over a year, interspersed with assignments to Berne, Bonn and Zurich.

During that time I was asked to write a *Functional Specification and Operating Manual for a Computerised Sports Package System* – basically this was a document to describe what the software needed to do and how to input the data. Writing and explaining something interested me more than programming and debugging did, so gradually my workload shifted until I was a full-time technical writer for the company.

In addition to finding my way into a new career here I had also met Will, one of the programmers, who later became my husband; he had a degree in Printing Technology and took to programming like a duck in water. He became the expert on 'magtapes' and was mainly sent on assignments to Scarborough.

After our marriage we moved to Cambridgeshire as we wanted to start a family and raise them away from the 'Big Smoke'. Will secured a job as a programmer with a firm in the new Cambridge Science Park. I applied for a job with Acorn Computers (remember them?) as a technical writer. On the day I was offered the job I also found out I was pregnant with my first child, and as was still the norm then I knew I would not want a full-time job once I had the baby, so I turned it down. Instead I took a temporary position as an executive officer at the Countryside Commission offices in Cambridge – I still get a kick when I remember the interview for that job because I was told there were over one hundred applications for it. Of course, I was overqualified for what amounted to moving papers around and answering simple enquiries on the telephone. Anything of any interest was handled by the three (male) commissioners, but it was not long before they sussed out that with my geographical and countryside knowledge I was able to write up their reports from their notes and carry out certain investigations for them. So I spent an enjoyable six months there and who knows where that might have taken me if I hadn't become a full-time Mum?

I liked being at home with my babies – I didn't want someone else bringing them up their way – I wanted them to learn from their own parents. I enjoyed playing, reading and talking with them throughout the day, going out for walks in our village and often taking them in the car to visit nearby villages to ring the changes.

But however much I enjoyed motherhood, and I did immensely, I also needed some intellectual stimulation and this led me to explore the extra-mural classes at our local Village College (a rather grand title for Cambridgeshire secondary schools). I chose archaeology and so I attended evening classes and the occasional day's field trip. There was also the odd bit of private tuition in maths I would give when asked by another parent.

After my second son was a couple of years old I started teaching maths part-time at one of the nearby village colleges; I used a combination of childminder and friends to look after the children while I worked, but I was still with them the majority of the time. It was important for me not to lose touch completely with the workplace, but inevitably I did, and I didn't ever go back to being a full-time teacher in a school in the UK.

Enjoying a fire in Wester Ross with Andy and James

Once again, after several years in Cambridgeshire, I got itchy feet; this time of all things, for the sea – the sound and sight of waves crashing against the shore, the taste of salt on my lips. We *could* get to the coast from our house but it was a long day out and usually reserved for bank holidays and 'special days'. I missed being near the sea, and also mountains or even hills, of which flat Cambridgeshire could not lay claim to. We had made good friends in our village and the cultural activities were a huge bonus to living near Cambridge, but my strong attraction to the countryside, which I now realised had to include more than just agricultural fields and the odd nature reserve, was pulling me away. After much deliberation and job hunting, we picked Dorset – as well as ticking most things on our list (except mountains) it was also closer to Will's family and where he had grown up.

So we moved to Poole on the south coast of Dorset. On meeting the headmistress of the primary school that my eldest son, James, was to go to, her first question on finding out that I was a teacher was: 'Would you like to do Supply work here?' I did not take up her offer but have subsequently on occasions thought that the opportunity to move into Primary School teaching could have been a prudent move. However, I had a toddler at home and was unfamiliar with any childcare facilities in my new neighbourhood so decided to allow a little time for us to settle in and find a house to buy.

A few months later once my youngest, too, was at school, a job advertisement in the Bournemouth Evening Echo caught my eye: 'Home Teachers required by Dorset County Council – must be qualified and have teaching experience.' So began for me a period of several years as a home teacher – my pupils had sometimes been excluded from their school for disruptive behaviour or possessing drugs; I taught several girls who had their tuition at home because they were pregnant; some had severe illnesses that meant that they couldn't attend school, occasionally the illness was terminal.

I covered most of the subjects on the curriculum at one time or another, which was great for my French, understanding of Shakespeare, reading other poetry, science topics and knowledge of history, but whenever there was maths to be taught I was often called upon because some of the other teachers didn't feel capable of teaching it. I felt grateful for having such an interesting job and one that fitted in so well with my family; in retrospect it was also the job that I held down for longest in my working life.

After a spell working abroad, more of that later, I found myself back in Dorset with the children and looking for a job again, now minus a husband whom I'd grown apart from and separated. While I'd been away Dorset County Council had re-organised their home teaching commitment and opened pupil referral units for excluded children which were now fully staffed; their pool of home teachers was vastly reduced and they were not recruiting, in fact, they already had a waiting list which they were not adding to.

The usual route for teachers in my situation would have been to take supply work but this had never much appealed to me – I liked having my own pupils with whom I could build a relationship and get to know their needs and I also like the stability of knowing what days and hours I would be working.

Once again I took on a junior administrative role, this time in the community Adult Education service, as an examinations secretary. There was nothing in the role to stretch or challenge my grey cells but I got to know some people working in this field, and as I've found before, other doors started to open.

I taught, first, an evening class in *Computers for Beginners*, then later, also a GCSE maths class which was the start of my teaching adults. I liked their keenness and motivation to learn, and an added bonus was their extreme politeness and undivided attention given to my lessons.

From adult classes in Poole it was a relatively short step to become a lecturer at Salisbury College – my roles there were quite varied – basically I was willing to try anything they thought I was capable of as long as it kept me in a job. My primary role was running an Alternative Curriculum programme for pupils at local schools who found it hard to follow an academic route five days a week – for one day a week a limited number came to the college and joined in one of our vocational courses, perhaps in the hairdressing salon, the motor vehicle workshop, at the engineering benches, in the restaurant kitchen or with the film and photographic group. It was my job to coordinate these placements with the school and our college, and keep a watchful eye over them when they were with us to check that everyone was reasonably happy.

On the whole it worked well but it was not easy to expand the numbers on the programme as we were accommodating them within our normal groups, rather than running dedicated classes for them. The pupils benefitted hugely from being alongside students who were working towards vocational qualifications, and could hopefully try to emulate their maturity and match the aspirations they saw around them. I felt I was part of a worthwhile scheme, but I was doing no teaching in this role and as that is the position I adopt naturally when in an educational establishment I looked out for opportunities and they came along.

My Alternative Curriculum programme was managed in the Foundation Studies Department by David, an experienced and exceptionally kind man, who excelled in teaching and being with young adults with learning disabilities. I knew this was not my forte, but there was a course titled *Choices*, which was for 16 year old school leavers with no qualifications. They were short of someone to teach Life Skills and so I took this on with gusto.

David always reminds me of the time when he came in to do one of his regular observations on my teaching and my topic for the lesson was *Birth Control and Contraception*; the resources required for the practical activities included bananas and condoms! I'd come a long way from what they had taught me about teaching geography and maths in Glasgow in 1975.

My friend, Carol, worked alongside David teaching young adults with moderate or severe learning disabilities at the College; her background was in Primary Education where she had reached managerial level, but she realised it was not for her and she changed direction for something which she found more satisfying. She and I shared an office with Karen who had a wicked sense of humour and we did a lot of laughing out loud together.

I looked forward to Friday lunchtimes, when the students training to be chefs served a three-course meal in the Wessex restaurant on the top floor to the public and staff for a very reasonable sum. Not many staff took up the offer, but John, a chemistry lecturer, persuaded Carol, myself and Gary, an EFL specialist (English as a foreign language) to join him at a table. It was a good opportunity for a chat and a laugh with colleagues while the trainee chefs practised their 'silver service' skills on us and we tried out their 'exquisite à la carte menus'. Looking at the current selection on their website brings back tasty memories – it does not seem to have changed much. My choice today might be:

Potato, Leek and Red Onion tart with a rocket salad

Confit of Duck with Lentils and Spring Onion Mash

Strawberry Bavarois, Chantilly Cream and Langue Du Chat

Filter Coffee

Fortunately my teaching timetable on a Friday afternoon was light and the college always closed half an hour earlier than usual. I used to like ending my working week by stopping off at Martin Down on the way home and having a forty minute run on the grassy chalk land reserve – my way of starting the weekend, getting some exercise and essential top-up from the countryside.

🚲 🚲 🚲 🚲 🚲 🚲 🚲 🚲

After the first day of my cycle trip Carol, John and I spent the evening at their house reminiscing and looking at photographs of their recent travels, including a cycle trip in Poland. They play musical instruments, sing and do morris dancing in the local Dorset tradition and have met many people in other countries through their shared interests.

Chapter Three

CALL OF THE WILD

I was entertained at breakfast the following morning, first by a procession of many species of birds flocking to the bird feeders just outside the window, including a pheasant pecking underneath, and then to an impromptu concert by John and Carol on their accordions. It couldn't have been a more wonderful start to my morning.

Carol cycled with me back to Salisbury, via the camel in the field (belonging to the Lady in the manor who enjoyed riding it). I decided I wasn't happy with my brakes after all the rain and mud so found a bike shop and left my bicycle in the hands of Pip, who replaced the pads with a better quality type. He was interested to hear about my proposed trip and donated his labour towards my charity-raising cause and noted down the name of my blog.

I said goodbye to Carol and John and continued east along the Clarendon Way, encountering frequent showers, but village bus shelters are a welcome sight to cyclists wanting a break and I used many of them over the following weeks. You can find out a lot about a village by reading the posters pinned up inside, everything from Zumba classes, preparations for the Best Village competition to dancing the night away at a Motown disco run by the football club.

Turning north along the Test Valley cycleway I found it harder going, the surface being gravel interspersed by puddles, but pleasurable nevertheless. I stopped in Stockbridge at a café to write my blog on my little computer and had the additional pleasant surprise of bumping into Janet, a friend who had trekked in Iceland with me as part of a group.

'Hi Enid, didn't expect to see you here. You look engrossed in what you're doing.' She was interested to hear of my tour and wanted details of my blog and charity-raising website. Over the coming weeks the kindness and support shown by everyone just blew me away.

Once the seed of an idea to do a long-distance cycle ride was planted in my mind, the details fell into place and knitted together to form a cohesive plan. I knew I wanted to cycle to somewhere in Scotland, my homeland, and where more fitting then the city I was born and grew up in? It would be like going back to my roots, and to combine this with visiting as many of my family and friends as I could en route would remind me of the journey I had been on to be the person I am today.

Several years ago I was visiting my friends, Sue and Roy, who live in Hampshire and as usual the topic of conversation turned to cycling. They are keen cyclists and since they retired have been on many long-distance tours in different continents and always have interesting stories to relate on their return. I mentioned that I would like to do longer rides also but as a woman on her own I didn't think I could manage it alone.

'I think you should read this, Enid,' said Sue and handed me a book.

I read out the title, '*A Bike Ride, 12000 Miles around the World* by Anne Mustoe. Sounds intriguing, thanks.'

That evening I started reading the book and was hooked from the beginning. Anne Mustoe was given a bicycle as a leaving present when she retired as a headmistress at the age of 54. In her own words she was somewhat overweight and unfit, without any idea how to mend a puncture but since a chance sighting of a lone European cyclist in Rajasthan she resolved to cycle round the world. She completed her circumnavigation in fifteen months; the resulting book included all the preparations, route-planning, packing and budgeting, as well as describing the riding. It was a fascinating insight into how a middle-aged woman took on a challenge and successfully fulfilled it.

Reading her book gave me both the inspiration and the hope that I could bring off a trip of my own, albeit on a much smaller scale. I started with a few days at a time, and built up to a week's cycling in Denmark then Germany. By now I felt ready to tackle a much longer trip.

As a woman cycling on her own I also knew I would find comfort in knowing that I would be staying with people I knew for parts of my trip. It was important to me that I didn't just do this trip just for my own selfish reasons and there was no doubt in my mind which charity I wanted to support. My eldest brother, Donald, died from a brain tumour, when he was just 44. The youngest of his four sons, Stuart, was marrying Natalie in Dryburgh Abbey in July and if I could organise my dates appropriately I would be able to attend their wedding at the end of my trip. This would be a fitting way to pay a tribute in memory of my brother. My second eldest brother had also died of cancer just three years ago and his wife, Anna, would be at the wedding too.

Therefore, raising funds for Cancer Research became another focus in the weeks before my departure, leading to an interview with the local press. As the donations and messages of support began to pour into my fund-raising website I realised just how many people were behind me and sending me their good wishes. Reading the messages as they continued to come in throughout my trip sustained me through the low points.

The timing of this cycle trip was in large part due to my beloved cat, Jack, who had died earlier in the year, aged 19, on Friday January 13th. There was no longer anyone at home dependant on me and I was free to travel. My love affair with cats started with the ownership of my previous cat, Teuchter (a Scottish word for a Highland dweller) affectionately always called Teuchy. She came to me as a kitten when I was living in a Glasgow flat which we co-inhabited with mice. My phobia of vermin was rampant during my student days when living in mice-infested flats. Going into the kitchen to be confronted with a dead prey in the mousetrap and feeling totally unable to go near it until one of my flatmates dealt with the offending object was a regular occurrence for me. Even further back in time I can remember my Dad with the axe in his hand chasing a rat out of the house. So perhaps my phobia stemmed from then.

As a child I used to ask my Mum if we could have a pet, thinking of a cat, but she always turned my request down, and I knew it was because nine people living in the house was enough for her to cope with. I felt this to be grossly unfair because she used to tell us about the cats they had in their family while growing up in London.

I spent a lot of time as a child reading books borrowed from the library. My local branch called Coldside, an immense Baroque concave-fronted building, sat proudly on a corner site with splendid wrought-iron railings. I used to wonder why these railings hadn't been sawn off to help with the war effort as so many of the others in my locality had been. The library is now a category A listed building so maybe they were saved from the chop because of its historic importance even then.

Coldside Library

Inside was a massive circular lobby with tall columns and a wrought-iron stair baluster leading to the reading room and reference library which for a long time were out of bounds to me. I can't remember whether there was a notice forbidding children to go upstairs or perhaps my parents warned me not to, but when at a much older age I did sneak up for a peep it was almost empty except for a few men. They sat in total silence reading newspapers which were mounted on boards, held by a cord down the centre page. Even more mysterious was a room on that floor which I was aware existed but didn't ever succeed in locating; it was a studio for the BBC but as far as I was concerned the programmes must have all been secretly recorded and broadcast because I never saw any action during my visits.

Downstairs was where my parents first introduced me the main lending library; it was open one evening a week until around 7pm and after tea my Dad would take us in the car so that we could all borrow books. However, it took Mum and Dad a couple of weeks to read their allocation of two books. I was limited to one book, so from an early age I was allowed to go there by myself – it was less than a ten minute walk.

One of my earliest encounters with the library staff was on a Saturday morning when I went into the library and chose a Noddy storybook. I went home, quickly devoured it, so took it back to the library that same morning to change it for another but was sternly told, 'You can't return a book on the same day as you borrowed it.' It was obvious to me that the reason behind this was that my library card was still on the borrowing counter, not yet on the returns' side where I was standing with my book. To find my card would have meant the librarian going over to the other counter and she wasn't having an avid young reader mess up her administration system so she sent me home with my book to read over and over again until Monday.

It didn't stop me though, one at a time, working my way through the children's books, especially Enid Blyton's *Famous Five* and *Secret Seven* stories and then on to teenage girls' novels such as *Cherry Ames District Nurse* (one of twenty seven about Cherry Ames) and *The Chalet School* series which consisted of an incredible fifty eight books. From there I progressed on to the Adult non-fiction section, attempting to use my children's library card, which caused a further disruption to their administration but this time they decided to issue me with my first non-fiction card and so I could at long last take home *two* books.

I started with accounts of the great explorers: David Livingston, Captain Scott, and was enthralled by their adventures. I followed the expeditions of big hunters in Africa and climbers' repeated unsuccessful attempts on Everest. It was somewhere amongst the reading of these intrepid tales of derring-do that my desires to explore beyond my own backyard were born, in particular to go to Africa.

When I became the owner of a beautiful ginger and white tabby cat while living in Glasgow, it was my substitute for an African lion, and as I moved house seven times in the next fourteen years Teuchy was my constant companion; eventually she died peacefully in Dorset during her twentieth year.

I realised my dream of visiting Africa in my late twenties with a Safari trip to Kenya, and I was elated at seeing lions, elephants and many more animals wild in the savannah. I knew I would return to Africa one day. It gets into your blood and doesn't let go.

Chapter Four

'AND WILD WAS THE SURGE, OF THE DARK ROLLING SEA'[1]

My second night was spent with my sister and brother-in-law, Jean and Ian, in Andover, and the good news came in that my total raised so far for Cancer Research had exceeded one thousand pounds.

I had decided to write a blog of my journey and include my own photographs for illustration. As Ian had been writing his own blog since he retired a few years earlier (entitled 'It's what retired people do') I naturally had employed his talents to help me set up mine, and thus under his watchful eye I uploaded my photographs of the previous two days and posted my first blog of the trip. For reasons unknown to me my readers, with one exception, were unable to post comments, but instead many sent encouraging text messages which were always a thrill to receive. The exception was a comment from a guy in the United States who tried to sell me his latest invention. Looking at the blog statistics was fascinating as I could see I had followers in countries as far afield as Russia, Ukraine and Brazil, where to my knowledge I was unknown.

Lorna, Jean's eldest daughter, turned up in the morning with her two sons, Callum (a very keen BMXer) and Ross, to send me on my way. The boys' favourite item of mine was the tiny little mouse I had for my netbook: 'So cool!'

It was a gentle and pleasant climb up Coombe Hill and then down into the valley containing the Kennet and Avon canal. I had cycled along this during the previous Spring and enjoyed it so much I wanted to include it

---

[1] From 'THE ROAD AND THE MILES TO DUNDEE'

in this itinerary. However, that was without bringing the June 2012 monsoon into the equation. Heavy rain accompanied me all the way to Reading.

The towpath was a continuous series of muddy puddles and by the time I was close to the outskirts of the city, my bike, my bags and I were completely mud-splattered. As it was only 3 o'clock and Alex, the friend I was staying with that night would not yet be home from work, the thought of a cosy tea-shop entered my head.

Then, the familiar bump, bump – yes, another puncture! Or rather, as it turned out to be, the same one leaking air out of the side of the patch. I decided to fit my spare tube and was beginning to feel quite pleased with myself after getting the job nearly completed despite the dreadful weather and the soggy, muddy conditions under which the replacement was carried out. But with the bike re-assembled I couldn't get any air into the tyre and thought it must be the type of valve or my pump that was the problem. So I started walking along the track towards the road, about three miles away, and met the only other cyclist who was also mad enough to be braving the weather. He couldn't blow up my tyre either and suggested I might have nicked the new tube while putting it in.

Thanking him I walked on towards the road and seeing a relatively mud-free lay-by to stop in was encouraged to take the tyre off again and have another look. Sure enough, a further puncture, so I proceeded to mend it and got the bike reassembled once more. On the way into Reading I felt I was cycling through treacle, so when I spotted a branch of a well-known bike shop chain in I went with my bike where the mechanic immediately spotted the problem and re-aligned my wheel. Would I reach my destination that evening without any further complications?

Having contacted Alex who wanted to come and collect me and my bike and put us out of our misery, I doggedly cycled on, only for the chain to then come off. I succeeded in sorting that when Alex drew up alongside me and offloaded my panniers into his car. But I was determined to arrive at his house under my own steam. His comment when I got there: 'I wasn't expecting you so soon' gave me a little inner buzz.

It had been a long demanding day but nothing a warm shower and a beef curry couldn't put right. I even hosed down my bike on the forecourt, fixed the puncture in my spare tube and adjusted the following day's route to Oxford to avoid non-tarmac roads.

Alex and I got on to talking about where we'd first met.

'How different your trip is from Corsica. The problem there wasn't rain – it was the *lack* of it. We had to carry all our own water when we walked along the GR20,' recalled Alex.

'Yes, I remember. My favourite bit was sunbathing on the summit of Monte Cinto and the spectacular views from there. Mind you, the descent down to the GR20 seemed to go on forever and it was so hot in the valley, by the time we reached our campsite I was too exhausted to even put up my own tent. Mark took pity on my and helped me.'

Mark was the leader of our little group of six who were walking in Corsica in the summer of 2001.

On the summit of Monte Cinto in Corsica
(Alex on the far left, I am in the middle)

As well as reaching the highest point on the island at Monte Cinto (2706m), we also climbed Paglio Orba which was a proper scramble and Mark, again, came to my rescue as he helped me with where to place my feet both on the ascent and the descent. But it was worth it for the fantastic views of the sea and to look back at the mountains which we'd crossed.

Some nights we spent in remote refuges and others at farmsteads where we erected our tents. At the *Bocca di Conia Bergerie* after watching a herd of 250 goats being brought down the mountain and into the safety of an enclosure for the night, the Berger's wife fed us a gastronomic meal of five courses, including veal steaks washed down with wine and martini.

After two weeks of terrific mountain walking and convivial company we arrived at the west coast and were looking forward to the impending boat and snorkelling trip which was to be the climax on the final day of our trip – this would be my first go at this activity.

As a young girl I had learnt to swim in the cold freshwater of Loch Clunie, near Dundee, with my Dad holding me around the middle, then just with the support of a hand and finally, no hand at all. I wouldn't describe myself as a strong swimmer but I was competent in both the swimming pool and the sea.

We checked into our *gîte* and immediately all headed straight down to the beach for a swim. The large waves breaking on the shoreline made the going quite rough but we found if we headed out a bit further it was calmer and better for swimming. As we walked back up from the beach a dramatic thunderstorm broke out and we made a beeline for our gîte and dinner.

The following day we boarded our minibus and headed off towards Partinello to start our day's walk to Girolata where the boat was waiting to take us snorkelling. Soon after setting off Mark's phone rang and we heard a one-sided conversation in French from which we gathered our trip was in jeopardy.

'Sorry guys – the boat can't go out. The sea at Girolata is too rough.' Oh well, I thought, I could still enjoy the walk down to the coast.

After the long slog to get there we were hot and quite tired, so sat down on the beach which was composed of bark and wood shavings, to partake of our picnic before continuing on our way to Osani, the official end of the walking bit of our holiday. The shore here is part of the Corsica Regional Natural Park and particularly beautiful – it has hidden coves, long beaches of fine sand, sea grottos and high cliffs composed of blood-red porphyry.

But it is the next day which is indelibly printed in my mind. It was a Saturday, and it started with a swim in the hotel pool, a bite of lunch from a take-away and then on to our bus which took us to the Calanches, an area of large pink granite outcrops forming weird and wonderful shapes. By the time we reached our hotel we were in a relaxed mood and headed off down to the sandy beach for a swim.

When I entered the water Terry was the only one in my sight. The large waves were making it difficult for me to swim and I decided to come back out, but the strong undercurrent caught me and pushed against me and I couldn't make any headway. As the waves repeatedly crashed over my head and my attempts to swim back to shore were fruitless, I called out to Terry: 'I can't swim against these waves – can you help?'

'I can't either', came back his response.

I battled my hardest against the sea but I couldn't do it, every time I got my head up another wave came over the top of me and swamped me again – I was in deep trouble and so was Terry. We yelled 'Help, help!' (maybe it should have been 'Aidez-moi'?).

But there was no one else near us in the water and the crash of the waves drowned our cries. 'I can't make it,' I shouted and could feel myself becoming weaker as I was being pulled under. 'Keep swimming, think of your sons,' yelled Terry. But I had nothing left and thinking about my sons I went under...

'Enid, Enid can you hear me?' I opened my eyes and saw a couple of guys leaning over me. I couldn't say anything. I was completely spent and I was aware that I was hyperventilating. I vomited violently and they laid me in the recovery position on my side.

I was lying on the beach. Terry was kneeling beside me willing me to recover but I still couldn't say anything and continued to struggle for breath. I heard them contemplating bringing in a helicopter but they decided on a stretcher instead. I was lifted back to my hotel room and laid on the bed. The rest of the day is a blur – repeated vomiting, a visit from the doctor, flashbacks, the whole night long. I was in deep shock.

The following morning, Mark came into my room to see how I was. 'What happened?' I asked. He explained that two chaps on the beach heard my cries and pulled me from the water; they also helped Terry, who was still conscious, out of the water too.

He told me the two chaps were downstairs having breakfast. 'I need to go down and see them. I'll be down in a minute,' I said to Mark. I pulled on a T-shirt and shorts and walked unsteadily down to the dining room and over to the table where my two rescuers sat. What do you say to someone who has just saved your life? I thanked them as sincerely and gratefully as I could.

'We're just so glad that you're okay. We weren't sure you'd make it – whether your heart would cope with the strain. We're so happy we could help you.'

I lived to tell the tale. It changed me though. From that day on, my appetite for risky activities diminished and before taking part in anything nowadays I go through a mental risk–assessment of the dangers involved. I encourage my sons to do the same.

On that final day before we flew back to London, Alex and the others in my group rallied round me. I've kept touch with them ever since and we meet up regularly.

🚲 🚲 🚲 🚲 🚲 🚲 🚲 🚲

Staying overnight with Alex in Reading reminded me of the incident in Corsica, but he took my mind off it by telling me about his exciting plans for a forthcoming walking trip to Bulgaria with friends.

Chapter Five

'IN TIMES TO COME I'LL REMEMBER THE LADDIE'[1]

While cycling alongside the canal, accompanied by commuters making their way into Reading city centre the following morning, I heard the 'beep, beep' of a text message arriving.

> Just a suggestion, but as the forecast is for gales and lashing rain, you could take the train to Oxford, stay overnight, return to Reading by train the following day and do the ride then as it's predicted to be a dry day. Alex.

Right on cue the first drops started falling. My bicycle's own reflex response to this proposal was to obey the next sign-post to the railway station and I found myself queuing for a 'Return to Oxford, with one bike please.' I like quick decisions – they make life easier.

Sitting in front of a steaming coffee among the dreaming spires of Oxford, I was inspired to write more of my blog and catch up on my e-mails. A spot of sightseeing then took me to the resplendent buildings of Worcester College which form a frame to the verdant lawn mown into a perfect spiral shape. Then I visited the Ashmolean Museum, the world's first university museum built around 1680; in particular I was interested in viewing the Eastern art and ceramics collection – wonderful specimens from China, Egypt and the ancient civilisations.

Over breakfast at the youth hostel the following morning, I chatted to a family of three sisters, one husband and two children who were there to

---

[1] From 'THE ROAD AND THE MILES TO DUNDEE'

compete in a triathlon. Each of the sisters was running, cycling or swimming; the husband was there as the motivational coach and the little girls as cheerleaders. The smell of frying bacon was in the air as they stoked up their fuel tanks ready for the task ahead. I was glad to extend my good luck wishes to such a lovely extended family.

I returned to Reading by train in order to cycle the incomplete section of my route as proposed by Alex. It was a fine run, albeit into the wind for much of it. Living in Dorset we don't get to see red kites, so it was a marvellous sight to see so many of them swooping really quite low over me and casting me in their shadow as they passed above.

Picnic lunch was eaten by the Maharaja's Well, an unexpected Indian–influenced structure with gilded dome and elephant sitting astride the well in the village of Stoke Row. I was joined by a father with his two young daughters investigating its history. They told me it was built in 1864 with an endowment from the Maharajah of Benares, in appreciation to Mr Edward Reade, the local squire who had helped a local community secure a public well. It's always interesting to hear what other people are doing and they likewise are intrigued by my venture.

Further on and sitting by the Thames at Abingdon licking on an ice-cream, watching the boats go by and the swans glide effortlessly past, I rejoiced in seeing the water glinting in the sun's rays. The local folks were out and about this Saturday afternoon making the most of a break in the clouds and smiling at each other. The 'feel good' factor of the Queen's Silver Jubilee had stirred the nation, and bunting was strung between the lampposts alongside the river. Many of the villages I passed through were celebrating the anniversary with Union flags waving from almost every house and streamers of red, white and blue fluttering between. It was a joyful sight, almost as if I was the one being greeted. I wondered why some neighbourhoods displayed little commemoration and couldn't help thinking it was a little mean-spirited not to put out the flags at least for my benefit.

The remainder of the day's cycle along the towpath of the Thames was a gentle and relaxing entry into Oxford, apart from the frequent dodging of bikes ridden by families and students weaving in and out towards me. I vowed to myself to return to this beautiful and inspiring city for a longer break at some point. Perhaps rent a self-catering apartment for a week, arm myself with an informative guidebook and explore quarters steeped in history and interspersed with modern innovative structures. Of course, I would go everywhere on my bicycle just like most of its residents.

Back at the hostel, I located a bathroom hidden down the corridor and allowed myself a long soak, a reward for the 400 miles already travelled. A second treat that evening was a Jubilee Special roast dinner being served at the hostel for five pounds; the pork came with all the trimmings including the crackling.

The suggestion from Alex to delay today's cycle ride by one day just shows what an eminently sensible chap he is. That's what friends are for.

Next morning I was away bright and early and it was strange cycling through the leafy suburbs of Oxford past many buildings of great architectural merit without seeing throngs of cyclists making their way into the city and the colleges. There was just the occasional passer-by clutching his Sunday newspaper under his arm or walking her dog pulling at its lead.

On exiting the village of Hampton Poyle, I spied a squirrel nibbling on nuts at a feeder attached to a telegraph pole, so I stopped to say hello. 'Hello,' came back the reply and I looked over to the opposite side of the road to see a lady tending her garden. We started chatting and on hearing of my grand tour she right away offered me coffee and porridge. I accepted the former with gratitude and while the kettle was boiling noticed that the name of the house was *Jubilee Cottage*. On enquiry, Judith told me that in fact it was built in the late 17th century and still had some of the original beams and an inglenook fireplace.

'Come in and have a look round.'

I stooped low to move from room to room and was delighted to note the charming ornaments and decoration in each room. But the best was still to come, Judith a professional gardener, took me on a fascinating tour of her various 'garden rooms' showing me her delightful selection of plants. She had an extraordinary selection of traditional cottage garden flowers mixed with many uncommon modern cultivars, with plenty in bloom providing masses of bold colour. I especially liked her oriental, majestic poppies and took some close-up photographs of the blousy petals in pink, red and white with contrasting black stigma. Her husband, John, an amateur astronomer, had his telescope sitting in the conservatory trained on the skies where he had hoped to watch the transit of Mars across the sun the previous week but unfortunately the view had been obscured by cloud.

One of Judith's Papaver poppies

Concluding my visit with 'Beautiful garden Judith and thank you for the fine company,' I mounted my bike as Judith slipped me a five pound note. 'For your Cancer Research appeal. I'll enjoy following your blog. Goodbye and good luck.'

Thoughts of my gardening brother, Donald, arose as I pedalled off down the road. He was my eldest brother and older than me by seven years. There were seven children in all. Donald had polio at a very young age and possibly because of his hospitalisation, wearing callipers for a few years and consequential limp he tended to be rather quiet and thoughtful, which in our house was the opposite of everyone else where attention-seeking was more familiar.

But I was drawn to Donald who seemed to have time for me and I sought out his company and spent many contented hours with him. He had the most incredible number of hobbies and just listing them here doesn't seem to do them justice: constructing models from Meccano; playing with his John Bull printing set which consisted of little squares of rubber with numbers and letters which you pressed backwards into a holder block so that the words came out the right way once printed on the page; stamp collecting – including a large number of first-day commemorative covers; rug-making using a hook and pieces of wool – he made patterned ones for most rooms in the house – the one in the boys' bedroom had on it a wigwam and Red Indians; photography – in black and white of course, and I remember the day he handed on his first Kodak camera to me when he upgraded to a 35mm model; fret-sawing – this involves intricate cutting work often in tight curves – I remember the captivating little wooden sailor painted in red and silver with a calendar tab attached which he gave me for Christmas one year; riding his 'pedal bike'; riding a motor scooter on which he whisked me away as a pillion passenger one Sunday morning on the spur of the moment (with Mum's permission) for a weekend's youth-hostelling in Perthshire; and not least, gardening, which became his paid vocation.

His love of plants probably came from tending a small plot in our back garden which we were each given as we became old enough to look after one; I guess it was a clever ruse of my parents to save them from the labour of doing the whole garden themselves. But Donald's ambitions didn't stop at a three-foot square plot, his next step was to add a small greenhouse on to the shed, accessed through a doorway cut in its end wall, and the promise to my parents that he would make good the shed when his need for the greenhouse was no more. The extra protection provided by the greenhouse allowed him to grow tomatoes and I recall he used a ring culture method employing bottomless pots.

Following on from the success of his tomatoes he rented an allotment in our neighbourhood, and after an eight-hour day working as an apprentice gardener, cycling to whichever park in the city he was currently tending, in the summer he would then further put in an evening shift at his allotment. I often accompanied him there, and loved it especially when he asked me to help him harvest the fruit and vegetables. After he took them home he would present them to my Mum with a little invoice printed on his John Bull set to cover his growing costs – an amicable agreement for both of them.

Donald initiated an annual gardening competition for the family. This went by the name of *The Grand Gardening Show*, held in August and the notices would be pinned up around the house to detail the various classes of awards; all produce, of course had to be grown in our garden. There was one for the best flower arrangement, another for the finest pansy (the requirement was for a single specimen to be displayed on card), and one that puzzled me at first was a *foliage* arrangement. I learnt that this meant leaves only, and there was always fierce competition among us immediately after breakfast on the Saturday morning of the show to be the first out into the garden to choose and cut our preferred stems and branches before carefully arranging them in a jam jar or tin and placing it on the correct shelf in the shed. Mum assisted Donald in the judging and there was great excitement as the winners were announced and the prizes were awarded: 1st, 2nd, 3rd place certificates printed using the John Bull set; plus a 'highly commended' card for some exhibits (one more word to add to my vocabulary), with the top award 'Best in Show' being a hand-sawn wooden gold-painted cup on which the winner's name would be carefully painted.

After serving his long apprenticeship, he gained further experience both in Brighton and at a college in Yorkshire adding to his horticultural credentials. He married Barbara and they set up home on the Kintyre peninsula on the west coast of Scotland where Donald was employed in a nursery.

I was living in Glasgow at the time, working as a teacher in Easterhouse, then Europe's largest council house estate which had been built to replace the old tenement slums of the city. However, moving people out to the 'healthy suburbs' wasn't the panacea to the city's housing it was meant to be as no one seemed to realise that 40,000 people would need shops, doctors, banks and local employment; even worse, the houses built of concrete with metal-frame windows were cold, damp and expensive to heat.

When my summer holidays came along I was glad to escape on the coach heading north to Argyll to stay with Donald, Barbara and their sons (in due course four in total). I enjoyed tramping the heather moorlands with Donald and being shown around his nursery. Barbara would dress up for dinner (or tea as we always called it) in a long skirt and enjoy the extra company.

But Donald's ambitions lay higher still, and as a canny saver, he was eventually able to put down enough deposit to buy his own nursery in Acharacle on the Ardnamurchan peninsula in the Scottish Highlands. His dream was to cultivate many varieties of heather from cuttings; he produced a brand new variety from a seedling which appeared naturally on his nursery. He named it *Calluna Moidart Gem* in readiness to sell to specialist growers.

But tragedy was to strike within months of them moving to their own piece of land at Acharacle. His first job on moving there had been to erect a temporary wooden cabin for the family to live in until they got planning permission for a permanent house. Next came the assembly of polytunnels for his heathers and his progress in that short space of time seemed remarkable but perhaps he somehow knew that he had to get on with it, because he started getting headaches and losing the feeling in the fingers and toes on his left side, which he put down to his legacy from polio. However within weeks he was in Glasgow's Royal Infirmary receiving radiotherapy for a brain tumour. His letter to me written in hospital reads:

> *Just a wee note to let you know I am a patient in the Institute of Neurological Studies, Southern General Hospital, Glasgow. It all happened rather suddenly.* He continues ... *I don't enjoy hospital life one bit but keep thinking of all the jobs needing done back at the nursery.*

By now I was married and living in Cambridgeshire with two young sons, but there was no doubt in my mind what the priority for me was on hearing from Donald – to get a train up to Glasgow as soon as I could arrange it. I remember the journey to get there, sitting in one of the outdated train compartments for six, with three or four young men who were discussing a gig they were playing that night in Glasgow – I found out later one of them was Elvis Costello.

I walked up to the hospital and saw a sign pointing to the Oncology department and made a mental note to look it up in the dictionary later. I saw Donald in a bed at the far side of a small ward and a sudden chill clutched at my heart as I realised I was looking at a very sick man. I sat close to my brother and he spoke to me of his future plans for the nursery and showed me a magazine article in which he said his name was mentioned as the grower of a new heather cultivar, but I couldn't see his name anywhere (was his brain already imagining things?), so I nodded and agreed how wonderful it all sounded.

I left him to get his lunch and an afternoon rest, while I made straight for the nearest book shop in Byres Road and headed to the Medical shelf, where I looked up brain tumour. Maybe it is because it was more than twenty years ago or perhaps I wasn't seeing the pages very clearly but all I could see were references to brain cancer and it didn't seem to me that that was the same as a tumour, so I didn't read on. I was able to visit Donald again that evening but it was hard when it was time to say goodbye.

A couple of letters from him over the next few weeks included requests to my husband to use his computer skills to design, print and photocopy a small pamphlet to advertise his nursery, the new heather cultivar and various other plants for sale. Will readily completed this and a further job followed on. Donald was intent to keep on planning for his future. He mentioned in another letter that the radiotherapy was beginning to give him some feeling back in his left fingers and every day he could clench a little bit harder.

However, he only lasted a few more weeks, and when the family gathered at the nursery in Acharacle to bid him the final farewell, it was the first time that I saw the work he had put into his life's dream on his own nursery. We buried him in the churchyard overlooking Loch Shiel. It was one of the saddest days of my life. He left behind a wife and four small boys, the youngest of whom was Stuart.

Donald and Barbara with their three eldest boys, and my James on the far left.
A picnic in the Scottish Highlands together.

Some 23 years later Stuart was getting married and I was cycling to Scotland to raise money in remembrance of his father. As I pedalled along, the phrase 'and the good die young' came to mind and I couldn't think of a convincing reason for his short life.

Chapter Six

CHARITY BEGINS BY BUILDING A HOME

On this pleasant Sunday morning I continued cycling along small lanes in a north-easterly direction, to the historic town of Bicester and emerged into its quiet market square from Sheep Street. Finding my way into a town or city was usually not too difficult as the centres are well sign-posted. However, it was often tricky to locate my desired route *out of town*. This was where my GPS fixed to my handlebars was of use, as a single tap to the screen 'woke it up' and the blue arrow displayed the direction I needed to take, so at the next junction I knew whether to go left, right or straight on. I had been on a lengthy learning curve to achieve this level of competency with my GPS but I was glad I had persevered as it helped me enormously with my route-finding.

After a previous solo cycling trip in Germany I had mentioned to James, my elder son, how many times I had lost my way and covered extra miles finding my way back on to my proper route. This was certainly not the fault of the excellent cycling maps or dedicated cycle lanes in Germany which make travelling by bike a pleasure there. Simply, once I got going on a particular road it was all too easy to miss a turning if I was free-wheeling downhill at the time and didn't want to stop to locate my exact position on the map to see where I needed to be going next.

So it was a pleasant surprise on my next birthday when I received a GPS with a bike-mounting attachment from James. I had used a digital-mapping programme on my computer for some time: this allowed me to plot a route on a 1:50000 Ordnance Survey map and then print a copy to take with me either for a country walk or bike ride.

With the GPS, theoretically, I would now be able to download the route on to my GPS. One of its initial teething troubles was its short battery life but I overcame that by changing the power settings and using either rechargeable or lithium batteries (relatively expensive). But a bigger problem arose when I couldn't get my GPS to accept any route other than a short simple one with few waypoints, and certainly not multiple routes. So I made a few phone calls to the technical support department of my digital mapping software. It felt like I was talking directly to the computer whizz kid who had invented the product and he explained that with new models of GPS coming out every month it was difficult to ensure that they had allowed for everything. But his suggestion of 'fixing' this shortcoming in their system using a crafty little method to download my routes did the trick and from then on I was up and running with it.

One of the most time-consuming tasks, but eminently enjoyable for me, was planning my route in the months before my setting-off date. I decided to use SUSTRANS (*SUStainable TRANSport – the pioneer of safe cycling routes in the UK*), which has a well-signed network of routes throughout the country (National Cycle Network or NCN for short). These are either quiet roads or lanes, traffic-free paths or signed on-road routes on busier roads.

So sitting at my table at home, with my laptop running my digital-mapping software, and alongside my newly-purchased compact netbook computer (small enough to take with me) displaying the relevant NCN routes for the section I was planning, I mapped out what looked like a suitable course. Other points to take into consideration were overnight stops and daily mileage; I reckoned on doing an average of about fifty miles each day. Once I was happy with my plotted route I transferred it to the GPS and printed a map at a suitable scale. To cut down on space and weight I trimmed down my maps to include just a wide-enough 'corridor' of my route to give me a slightly wider perspective than just the track I was on.

After finding my way out of Bicester I headed towards Milton Keynes, on quiet roads and traffic-free tracks. It was along one of these tracks that I stopped opposite a large house to have a short rest. I was just wondering who lived in the old house when two lads appeared from behind a hedge, 'Hi, do you know anything about this house?'

When I confessed to knowing nothing, they were more than happy to fill me in on their reasons for being there that afternoon. 'We often come out here to explore this house. The owner, an elderly man, died a little while ago and since no relatives have come forward it's still empty. It gets vandalised and what we want to do is 'save' it from council demolition and 'do it up'. Only a couple of the rooms are damp, so we reckon if we can get the roof fixed and redecorate it, it'll be habitable. If necessary we'll squat in it to stop anyone else getting in to vandalise it. It's a great project for us – we come out at weekends and it'll give us something to do over the summer. Hey, turn round a second – what's that say on your back? *Cycle Dorset to Dundee* – wow, that's amazing! Have a good trip.'

I wished them well with their venture, and cycled the short distance into Milton Keynes, leaving them to their 'castles in the air' dreams.

I once helped build a house – in Romania. The Norwegian school I was working in at the time took part in a Habitat for Humanity project. The students raised $60,000 (through clearing snow from driveways, packing groceries in supermarkets, and selling home-made waffles) which was enough to buy the materials needed to build one house in Romania. A group of 21 teenagers, myself and our leader Jacques, travelled to Beius in a sparsely populated part of rural Romania and spent two weeks building the house. A couple with one young child and another on the way had been selected from many applicants to be the recipients of this house – various criteria were used in the selection process – they needed to have an income, pay some of the costs back and help with the building.

Under blazing hot skies we worked our socks off every day, directed by a couple of Romanian builders. From the foundation up we erected the timber frame, clad the walls, tiled the roof and decorated inside. My last day was spent tiling the bathroom. We were accommodated in the town by local families and in the evenings were often entertained by the school or local community who put on cultural events for us. You could see that they took pleasure in hosting us. The communication with Jacques' and my host family was in French – needless to say Jacques (a French Canadian) was more fluent than me.

On the final afternoon the house was handed over to the family and it became quite a celebration, attended by the town's mayor, press photographers and TV camera crew. To watch as the couple tried to express their gratitude to all involved was a most humbling experience.

There was not a dry eye in the house – this was a life-changing event for this family and no words could convey their joy that afternoon – it was written all over their faces. This house-building project remains for me one of the most satisfying deeds in my life and one that I was glad to be a part of.

Building the house in Beius, Romania (I am on the far left hammering in nails)

🚲 🚲 🚲 🚲 🚲 🚲 🚲 🚲

The ride into Milton Keynes – or MK as its residents call it – was along cycle paths segregated from the traffic, and so I was able to enjoy the parkland and lakes along the way. MK was designated as a 'New Town' in 1967, deliberately located equidistant from London, Birmingham, Leicester, Oxford and Cambridge so that it would become an independent and industrial centre in its own right. It was planned as an overspill with the aim of relieving the housing pressure in London. The target population was 250,000 and according to the 2011 census it is very close to reaching it.

I found the hotel near the town centre where I had a room booked for one night. I did this using the online facility before I left home and it was no more expensive than a shared dormitory in a hostel, of which MK had none anyway. A request to the receptionist to give me a ground floor room was granted, which allowed me to wheel in my bicycle with me.

The room was fairly large and I took advantage of my early arrival to wash clothes and hang them on chairs around the heater to dry. Then I took a short walk to the nearest supermarket to stock up on food for my evening meal and breakfast the following morning – I feasted well on pasta, salad, fruit, yogurt and chocolate. The rest of the evening was spent catching up on e-mails, writing my blog and watching some TV, including the weather forecast: *Rain in the morning, drying up by midday.*

Chapter Seven

'SHE APPEARED LIKE AN ANGEL, IN FEATURE AND FORM'[1]

In view of the thoroughly wet and dismal weather I saw through my window the following morning, I took advantage of the hotel's midday 'throwing out rule' and stayed in my room. Detailed work on my route for the days ahead was still needed so I spent the morning at my computer quite happily looking at maps and plotting daily routes. I deleted the old routes on my GPS and downloaded the new ones.

I couldn't delay my departure from the hotel any longer – it was noon, but still raining hard. Despite the comments one frequently reads about cheap hotel chains, I'd enjoyed my little break and found the room comfortable – it served my needs admirably. I was glad of MK's pedestrian-friendly covered walkways as I pushed my bike into town and into the longest shopping centre in the world, as verified by the Guinness Book of Records. My plan was to wait around a bit longer as I was confident of the weatherman's forecast that the rain would ease off by the afternoon.

A newspaper and a coffee occupied me for a while but then a quick calculation of the mileage to cover that day meant I had to get on my bike and get going. So I donned full waterproof gear and started pushing my bike, only to be reprimanded by a security/information gent who informed me 'no bicycles allowed inside,' and pointed to the nearest exit.

I headed off along a cycle path in a promising direction and after a while looked down at my GPS to ascertain my correct route out of town.

---

[1] From 'THE ROAD AND THE MILES TO DUNDEE'

Looking though a rain-splattered screen I made out the words:

```
Error - no data.
```

I found out later that my GPS could not cope with my deleting just some routes and it had deleted *all* the other ones in that 'set' too, including today's. I still had my map, but it was very difficult to make much sense of the myriad of cycle paths in MK's suburbs in the lashing rain. I felt at a big disadvantage trying to navigate without the aid of my GPS.

Eventually I made my way into the countryside and found myself battling a headwind as well as heavy rain. This began to get me down seriously. However, at this point I had no choice; nobody but me could get me out of this situation, so I rode on. My chosen route led me into Cranfield Nature Reserve, but the only wildlife I was likely to see would be frogs frolicking in the puddles. I knew I was missing out on an unspoilt woodland scene but I was unable to appreciate it in the current conditions. As the waterlogged track took me further into the woods I wasn't sure if it would be passable. I got off and squelched my way through the deepest mud, then along a flooded concrete path, eventually emerging on to a road again.

Looking at the map now in retrospect it is easy to berate myself for not choosing to stay on a tarmacked road, but I was still a relatively new follower of NCN routes and blithely went where they took me. Much later on, when I chose not to follow NCN routes wholesale, I made some better decisions, but for this day's route I stuck to my plan.

I crossed the A421 by a bridge and watched the traffic underneath me slowing down to negotiate floodwater across all lanes. There was a lot of standing water down there. Finding my way through the village of Marston Mortaine and the back road to Bedford in the worsening conditions and with no GPS took me an age, and it was with some relief when I spotted the outskirts of Bedford a few hours later.

Much of the cycleway through the town was by the river and once again I could see that it should have been a picturesque part of my day's ride. I made a mental note: another place to revisit on a more temperate day. I stopped in a park and sat down on a bench to draw breath and for a bite to eat. It only made everything wetter fumbling under waterproof covers to extract a muesli bar in torrential rain but I needed sustenance before I could continue. A gentleman walking his dog noticed my bedraggled form on the park bench and paused,

'No, not a good day for cycling is it? I'm a retired teacher. I cycled to school along this route every day and I only ever remember a few wet days in all those years. What's happening to our weather? Are you going far?'

I heard my phone beep and groped with wet hands deeper into my bag to see who was texting me. It was from Jean, my sister, sympathising with me regarding the dreadful weather. This made me feel even sorrier for myself and a few tears welled up in my eyes. But there was nothing for it but to continue, rain or not.

My final segment for the day has the following description on the website:

> This high-quality off-road section of the NCN routes 12 and 51 from Bedford to Sandy follows the disused railway line - perfect for walking or cycling. The ride is very flat and the main highlights are lovely views of the River Great Ouse and a spell through Priory Country Park. It is an ideal family and starter route.

Needless to say these were not the conditions in which I found myself tackling this stretch; the rain blotted out any view and my eyes tried to focus on the sloppy trail in front of me as I attempted over and over again to dodge the many hurdles along the way. Calling on every last ounce of energy I battled through more rain, more mud and more puddles. My thoughts were of only one kind – get to the end of today's ride and then give up on the whole idea of cycling to Dundee. This was not for me. What point was there in struggling like this? I did not have to do it. I could stop any time I wanted to.

When I crossed the main A1 road I knew that the town of Sandy and my bed for the night were not far away. The end was in sight.

That evening as I sat in the little chalet at the back of the pub, I questioned why I was putting myself through such misery. I was spent. It was easy for my son to tell me to not to give up but what reasons did I have for carrying on?

I knew I would feel a fraud if I gave up now because so many people had supported me through my fundraising webpage and were following my blog, and *they* expected me to complete the ride. They expected me to succeed.

I had started off with high hopes. I had planned my route, split it into realistic daily chunks, arranged all my accommodation in advance and had chosen June to do it because it's normally pretty decent weather then. But the unseasonable rain and the resulting ground conditions had made the going unbelievably difficult. Not having the route on my GPS today had made route-finding time-consuming and an extra burden with which to fight the elements. It was too hard. I wasn't made of tough enough stuff. I should stick to short bike rides in fair weather in future. I had bitten off more than I could chew. My supporters had all wished me good luck but all the luck in the world had not prevented it being the wettest June on record.

I phoned my good friend Lizzy back in Dorset and told her I didn't think I could carry on. I knew it would mean letting everyone down but it was beyond me and I didn't have it in me to carry it through.

'Enid,' she replied. 'This is your journey, not theirs. Nobody wants to think of you battling away and suffering day after day just to say that you did it. It's up to you how you do it. You can make it as long or as short, as easy or as hard as you want. If you want to get on a train for a section then that's your choice. There are no prizes for sufferance.'

That was a turning point for me. What Lizzy said to me made a lot of sense. It would be one day at a time for me. I have been advised that the way to eat an elephant is one bite at a time. I would chew it slowly and deliberately. If I took on board this advice and guidance, maybe, just maybe, I could keep going and get to Dundee.

The words of the old Scottish ballad 'The Road and the Miles to Dundee' came into my head:

Cauld winter was howlin', o'er moor and o'er mountain
And wild was the surge, of the dark rolling sea
When I met about daybreak, a bonnie young lassie,
Wha asked me the road, and the miles to Dundee

I hadn't chosen an easy way to commemorate my sixtieth year on the planet, but if it was easy, everyone would be doing it. At times the long road I had chosen would be arduous and demanding. But it was my journey and one way or another I now knew I could do it. My determination was back, failure was not an option – it felt good to have made the decision to carry on. Thank you Lizzy for your wise and perceptive message. It was what made the difference on that day and influenced my decision to carry on.

My mind went back to an earlier event in my life when I had also to raise my game to complete a challenge I had set myself.

🚲 🚲 🚲 🚲 🚲 🚲 🚲 🚲

Several years ago, I had a week to myself when my sons had gone off camping with their Dad. I headed north to Scotland in my car, stopped off in Acharacle in the Western Highlands for a couple of nights and spent a few hours catching up with Barbara, my sister-in-law (Donald's widow) and my nephews John and Stuart. They lived on Dalilea Nursery in a house which another of my brothers and a brother-in-law had helped to build after Donald's death. It had not been possible for Barbara and her young sons to keep up with all the work needed on the nursery and it had become somewhat overgrown. The middle two boys, Grant and Gary were away at school in Fort William as weekly boarders and came home for weekends on the bus. Stuart, the youngest, attended Acharacle Primary School where part of his curriculum was taught in Gaelic. John, the oldest, helped out at the local salmon fish farm on Loch Shiel.

The following morning was a gorgeous day, hot and sunny, too good not to take full advantage of and go climb a hill! So I rang John and invited him to go up Ben Resipole with me, a mountain I'd had a clear view of from their house and always wanted to conquer; I knew he'd be familiar with it and could act as my guide.

It was a long and strenuous walk, getting steeper and steeper towards the top; the strength of the sun made it hot work but there was a nice breeze at times and it was more than worth the effort when we reached the summit. We were at 845m (2773ft), the highest peak on Ardnamurchan with spectacular views of Loch Shiel, Loch Sunart, the island of Skye and some of the smaller isles. I enjoyed having the opportunity to spend some time with John. We almost ran back down. It had been good.

For me it served as a training day for the big challenge I was set on doing – an ascent of the Five Sisters of Kintail, a classic ridge walk taking in three Munros (Scottish mountains over 3000 feet) and two tops (also over 3000 feet but not classed as separate summits). Why were they called the Five Sisters?

Legend tells us that the local Chief had seven daughters. He agreed a deal with two Irish Princes that after marrying his two youngest, they should fetch their five brothers to wed his remaining five daughters. Unfortunately the tale tells us that these two Princes were caught in a vicious storm while at sea, their ship capsized and they never made it back to Kintail. The five sisters waited and waited but to no avail. They asked their local Grey Magician to preserve their beauty into the after-life while they waited and he did this by casting a spell and turning them into the mountains that we see today.

The following morning, before leaving the village I visited Donald's grave in the churchyard to leave flowers and spend a few quiet moments with him – a beautiful spot overlooking the hills and loch below.

Then I continued my road journey to Glenelg, on the mainland opposite Skye. I checked into a comfortable Bed & Breakfast on the sea front and kept an eye open for otters on the stony beach, but with no luck. Later on I chatted to my hosts Mr and Mrs Cameron, and found out that they visited an old lady who lived in a cottage a few doors along. Her name was Miss Robertson and she was a retired teacher from Dundee, and on further discussion I concluded that she had been one of my Primary School teachers so I arranged a visit.

I knocked on the door of a glass porch and an elderly lady opened the door to me: 'Hello, come in, you must be Enid.'

She gestured for me to sit down in an armchair in the porch and while she filled two glasses with sherry I took in the view across the narrow strip of sea towards Skye, less than a mile away. Miss Robertson and I then had a wonderful chat about Dundee; it turned out she had not taught at Downfield, my old primary school, but at Rockwell, not far from my house. It didn't matter at all though. She talked enthusiastically about living in a Highland village, and how retirement now gave her the time to read and reread the many books she owned, which was not possible during her working life.

I left her with her splendid views and books and made a silent wish that if I was still alive in my nineties that I would have faculties sufficient to enjoy life like Miss Robertson.

I talked over my plans with Mr and Mrs Cameron to walk the Five Sister's ridge the following day; 'Och, are you sure lassie? You're not going to do that alone are you? What will you do if you have an accident? We'll worry about you.'

I tried to reassure them that I wasn't new to the hills, that I had begun hill-walking with my Dad when I was knee-high and as a teacher in Glasgow I helped to run the school hill-walking club. I promised I would take my mobile phone with me as there was a good chance that I would receive a signal on the ridge. And I agreed a time with them that I would expect to be back by.

So the following morning after feeding me a huge plate of bacon and eggs they waved me good bye: 'If you are not back by 8pm we'll contact the Mountain Rescue. Good luck and take care!'

After parking my car in Glen Lecht I walked three miles up the glen before ascending the first bealach[1] and then started along the ridge in a north-westerly direction. One by one I ticked off the summits, which involved quite a bit of scrambling. It was airy stuff – I was more than 3000 feet high with precipitous cliffs on either side of me. I felt on top of the world – what a grand day out I was having.

I stood at the top of a particularly steep rocky buttress on the last but one of the peaks and could not envisage how on earth I was going to get down it. It looked harder than anything I'd come down already. I had only seen a few other walkers all day and no one for at least the past hour, so there was no one I could wait for and tag along with. Returning by the way I had come certainly did not appeal – I had already been out for about eight hours. Mmm... what was I to do?

'Okay Enid, take a deep breath, take it slowly, step by step, you need to be able to do this.'

---

[1] pass

Trying to overcome my fear, facing away from the rock, not the recommended technique but the only way I was able to do it, I gingerly made my way down the crag. I got down. I had made it!

I continued along the remainder of the ridge and then started on my descent down 800 metres of grassy slope. By this time I was tired and my legs and knees were complaining at the steepness, so I sat down and slid on my bottom! I returned to my car ten hours after leaving it. I went into the car-park café and celebrated with scampi and chips.

I drove back and reported in to Mr and Mrs Cameron who looked relieved, then beamed at me, congratulated me – I think were astonished

The Five Sisters of Kintail

at my achievement. I was fit only to lie down on my bed for the remainder of the evening – I was shattered. But I was a very happy person – I had completed a solo ascent of the Five Sisters, plus a sixth tagged on the end – not bad for a 47-year-old mother of two I considered.

᚛᚛ ᚛᚛ ᚛᚛ ᚛᚛ ᚛᚛ ᚛᚛ ᚛᚛ ᚛᚛

Sitting in my chalet in Sandy, my only thoughts now were to get a good night's rest and concentrate on taking it one day at a time until I reached my goal – Dundee. I was going to continue and I was going to get there – I had made my decision.

Chapter Eight

TOP GEAR CHALLENGE REPLICATION

In the morning I listened to the radio reporting the previous day's deluge:

> *Some areas of the country got a month's worth of rain in just 12 hours. The road between Bedford and Milton Keynes had to be closed after water blocked both carriageways, and elsewhere, some drivers had to be rescued from their cars. Heavy rain continued to batter parts of the region overnight, bringing the risk of further flooding.*

Today was overcast but dry and I was looking forward to reaching Cambridge where I would be staying with my friend, Joelle for a couple of nights. But first what to eat for breakfast? I had assumed my relatively expensive overnight deal included a bite to eat but discovered that wasn't the case, so I packed up – by now I knew where everything went in my bags – it all had its own place. I wheeled my bike out from the shed and as I was attaching the bags on the landlord appeared and wished me well on the remainder of my journey. From behind his back he produced a small carton of orange juice: 'You'll be needing this for the miles you'll be doing.'

Fortified by the thought of the extra oomph the juice would give me I set off to find a shop where I could buy a Danish pastry to go with it.

I had deliberately kept my mileage for today comparatively low as I wanted to have time to visit the Lodge, the headquarters of the Royal Society for the Protection of Birds with its extensive nature reserve. So I spent the morning exploring its woodland, heath, grassland areas and beautiful gardens. I used my binoculars to watch birds from the various hides around the reserve. I especially enjoyed seeing the greater spotted woodpeckers feeding from the peanuts and squirrels performing acrobatics moving around the branches.

Funnily enough over the last few days *green* woodpeckers had been a common sight for me as they took off in front of me making their loud laughing-like mocking call, giving them the name of the 'yaffle'. I like to think they weren't laughing at me.

I then continued eastwards and before long began encountering familiar sounding village names – Gamlingay, Bourne, Toft, Comberton, Barton and Granchester. Cambridgeshire was where we had lived for nearly eight years and where both my sons were born.

After Will and I got married in London we had moved to Cambridge as we wanted to bring up our family in the countryside. Our first-born, James, was born at the old Rosie Maternity Hospital in Cambridge and we took him home to our newly bought house in Cottenham, a village seven miles north of the city on the edge of the Fens. He had fair skin, blond hair and was blue-eyed, which surprised and delighted me as I was a brunette.

Village life in the 1980s with a toddler consisted of National Childbirth Trust (NCT) meetings where I could get together with other young mothers to discuss our offsprings' feeding, sleeping and toilet habits. I went everywhere on my bike, an old one bought from the hundreds for sale every week from students in Cambridge. It was a common site in Cottenham to see mums on bikes with a baby strapped into a moulded plastic seat behind, and a toddler sitting on a seat across the bar in front. I cycled around the village with James right up until my second baby was due.

Andrew, expected on the 30th November (St Andrew's Day), was named after the patron saint of Scotland even though he came three days early. His middle name is Donald, named after my brother who was then working in the Highlands of Scotland. He took after my side of the family with his brown hair and a darker complexion.

I stayed mainly at home and looked after the family in the early years, as did most of my friends. We met up in each others' houses for the children to play with each other and for us to chat about everything and nothing. There were four of us in particular who were good friends and we also all got together to socialise with our husbands. I remember dinner parties in each others' houses and in the summer, barbecues in our gardens.

Two of our group, Bernie and Steve, had the use of their family chalet in the Norfolk Broads and one summer weekend we were all invited to join them. My memories of it were as an idyllic time messing around on the boat, watching the children play together and relaxing over cool beers together in the evening as the sun went down over the reed beds.

The children punting on Hickling Broad (James on the far left)

But nothing stays the same and life moved on taking us with it. Of the four of us mothers, none of us still lives with the father of our children; three of their husbands have since died and Will and I are divorced.

🚲 🚲 🚲 🚲 🚲 🚲 🚲 🚲

Joelle, a friend from that time, moved from the village of Cottenham a few years ago and now lives in Cambridge and it was to her house that I was heading for a two night break. I felt very tired after cycling for three days through quite gruelling conditions at times and was glad that Joelle had left the key for me and wasn't due home for a couple of hours as it meant I could get myself cleaned up and rested before she arrived.

We spent a pleasant evening chatting over a meal. When we heard on the News that evening that it was now officially the wettest June for 48 years in England, Joelle commiserated but added:

'Enid, it makes it even more of a feat what you're doing. You're an inspiration to others.'

She asked for details of my blog and also my fund-raising page, and book-marked both. I was pleased to be with a good friend and looked forward to my 'day off'.

Wednesday morning in Cambridge; it was dry and I planned to ride my bike along to the nearby cycle shop in Cherry Hinton to have them adjust the brakes. Mud and grit play havoc with these mechanisms and I am no mechanic. I wheeled my bike out from the shed, but oh no – another puncture! Well, at least I could hand it over to the expert to fix. After about half an hour's walk I stepped into *Blazing Saddles* which had a sign in its window advertising SAME DAY REPAIRS. Its owner, Mark promised to do whatever needed to be done to my bicycle:

'I don't repair punctures – not worth my time – I'll put in a new tube and look at the brakes. Leave it with me, and come back in a couple of hours.'

I walked along to Hills Road and opposite me was *Elajé*, a Hair and Beauty salon. I found myself opening the door and was welcomed by Samantha: 'Hi, how can I help you?'

'Do you have anybody who is free now to do a back, neck and shoulder massage?'

'Yes, I can do that for you,' and with that she asked me to sit down on a very comfortable armchair while she prepared a therapy room for me.

'Is it okay if I call you Enid? Good. What type of massage would you like today Enid?'

I explained my mission and just like Mark at the bike shop who had promised to sort out my bike, Sam promised to do the same for my upper body.

After she got me lying face down on the bed she started kneading my aching muscles. It began to hurt as she worked deeper into the tight tissue, but the more she continued I could feel the whole area softening up and by the time she had finished I was ready to float away. I paid up, thanked Sam and bid her farewell. She, in turn, wished me well on the rest of my journey.

I continued into the city centre. It felt very familiar. While living in Cottenham I had probably come into 'town' most weeks with the children or by myself, to buy fruit and vegetables at the Market and to purchase clothes and other items that a growing family needed. Even after we had left to live in Dorset we had returned a few times to visit our friends here. These trips continued after Andy, my youngest son, was offered a place at Cambridge University to study mathematics.

It had been his Comprehensive School that had suggested him applying to Oxford or Cambridge, but because of his birth association with the latter he chose to have a go at trying to get into Cambridge. We had no knowledge to offer him about which College to apply to as no one we knew had been there. However, one of James' friends from the same school was at Churchill College studying maths and enjoying it so that was where Andy applied and was successful in getting a place.

I remember his first term there and the phone calls home. 'Mum, I'm finding the maths really difficult – the other boy in my tutorial is the class boffin and basically I'm out of my depth here.' At his school, Andy had outshone the others at maths so had never encountered anyone better than himself. In some ways he had not had to really stretch himself as it had come fairly naturally to him. The goalposts had changed now and he would have to up his game if he was going to succeed.

I tried to reassure him that he would not have been accepted on the course if they had not thought he was capable of it and to keep ploughing away at the work. I had studied maths for two years as part of my BSc course at Edinburgh University and I recalled to him how I struggled dreadfully at first but with a lot of hard work things did start to fall into place eventually. So it was with Andy – in his second term he was paired up with a different student for his tutorials, one who was of a similar ability, and from then on his confidence grew and he blossomed. He loved his time in Cambridge and made many good friends who he keeps up with today.

🚲 🚲 🚲 🚲 🚲 🚲 🚲 🚲

I took the bus back to *Blazing Saddles* and true to his word Mark had my bicycle ready for me. We chatted for a while about my trip and my bike I asked his advice on which oil was best to use. I now realise that for every bike mechanic you ask you'll get a different answer – they each have their own preference and can justify it. We discussed raising money for charity – he had a box on the counter.

'I get people bringing their bikes in all the time with flat tyres and asking me to pump them up. I'm happy to do so but I ask them for a donation to my charity box. I raised over fifty pounds last month!'

We wished each other well with future fund-raising and I cycled back to Joelle's house. It was good to have wheels again. Cambridge was a great centre for cycling and it had been fortunate for me that my schedule allowed for me to have my bike maintained while there.

We met up that evening with Noreen, a friend of Joelle's for a meal out and I was able to use a restaurant voucher given to me by my friends, John & Jacquie, sent with their donation for my fund-raising with the message: 'You'll make better use of this than we can – enjoy!' So it was to Prezzo's we headed and basked in a fine evening of food and conversation.

Four years earlier Joelle had taken me completely by surprise with the suggestion that we should drive from Norway back to the UK the 'long way'. I was living and teaching in Sandefjord, a delightful town on the south coast of Norway at the time, and Joelle and Dorothy, also a friend from Cottenham who now lives in the Lake District, were over for a long weekend to visit me. It was a great opportunity for a reunion as the last time we had been together was seventeen years previously. It was March and there was a lot of snow still on the ground – I managed to borrow cross-country skis for us and we messed around on them at the nearby recreation ground where there was a marked trail. Actually it was really a glorified photo-shoot for us as we posed for each other to take 'action shots' in the snowy landscape –well, sometimes one just needs to impress the folks back home.

Probably spurred on by our skiing efforts, Joelle came up with the idea of her returning to Sandefjord in June to drive with me in my car back to the UK. When I first started working in Norway a ferry sailed from Newcastle to Kristiansand which left me only a 200 kilometre drive to Sandefjord – ideal while it lasted. However, within a year, Kristiansand was no longer on the route, and Stavanger was the only Norwegian port of call. That was a more serious day's drive of 440 kilometres but still manageable. Then it was curtain-time for any ferry service between England and Norway – maybe Ryanair's ridiculously cheap fares were to blame – sometimes it was possible to get one for a mere 99 pence! The shortest alternative by road was then to take the short ferry crossing over to the northern tip of Denmark, then drive through Germany and the Netherlands and another ferry across the North Sea or Channel to England. I took this route subsequently several times over the next couple of years. However, Joelle had seen one of *Top Gear's* challenges in which Jeremy Clarkson & Co. had driven from the UK to Norway via Sweden over a long bridge from Denmark and this caught her imagination and pioneering spirit. Well, I was always up for a challenge so it did not take her long to persuade me and I agreed to her plan.

The distance to cover was around 2200 km but we decided not to try to beat Top Gear's time of less than 48 hours, and instead to relax and enjoy some of the places we would pass through. So we allowed ourselves six whole days and booked a ferry crossing from the Hook of Holland to Harwich accordingly. We crossed from Sandefjord to Strömstad, in Sweden, by ferry but visibility was almost nil due to the fog so we didn't venture out of the warm lounge below decks. The sun came out on our way down the E6 towards Gothenburg where we overnighted. Our next sea crossing was over the Øresund Bridge to cross the strait between Malmo and Copenhagen, a total distance of 8 kilometres – the longest bridge-tunnel in Europe. It was a spectacular bridge to cross. On reaching Danish dry land we immediately turned off down a side road which led us down to a beach and we did a spot of sun-bathing with the view of the bridge in the distance. Our next stop for the night was in a campsite at Korsør on the west coast of Denmark's main island. We were given the use of a charming wooden cabin and invited to join in their Midsummer celebrations which were taking place that night.

We watched as a gigantic bonfire, on top of which was an effigy of a witch made out of straw and cloth, lit up the night sky. It was a happy affair and families enjoying their summer holidays joined in. Afterwards we sat on our balcony and relaxed with a glass of wine – we had covered a good distance so far and were enjoying the trip.

A few more bridges took us on to Jutland – the sticky out bit of Denmark – and a most interesting visit to Ribe, the country's oldest surviving city, and its beautiful cathedral. We spent that night close by Glücksburg Castle, a fairy-tale white building on an island in the middle of a lake, so photogenic in the pink floodlights that Joelle had to pull me away or I would have stayed there with my camera all night.

The next morning the geographer in me blurted out: 'I've always wanted to see the Kiel Canal – let's make a detour to get a look it.' So we did and it was every bit as thrilling for me as I'd imagined to see the famous waterway that I'd only read about in my geography books. Even better, the quays were lined with Tall Ships preparing to take part in a race. What I love about having studied geography is that it comes alive for me as I travel to different places.

Then it was Joelle's turn: 'I'd like to visit Lübeck – I've heard it's a beautiful old city.' So we went there too, and it also was every bit as enchanting as Joelle had hinted at, with its Hanseatic old merchants' houses and narrow winding cobbled streets.

After our meanders to places that took our fancy we needed to take advantage of the German Autobahnen and quicken things up – there is no speed limit but the advisory limit is 130 kilometres per hour (81 mph). We both took a turn as our nerves could not take too much of the ridiculously fast cars coming past us on the left and making it life-threatening for us to attempt to pull out and pass the endless row of trucks. In this way Germany sped past in a blur and it was not until the Netherlands that we took in our surroundings again. We pulled into a smart-looking town for a walkabout to stretch our legs and stopped at an ice-cream parlour where we were mesmerised by the number of flavours to choose from. A further stroll took us into a shoe shop where we both ended up buying a pair of leather shoes – mine were high-heeled, extremely well-made and amongst the most comfortable I own today.

Next stop was the ferry terminal at the Hook and an overnight ferry over to Harwich (an upgrade to a superior cabin with large window was gratefully accepted), from where it was short run to Cambridge to drop off Joelle before I continued back to my house in Dorset. However, I was only there for 30 hours because I had to return to Cambridge for Andy's graduation.

His Dad and I put on a united front at the dinner in his college the night before the ceremony. Immediately following the meal my phone beeped and I read the message:

    Waiting in the lobby upstairs, James.

He had just flown in from Dubai, where he had been working as a civil engineer since January, but he had not been sure whether he would be able to make it back in time for the graduation. I dashed upstairs to greet him and lead him back to join the others. It was a high point for me when we all came together to celebrate this momentous occasion and I savoured every moment of the weekend.

Andy on the right with his parents and brother on the eve of his graduation from Cambridge

🚲 🚲 🚲 🚲 🚲 🚲 🚲 🚲

On the tenth night of my cycle trip and just under 300 miles clocked so far I went to bed at Joelle's and smiled, remembering the fun we'd had on our adventurous European drive. Our next planned venture together is to take the train to Venice, but much as we would love to travel in style on the Orient Express I expect our pockets will dictate something less grand, but whatever it is I'm sure it will be fun.

Chapter Nine

THE WIND IN MY SAILS

Feeling rested after my break in Cambridge and a good night's sleep, I was packing my bags when I heard Joelle call from downstairs, 'Breakfast's ready, Enid.'

The aroma of coffee filled my nostrils as I sat down with Joelle – a French *madame* does not leave for work in the morning without at least one cup of well-brewed coffee and although a Scot, I too, had learnt to appreciate a decent cup. I sipped my coffee while Joelle chatted, 'How far are you going today, Enid?'

I outlined my plan for the day which was to be the longest ride of the trip, about 70 miles. Heading north through the Fens would be relatively flat and in any case I had not been able to find any affordable accommodation before Long Sutton, so with an early start and a prayer that I would not have to cycle into a head wind I had scheduled it into my itinerary as I felt it would be just manageable.

'You are brave, Enid. Let me know when you arrive tonight – I want to know you are safe. Let's go into the garden and have a photo of us together.' Remembering the skiing, photo shoots were clearly important to Joelle. I balanced the camera on the edge of the garden table and set up the camera to take a picture of us with my bicycle.

'Send me a copy please. I must go now; you know where to leave the key when you go. Good luck.' Joelle was the last person I would see that I knew between here and over the border in Scotland, so after giving each other a hug she went off and I knew I was on my own once more, this time for a few hundred miles. Staying with friends and family over the past week had meant a lot to me and it had been heart-warming to see them become so involved in my trip. Knowing that a growing number of people would be following my blog made me determined to keep writing and posting photographs as I progressed.

I pushed my laden bicycle out to the street and set off to join the morning crowd of commuting cyclists heading into the town centre. After crossing Jesus Green I came alongside the River Cam and thought I would stop to photograph some punts – a recognisable Cambridge feature to put in my blog. However, on feeling for my camera in my handlebar bag where I always kept it I could not find it. A thorough search was needed so everything came out of my panniers on to the ground but there was no sign of it. Mumbling 'drat' or perhaps something stronger, I realised I must have left it at Joelle's. Feeling annoyed with my own carelessness I turned around to return and retrieve it from the garden where I must have forgotten to pick it up. As I cycled back the way I had come I was mentally calculating the extra mileage and whether it would push me over my physical limit.

Back at the garden I could not see my camera anywhere obvious but said to myself, 'You've come all the way back here for it, you're not leaving here until you find it', so I began systematically searching among the shrubs but to no avail. I was flummoxed by its refusal to show itself but after half an hour of a thorough rummage I could see no sign of it, so knew I would have to go without it. I texted Joelle to let her know, and once more went on my way.

I pedalled furiously trying to make up for lost time, castigating myself over and over again for being so inattentive over the camera issue. I made my way north through Histon and on into Cottenham where we had lived for several years. I stopped on the Green and sat down on a bench to take in what had changed – not a lot as far as I could see – the wool shop had gone, but the rest looked the same. There were not many people about, a mum with a pushchair, a dog walker and that was it. The villagers used to all gather on the Green before Christmas to sing carols by the glow of the tree decorated with lights. The children would wait excitedly for Father Christmas to arrive and hand out presents, while the parents sipped a glass of mulled wine.

The street where our house was led off the High Street and I could not resist taking a peep. The first thing I saw was the conifer hedge we had planted all around the corner of our house to give us some privacy in our garden. Of course, we had planted a fast-growing variety, which was now totally unsuitable for its location and would give a lot of hard work to the occupants. As I rounded the corner I was surprised to see a large furniture van parked outside and it was obvious the occupants

The day we moved out of our Cottenham house in 1990

were moving out that very day – perhaps the hedge-cutting had got too much for them. Across the road was the house which our friends, Stephanie and Ian, had rented before moving out and buying their own.

The four of us had arranged babysitters and gone out for a meal together in a nearby village to celebrate and say goodbye before they moved. It was a night to remember. As it turned out it was fortunate that Stephanie was a nurse.

In the restaurant I ordered venison steak – I do not remember what the others were having but it clearly didn't take the kitchen so long to prepare as their meals were served and I had to wait for mine. I told them to start and not let it get cold, as one does. When my steak arrived I got straight into it not wanting to still be eating long after they had all finished. Big mistake. A chunk of meat lodged in my throat.... I could not speak.....nor breathe.....time stopped.....inside I was panicking but could make no sound...

Stephanie was sitting opposite me – she watched me slowly stand up, eyes bulging, face reddening – summed up the situation immediately and came round behind me, put her arms round my chest and thrust her fists upwards. Out popped the offending piece of venison and I gulped in air. By now our husbands both realised what had happened and were staring at me. I wish I could say that was the end of it and we got on with the rest of our meal and quickly forgot about it. However, that was far from how it was – it had been an absolutely traumatic moment and if it had not been for Stephanie's quick thinking and skill I am not sure the outcome would have been a happy one. We went over and over the sequence of events and I learned that Stephanie had carried out the

Heimlich manoeuvre on me, very effective in dislodging an obstruction which is completely blocking the airway. She had used it successfully on a previous occasion and turned to me and said, 'The manoeuvre can often bring up all the contents of the stomach, it can be messy.' There are some things to be grateful for.

I knew how lucky I was that Stephanie was there and expressed my gratitude as best I could to her. For years afterwards I was acutely aware of chewing up my food into small pieces before swallowing it and it is a rare occasion even today that I will have a steak– it just does not appeal.

🚲 🚲 🚲 🚲 🚲 🚲 🚲 🚲

I took a back road to Ely, not wanting to risk my life alongside the juggernauts on the main A10. It was a short climb up to the ridge at Wilburton but it was the only 'hill' of the day. Also the wind was from the south east so it was a grand help in pushing me along. Ahead of me I could see the *Ship of the Fens* rising up and towering over the low-lying fenland – Ely Cathedral's octagonal tower. This fine Norman cathedral took 300 years to build and even today one can see why the market town is called the Isle of Ely (or island of eels), only accessible by boat until the water-logged fens were drained in the 17th century, and today still a prominent landmark for miles around.

I stopped by a café in the Square and sat at a table outside, much easier to keep an eye on my bicycle. The town was familiar to me as I had often brought the children here for an hour or so while I did a spot of shopping followed by a walk and a picnic by the Great Ouse River.

On the map the next bit looks weird – there are two parallel almost straight channels continuing for a distance of 20 miles. This is the Hundred Foot Drain, so called because the man-made channels were built one hundred feet apart. In winter the gap between them floods and is an ideal habitat for wildfowl. I planned my route to follow this feature as it looked interesting but what I had forgotten is that the massive embankment which is between the road and the channel along its entire length blocks any view of the water. But I was happy to be sailing along a relatively quiet road and enjoyed the peace and huge skies the Fens offered.

I stopped at the Welney Wetland Centre and went into its eco-friendly visitor centre. Sitting upstairs in the Widgeon Café to eat some sandwiches, I then ventured out on to the balcony which overlooked lakes and marshland habitat to view any wildfowl visible through my binoculars. However I was met by such a gust of wind that I quickly went back inside. Because the wind had been behind me while cycling I had not realised its strength – but I would later in the day on some of the more easterly stretches. I was surprised to read on the information board that the tide reaches up as far as Welney even although it is 19 miles from the sea.

My plan was to cross the two wide channels at the Denver Sluice, a massive series of gates at the confluence of five watercourses. As I crossed over the first bridge I looked for my route going off to the left over the main channels but could not see anything that way except for water so I cycled on to the next bridge and again had a good look around there for my road but again nothing to see. The route I had plotted and was in front of me on my GPS screen clearly pointed to a route crossing the river, but after cycling back and forth for thirty minutes looking for it, I had another very close examination of the map and realised that there was no bridge here – it had only looked to me as if there was. I would need to take a detour of five miles in an easterly direction, then go through Downham Market before I would get to a crossing point and return to the road opposite Denver Sluice where I wanted to be.

At least it was flat but it was tough against the wind. I was glad when one hour later I eventually got back to heading in a north-westerly direction again. On a flat surface with the wind behind me I could see my speedometer reaching well over 20mph so my progress on these roads was good.

The next milestone on my route was in Wisbech where I joined the North Sea Cycle Route (NCN Route No. 1) which I would follow much of the way to Dundee. It had been a long day but I cycled into Long Sutton about 5.30pm having travelled a total of 77 miles. I was proud of myself for covering that distance and felt that it wasn't going to be distance that would be the hard bit in the days ahead, but it would be the hills further north that would really test my fitness. I booked into the pub where I had reserved a room and was pleased when I was upgraded to a larger room off the courtyard.

I was behind with my blog and e-mails so spent a while catching up on them. I'd taken a few photographs using my mobile phone but the quality was too poor to post on my blog. Then I heard the 'beep beep' of a message coming in:

> Hi Enid, I found your camera under the shrub. Love Joelle.

What relief I felt!

We had a chat on the phone and Joelle arranged to send the camera on to Scarborough where I was booked into the Youth Hostel in six days time – I could not risk her sending it to an earlier point on my route in case it got there too late.

I celebrated my good fortune and record mileage with the pub's Thursday Special, a roast dinner – it was obviously a hit with the locals as the pub was packed. It was a bit strange because unusually for me I did not find myself striking up a conversation with anyone. In fact, for the next few days this was the case and it wasn't until I progressed further north that I noticed a palpable difference in the friendliness and openness of the people I encountered. I took a walk around the small town to get a feel for the place and admired the fine Georgian architecture and tall timber spire of the church.

On returning to my room I reflected on my journey so far. I was pleased to have had some respite from the previous wet weather and awful conditions that it had brought and even although I'd pedalled like a bat out of hell at times today I'd enjoyed the cycling and the changing landscapes I'd passed through. But I promised myself to be more careful about looking after my possessions. For much of the day my thoughts had been obsessed with my negligence over losing my camera. On previous days, substitute camera for rain, punctures, muddy puddles, no route on GPS, and I could see that it seemed impossible for me to have a day's cycling without my mind being preoccupied by some matter which was unsettling me. What I wanted to strive for in the days ahead was a calmer mind, to refuse to allow these negative thoughts to consume my attention, and instead to enjoy what I was experiencing. It wasn't necessary for me to dwell on my failings or the unfairnesses of life – they would always be present to some extent and I could not expect to eliminate them completely. What would matter was the way I reacted to them. I had to learn to let go of how I thought it should be and to accept whatever came my way – perhaps the challenges that were presented to me would open up new possibilities for me and allow me to find more freedom. Instead of finding someone or thing to blame for anything that went wrong on this trip, whether it was self-incrimination or lambasting the abnormal weather patterns, there was no mileage for me in dwelling on it. As long as I felt that I was doing my best I had no reason not to be satisfied with myself.

My daughter-in-law, an Iranian by birth, has spoken to me of Rumi, their famous poet. He said, 'I want to sing like birds sing, not worrying who listens or what they think', and 'If you are irritated by every rub, how will you be polished?'

I resolved to try harder to embrace setbacks and see them as opportunities for spontaneity. But most of all to enjoy the fun and the delight around every corner.

Chapter Ten

UP THE STUMP

Breakfast was served in the bar which was noticeably emptier than last night – only one other couple and me. Back on the road the signs for Route No. 1 were easy to follow and I could see that it would take me on back roads, definitely not the shortest way to Boston, but as it was flat and I didn't have far to go today I didn't mind. I pottered through various villages – Gedney with its church dedicated to St Mary Magdalene and its unfinished spire ending abruptly in a stump; Fleet whose church is also dedicated to the same saint but this one has a 120 foot spire.

Villages take on a new life for the pottering cyclist – motorists and racing cyclists whizz through, but we stop and look over the church wall, read the parish notices, pop into the shop (if there is one) to buy a snack, sit by the duck pond until a coot or a moorhen appears (they usually do), listen to the children in the nearby playground and admire cottage gardens, perhaps even getting the heady scent of roses or lilac as we go past. They break the ride into natural sections and by taking our fill of what we see, hear and smell we soak up the unique atmosphere of each of them.

The Fens fascinate me, even before I lived in Cottenham, I thought of them as a mysterious place – what would a flat landscape look like? I'd learnt about their geography in school books and in the whole of Britain they seemed to be the most different from what I knew around Dundee – I was familiar with hills, glens, rivers, woodland, coastline, cliffs. Here it was all fields, surrounded by ditches and isolated farm houses. The people I passed did not say hello, nor often even meet my eye. I don't like to generalise but I heard it said, 'The flat open spaces between houses give them ample time to spot strangers approaching and decide not to be at home.'

This could explain the lack of conversations I was having in this part of the country. However this was about to change; as I sailed along Holbeach High Street and took a right turn I noticed another cyclist with panniers on his bike stopped at the cross-roads; this had been a rare sight and I wondered which way he was going, but I was round the corner and a hundred yards down the road before this thought got through to my brain and activated the 'why don't you stop and have a chat button?' So I kept going. The wind was in my sails this morning and I was enjoying the ride, going with the flow and did not want to break it up so I kept pedalling.

I spotted that the River Welland flowed out to the sea not far north of where I was and as usual in the Fens this river would be hidden from sight behind huge embankments, but my map sported a blue duck by the river which indicated a nature reserve. I saw that this could be accessed by a track leading off my road just before a left-hand bend. Although I was watching out for the junction I must have reached it sooner than I expected because before I knew it I was speeding west fairly fast, pushed along by a strong wind. My urge to sit by the river for a while was equally strong so I applied the brakes, did an about turn and pedalled back into the wind. Approaching me was the other cyclist I had seen at the cross-roads. He shouted 'Hi! Are you lost?'

'Hi! Yeh, I suppose it must seem like that, but I saw a nature reserve on my map which I want to go to but missed the turning so I'm going back to it.'

Fortunately it was a quiet road with little passing traffic and as we stood on either side of the road we chatted about our journeys. Peter told me he, too, was cycling the North Sea cycle route, having followed it through The Netherlands and joined it again at Harwich; he was heading for Berwick-upon-Tweed. We commiserated together about all the rain we'd suffered then he asked where I was heading for today.

'Oh, not far, only Boston – it's a short ride for me today'. He continued, 'Last night I paid seventy pounds for a B&B in Wisbech – the breakfast was good but I can't afford that every night.'

I told him I was booked into a guesthouse in Boston and gave him the name and number to phone – there was no phone signal where we were so he said he'd try it later. We waved each other good bye and for some reason I noticed a pair of sandals hanging from his panniers by their straps.

This time I found the track heading towards the river and was able to take my bike through a gate at the end of it and push it along a path on the edge of woodland until I reached the embankment and climbed to the top of it and sat down. What was there to see? Not a lot; a wide grey river and fields stretching away on both sides. But swallows were zipping past me, swooping down to the water surface to snatch a fly or two and a quick bite to eat. It was peaceful and I soon relaxed, enjoying the quiet of nature and the escape from the hurly burly of everyday life.

This was the attraction of cycling for me. It allowed me to explore side roads away from the main routes and access hidden places where I could be alone and observe what was around me. It brought together my passion for reading maps with the need to find new places to add to my mental 'picture library'.

Through my adult years as I moved around and lived in different parts of the UK my opportunities for cycling ebbed and flowed, but were never very frequent. It was not until we came down to Dorset to live and I was living on my own most of the time, now divorced and the children away at university during term-time, that I got 'back on my bike'.

It wasn't long before I realised five gears in Dorset wasn't going to get me anywhere very fast, so I upgraded to my first hybrid which was a cross between a mountain and a touring bike. To begin with I'd go out with a friend but that wasn't always easy to arrange and so I'd cycle alone. The old sense of freedom on the road came back, but this time it was the Dorset countryside I explored. The only real difference from Angus in the 1960s was the increase in the amount and speed of the traffic, so I sought quieter lanes and byways, for which the hybrid was ideally suited.

Soon Dorset wasn't enough and I felt ready to widen my horizons in the saddle. The Scottish islands have always been a magnet to me and as I'd never visited the Orkneys I took a flight there in May one year, stayed at the youth hostel and hired a bicycle. During that week I enjoyed reasonable weather, at times fighting a strong headwind, but it felt wonderful to visit well-known sights that I'd long-heard about:

Skara Brae, a stone-built Neolithic settlement, older than the Pyramids; the Italian Chapel, a highly ornate building constructed from two Nissan huts by Italian prisoners of war during the Second World War; the island of Westray to the north of Mainland Orkney, its cliffs teeming with thousands of fulmars, kittiwakes, black guillemots and the 'Bonxie' or Arctic Skua, a constant marauder of the eggs and young chicks; the numerous chambered cairns and stone circles usually devoid of other sightseers.

On my final night there was great excitement in the hostel which was fully booked with visitors to witness an annular eclipse of the sun – a rare event where the moon covers the centre of the sun but not its edges so that a ring or annulus of light appears around the moon. Alarms were set for 2.00am so that we could walk over to Deerness where the local farmer had opened up a field in an ideal position for viewing the eclipse.

However, when the time came, we were all bitterly disappointed because the clouds overhead stayed put and obscured the main show. One consolation was that we were in good company for Sir Patrick Moore, the veteran astronomer, was being filmed by the BBC not far away. He summed up his visit by saying: 'We are delighted to be visiting the north for this unusual event which is well worth watching. It's unlikely that you will see another in your lifetime.'

This trip whetted my appetite for seeing different places by bike. Next on my list was a trip to Hungary, recommended by John, a fellow lecturer at Salisbury College where I was working at the time. The tour was led by a young Hungarian couple, Pieter and Marietto, who met us in Vienna with bicycles. The group consisted of a few Brits, a few Italians and lots of Germans – the latter favoured three-speed 'coaster' bikes with brakes activated by back-pedalling, whereas the rest of us chose 21-speed lighter models.

We followed Pieter on a two-week meandering route that took us over hills, across plains and through the forests south of Lake Balaton, and finally to Budapest. Pieter and Marietto were brilliant hosts; by the time we arrived at our lunch stop each day Pieter had a cauldron of goulash bubbling away on a fire, and we were treated to a three course meal washed down with wine. This was followed by a long siesta under trees lying on mats provided by Marietto; the midday sun was a raging

40 degrees but even the Brits were not for going out in these temperatures. On our final day we were treated to caviar and champagne – not the usual cyclist's nosh!

Pieter stirring the goulash

This was the first time I really found my 'cycling legs'. About three days into the trip I realised I was coping well with the 40 plus miles we were doing each day, and one entry in my diary reads:

For the last several km up a hill, five opted to go on the bus. I followed the bus using only my two top gears – what a difference in my cycling!

Summing up at the end of the holiday:

Fantastic cycling – this has opened up a whole new way for me.

🚲 🚲 🚲 🚲 🚲 🚲 🚲 🚲

When I was planning my present trip however, I realised I didn't need to leave this island of ours to find routes that would provide me with plenty of interest. Although I had travelled the length and breadth of the country many times, it had been by car, train or plane and none of these forms of transport encourage the close scrutiny of backroads which is so easily accomplished with a bicycle. I knew that I would enjoy hunting out new places with the aid of my map and so here I was, in my element, sitting on the embankment overlooking the Welland River. My mind was quiet for a change.

However, I could see dark clouds looming and knew that we were in for showers so I re-joined the main road and continued through the Fens. Guided by my GPS I found my guesthouse in Boston quite easily and was made welcome by Mr Lynch. He was a bit puzzled by a phone call he'd received earlier: 'A chap who said he knew you wanted a room but I'm full up and had to turn him away.'

I explained how I'd bumped into him earlier on and passed on the phone number. I still had most of the afternoon left so after depositing my bags in my room I asked Mr Lynch for his recommendations on what to see in the town. He helpfully handed me a small tourist guide, 'The Stump is worth visiting and if you get there before 3pm you can climb to the top and you'll get good views.'

So I cycled into the town centre and found the church next to the square – this was St Botulph's church but was affectionately known as The Stump by the locals because of its extremely high tower, 272½ feet tall. The lady in the gift shop took my money and showed me which door in the wall to go through to access the stairs. 'When you come back down make sure you follow the signs to come out at that door over there, otherwise you'll find yourself up against a locked door.'

I read in my handy little guide when I had reached the top that there were exactly 365 steps up to the tower, corresponding to the number of days in the year, but the numerology didn't stop there. Being a bit of a numbers geek I was fascinated to read that the roof is supported by 12 pillars (months), the church is illuminated by 52 windows (weeks) and has 7 doors (days of the week). There are also 24 steps to the library (hours) and 60 steps to the roof (minutes and seconds). I loved the proportion of these dimensions and wondered about the architect who had designed them into this finished masterpiece. As promised the views from the top were extensive and let me view the whole town, surrounding countryside and the rivers and drainage canals flowing across it and out to the sea. Descending down the steps I was careful to take the stairs signed EXIT as I definitely did not want to be locked in the tower overnight.

The other attraction on my 'to visit' list was the ancient Guildhall, built in the1390s, and open to the public. Unfortunately that didn't include 4 o'clock on a Friday afternoon, so I had to be content with a cursory look over the wall. Then I examined my tourist map for other places to see and noticed that the River Witham has a cycle path running alongside it all the way to Lincoln cutely named *The Water Railway*, a traffic-free route of 33 miles, following the former railway. I spotted that it ran through a country park on the outskirts of Boston and that there were sculptures dotted about it so that was a good enough reason for me to make my way to it. I spent a pleasant hour or cycling by the river and looking for sculptures, none of which were memorable enough to have stuck in my mind, but I do remember the 'butterfly corner' where I rested for a while, but I reckon all the recent rain had drowned any butterflies that would normally have enjoyed the long grass and shrubs in the park as I didn't see any.

I made my way back to my B&B and later walked along to the nearby chippie – there's nothing beats a good plateful of fish and chips. Back at the Edwardian house belonging to my hosts, I checked my fund-raising website and was heartened by the number of donations coming in and the accompanying messages of support. It had been a good day, just the sort of day I had imagined having before I left on the trip, so I felt buoyed up and mentally prepared for the fifty miles I had planned for the next day which would include some hills at the end of the day, something I hadn't encountered for the last few days.

Chapter Eleven

THE YELLOW PERIL STRIKES AGAIN

After a typical hearty B&B breakfast I packed up and was away from Boston by nine o'clock heading east. My end point today was a youth hostel in the Lincolnshire Wolds, a new part of the country for me, where I was booked in for two nights so that I could have a rest day doing very little. I planned to deviate from NCN Route No.1 which follows the Water Railway to Lincoln inland before turning north to Hull. I wanted to stay closer to the coast so had planned my route to go via Skegness, a town I had never visited before; the only fact I knew about it was that it had a Butlin's Holiday Camp.

The wind was mainly behind me as I crossed the coastal plains of South Lincolnshire on back roads, but I could not find a lot to enthuse about as I passed through a series of dull and provincial-looking villages with the sea nowhere in sight, because it's this strange phenomenon on these coasts where nothing can be built close to the sea, presumably because of the risk of flooding. This was very unlike the environments I was familiar with where the coastlines were clearly marked by attractive beaches or cliffs.

My entrance into Skegness gained no further inspiration from the grey skies overhead. I pulled into a supermarket car-park to stock up on supplies for the next couple of days which I would be spending in the Wolds' outback. My timing was perfect as the heavens opened at the exact moment I padlocked my bike under the trolley shelter. I admit to pottering around the aisles taking advantage of the roof over my head while choosing foods which wouldn't weigh too much but were wholesome. By the time I reappeared outside the rain had stopped and I stowed my shopping in my cycle bags and made my way to the promenade.

There it was, my first proper sighting of the North Sea on this trip – I had cycled 450 miles to get here – and now all I had to do was keep the sea on my right and I'd reach Dundee. There were a few hardy souls of Skegness braving the wind, but no smiles from anyone. I sat in a shelter facing out to sea to eat the tub of pasta I had just bought. However, a few minutes of the bracing wind was all I could take and I soon carried on along the prom to a café at the far end where I ordered a nice hot cup of tea. I don't usually fall into prose but something about Skegness tempted me to put pen to paper and I came up with this little ditty (with apologies to anyone who may not agree with my sentiments).

Today I cycled for miles over land to Skegness.
It was as I expected, more or less.
Round and round went the rollercoaster train
While the grey over clouds threatened rain.
The beach was deserted, not even a sandcastle
Or girls in their swimwear, all a dazzle.
The air was thick with deep-fried donuts,
Fish 'n' chips, burgers and ketchup,
While out to sea were lines and lines
Of tall revolving wind turbines.
I cycled on, those scenes I had passed
Of Skeggie and Butlins, I knew were my last.

With my thoughts down on paper I left Skegness and after a few more miles along the coast I turned inland and hit both the hills and the wind at the same time. As I wasn't used to the climbing I found it hard, particularly once I reached Alford where it started raining again. When I realised the rain was settled in for the rest of the day I donned full waterproof gear including my large yellow cape. As the hills got steeper and the rain was coming at me horizontally I wondered if I had made a huge mistake in arranging to have a rest day here. What would I do in this desolate and inhospitable backwater for the remainder of today, never mind the whole of tomorrow? The water was running in rivulets down the hill and I took shelter under a tree on the verge – there was barely enough room for me and the bike but we had become close friends so we squashed in together. There was no sign of the rain easing, but never mind I thought, I only need to get to the top of the hill, the hostel is not far after that and I'll soon get into dry clothes and be warm again.

Eventually I reached the highest point and saw a sign to Woody's Top Hostel, aptly named, and not long later I saw a small brick building and stopped beside it. The door was shut and a notice stated that it opened at 5 o'clock – I looked at my watch which told me I had an hour to wait. I tried the door, it opened and led into a very small porch, but at least it was dry in there; the door to the interior was firmly locked. I unloaded my bags and transferred them inside but had to leave my bicycle in the rain. It didn't take me long to read the few leaflets on the shelf and then there was nothing to do but wait and shiver.

Now I knew for sure that it had been a very foolish idea indeed to have booked in for two nights – I would be forced outside at 10am the following morning and not allowed back in for *seven hours*. I would certainly be bored with no one to talk to either in the hostel or all day; it seemed unlikely that there would be a hostel-full of people. I was in the back of beyond here, any footpaths would be waterlogged, it wasn't exactly warm and don't even mention buses – the timetable on the wall had already informed me that there was no public transport on a Sunday in these parts. I imagined myself putting on all the dry clothes I had with me, donning my waterproofs and hoping to find a cave somewhere close by where I could spend the day. Maybe I could write some more prose – I already knew how it would start:

The mist and rain-covered Wolds ....

Why oh why hadn't I planned a rest day in Hull, my next stop? Now what is interesting here is that I didn't feel I could change my itinerary at this point. I can't remember what my over-riding reason for this was. Did I not think of it? Did I not want to risk forking out at least seventy pounds for accommodation found on spec in Hull? Did I not want to throw away the fee I had already paid for the second night in the YH and wouldn't be refundable? Did I feel I needed a rest day before I could go on? Whatever the reason was I stuck with my plan of two nights staying at the top of a hill with the prospect of nothing to do.

After a while a man's face appeared at the window through to the inside of the hostel – I don't know who was more surprised, but I heard his voice through the glass, 'I'll go and get a key and let you in.' He soon came back, unlocked the door, took in the sight of one very wet hosteller and kindly said, 'I don't see why I can't just let you in, even although we're not open yet.' He introduced himself as Andrew and said that his wife Jenny was just unloading the car and would be in soon. 'We've just arrived ourselves. We're here as volunteer wardens for the week. What's your name?'

'Enid, I'm booked in for two nights,' I said as I lifted my bags inside.

'Let me ask Jenny what room you've been booked into and then we'll see if we can find out how the water heater works and also get some radiators on. You look as if you'll need a warm shower and somewhere to hang your wet gear.'

Jenny appeared and looked at the hostel booking sheet which informed her there were three female guests and one couple booked in for the night. The three women were all booked into dormitory two, which she showed me in to. It didn't take Andrew and Jenny long to figure out the heating systems and Jenny was insistent that I use any of the radiators to dry my stuff on. She also added, 'I can't see any reason why you can't have this dormitory to yourself, then the other two ladies who are arriving together can have their own one too. It's just the booking system that they have at head office which allocates the rooms to use as few as possible.'

My washing drying on the line at Woody's Top hostel

I expressed my gratitude and went off to have a warm shower and wash some clothes – I even was able to hang them outside to dry once the rain had passed over. What bliss, to put on dry clothes and have a whole room to spread out all my wet belongings. I was cheering up already. Andrew and Jenny seemed friendly and there was only one kitchen cum dining area cum lounge so we would all be sharing the same space together which would mean I would have company.

Freshened up and feeling human again I ventured into the kitchen. Jenny immediately piped up, 'Enid would you like a cup of tea?' I sat down with them and we chatted about our reasons for being here. They were keen hostellers and travellers and having recently retired and become volunteer wardens they could stay in different parts of the country with accommodation included and meet a wide variety of people.

They were interested to hear about my trip and Andrew also talked about his recent venture: 'Last summer I cycled along the watershed in France from the Channel to the Mediterranean.' Jenny had provided back-up support from the car for part of it but had also joined him for some of the route. It turned out we had a lot in common and there was plenty to chat about. They were a no-nonsense couple whose conversation was not filled with trivia or dotted with well-worn clichés. Later on when I was updating the maps from my computer to my GPS, Andrew was keen to learn what software I was using and to see how it worked.

The other two females who were expected, soon arrived and introduced themselves, 'Hi, I'm Paula and this is Audrey. We've been at a funeral of a relative in Lincoln today and thought we'd spend a night here as the drive back to Liverpool is too far to go tonight.'

A young couple also arrived and were given a room on the other side. They appeared to appreciate its privacy and although friendly, they kept themselves pretty much to themselves. They were booked in for several days – just as well they had come in their car I thought as they would need transport here.

We all set about cooking our evening meals – mine was a large plate of pasta, a tin of tuna and finished off with a tasty sauce. After clearing up Audrey looked through the pile of magazines and games on the shelf and lifted out a box of Scrabble: 'Anyone for a game?'

'I'll join you,' I replied, as did Paula, and so the three of us competed for the Master (or Mistress) Scrabble champion of Woody's Top. I seem to remember it wasn't me but not sure which of Paula or Audrey grabbed the title. It was fun and there was plenty of natter between us in between goes.

Before going off to my single-occupancy bedroom Andrew and Jenny asked what my plans were for the following day and mentioned that they thought they would drive down to Woodhall Spa and find something to do there. Not missing my opportunity and without knowing anything about Woodhall Spa, not even how far it was, I quickly got in a request: 'Would you mind giving me a lift – I'm sure I'll find something to do there too. I need a day off cycling.'

'Of course. Let's hear the weather forecast in the morning and we'll make plans then.'

This was turning out better than I could have hoped. I'd spent an unexpected enjoyable evening with sociable and friendly people, had fixed up a lift to 'somewhere' tomorrow and did not have to listen anyone else's snores tonight, only my own.

Situations can often turn out to be different from one's expectations, sometimes better, sometimes worse. I remember on the first night of my holiday in Hungary, when Peter and Marietto gathered the group together to introduce themselves and tell us about their plans for the forthcoming cycle trip. Peter started us off by saying, 'We'll go round the room in turn and you can each tell us your name and what your expectations for this trip are.'

Various people mentioned things like 'see the Hungarian countryside', 'learn about the country's history', 'meet people', 'try local food and wine', 'get fitter'. When it came to my turn I said, 'I'm Enid. I'm Scottish but now live in Dorset on the south coast of England. My expectations for this trip? I don't have any. I want to just see what happens and enjoy my time here.'

Now, I don't know what made me say that, because having high expectations of myself and everyone else around me has always been one of my biggest defects. I expect I couldn't think of anything different to what those before me had said and these were just the first words that came out of my mouth. Or maybe I thought it would make me look sensible or clever or something like that. What I can't believe is that I didn't have expectations of myself such as 'don't make a fool of yourself by being the slowest and at the back', 'try to make an effort to get on with other people and don't judge them critically before getting to know them', 'don't fall out with anyone'. Also my expectations of other people surely would have included 'I hope our leader doesn't make us cycle in one line all at the same speed', 'the lunches will probably consist of a sandwich if we're lucky, made from stale crusts and cold meat past its sell-by-date', 'the Germans will be loud and push to the front all the time' and so on.

As it turned out the holiday exceeded all of the above expectations and more besides. But if it hadn't then I would have measured it against these expectations and by judging it in that way it would have failed in my eyes. I would have gone home and told my family and friends 'the leaders couldn't lead', 'the food was disappointing', 'the Germans spoilt it for everyone' and my lasting memories of that holiday would have been 'not a success.'

I used to feel that by expecting a lot from myself I could equally expect other people to deliver a lot. This led to many disappointments, humiliations, frustrations and much more. I was a slow learner but over the years I'm learning to expect less from others around me. This has led to some nice surprises as a result, and a lot less unpleasant ones. Harder to do is too expect less of myself, but having desires and aspirations is not wrong. Like the old gold-panning prospector repeated to himself, 'There is gold somewhere in all this sand.' It's about getting the balance right and not always expecting gold.

When it comes to natural events then I can count on the unexpected to happen. An attitude of 'Why did all this rain have to fall on me?' is one which I still have to fight on occasions. I need to remember, 'Life is full of surprises and we seldom get what we expect.'

I wonder what tomorrow will bring?

Chapter Twelve

TAKING THE WATERS

I joined the others in the hostel day room to have my breakfast and looking out of the window I noticed it was dry if rather cloudy. Andrew and Jenny were well on with their various tasks as wardens, brandishing brooms, cleaning cloths and dusters. Jenny came over with a map of the area and outlined their plans to me, 'The forecast is for it to stay dry today, but deteriorate tomorrow and continue wet next week. We thought we'd get away from here by 10 o'clock and drive down to Woodhall Spa via Horncastle and do a walk from there. There are some Roman remains in Horncastle; it might be quite interesting to have a walk around.'

I knew they had their bikes with them and could see on the map that the Water Railway cycle path went through Woodhall Spa on its way to Lincoln, so I mentioned this as a suggested activity for them. On reassuring Jenny that the route would be mainly easy-going she proffered a proposal for me to join them.

I chuckled, 'No thanks, I think I need to have a day without my bike. I'll explore the town by foot.'

After loading the bikes into their car we set off for Horncastle about 8 miles away, and parked in the town square. As we put our money in the machine to park I saw a map of the town on a display board and examined it, 'There's a marked town trail which says it takes about an hour to walk around – do you fancy following it?' They readily agreed to this suggestion.

A sign-post directed us away from the square and we found ourselves crossing a canal – there were information boards giving us the history of the town and we learnt that the canal was disused but there was a local group hoping to renovate it for pleasure craft. The trail then took us alongside the river and past the remains of a Roman Wall. As we turned back towards the square we passed a sculpture-tribute to Sir

Joseph Banks, an early leading English botanist – it took us a minute or two of viewing it from several angles before we realised that it depicted a flower bud just opening to show its petals. Andrew soon spotted a quaint little tearoom by the stream, named *Tea at the Bridge* and suggested a coffee sitting outside in the gravelled

Sculpture-tribute to
Sir Joseph Banks in Horncastle

courtyard. In the middle of the stream I spotted a coot's nest with three eggs in it. Upstairs was an art gallery featuring local artists and *objets d'art* for sale, which I had admired but decided I had no room for on my bicycle.

It was only a few miles further on to reach Woodhall Spa and once there we looked for the Water Railway and found a parking spot close by. Next to us was the Cottage Museum to which we all decided to visit – it was packed with memorabilia and old photographs of the town and provided a good introduction to the town for us. Andrew and Jenny then cycled off along the trail waving as they went: 'We'll meet you back here at 4 o'clock.'

I followed the Heritage Trail for which I had picked up the leaflet in the museum. It took me to such great delights as the Kinema in the Woods which opened as a cinema in 1922. Today it features a unique back projection, and shows the latest movies as well as some favourite classics. Nearby is the Tea House in the Woods – I was half-expecting a Teddy Bears Picnic in the Woods as I followed the path through the pine woods. I walked slowly round the trail stopping to read every word on every information board as I realised I had four hours to kill. I found out that the town was planned as a fashionable Edwardian Spa resort for people 'to take the waters'. They could travel by train on a direct link along the Horncastle branch line to Woodhall junction, and stay at one of several luxurious hotels (sadly mostly either burnt down or destroyed in the war) or the Alexandra Hospital (still standing).

I walked past St Andrew's church and graveyard – built in 1943 because the original was too small for the burgeoning population. Then I bought a sandwich and sat in the Royal Gardens to eat it while viewing the Dambuster Memorial – the famous 617 Dambuster squadron used one of the town hotels as their officer's mess. After a detour to see some Victorian mansions the trail took me to the site of Woodhall Junction, now a car-park for a supermarket, but enough station features still remain to be recognisable as such. The town with its majestic old buildings certainly had an air reminiscent of a more grandiose age.

I had left visiting Jubilee Park until last, thinking I could hang around there for a couple of hours until it was time to head back to the car. It contained many features including a heated outdoor swimming pool, a camping and caravanning site, children's playground, picnic area, bowling green, croquet lawn, cricket field, putting course, tennis courts and a café. I had a look round them all but decided the ladies and gentlemen dressed all in white playing croquet was the most interesting spectator sport. As I was sitting there a boy came past with his pet ferret on a lead. I said, 'Hello, what's your ferret's name?'

'Megan,' he replied. He told me he walked her daily when he could and the park was his favourite place to take her.

It started raining so unless I wanted to get wet I would have to move. I walked back into town and found a tea room which passed away most of the remaining minutes until I met back up with Andrew and Jenny who had had a successful and enjoyable ride by the river.

Back at the hostel the only other guests were the young couple who disappeared off to their room soon after cooking and eating their meal. I took advantage of the evening to catch up with my blog. I found I was able to get a weak wi-fi signal if I sat close by the window, so I was able to send the blog out to my followers. Then I sat back on a sofa and watched a TV documentary programme about wildlife in the Arctic on my computer through the headphones – downloaded before I left home.

As it was turning dark Andrew came in from outside and said 'There's a good sunset tonight.' So I went out with my mobile phone and took several pictures but they all turned out rather fuzzy because the camera on my phone couldn't cope well with sunset pictures.

I repeated the well-known, 'Red sky at night, shepherd's delight. Red sky in the morning, shepherd's warning.' It was actually a piece of traditional weather lore that I held a certain amount of belief in, so my hopes rose for a dry morning the following day.

All in all it turned out that I had surprised myself and really enjoyed my rest day. I hadn't expected to make new friends and spend a day sight-seeing towns I had never even heard of before. Another lesson learnt; expectations are best left at home. The unexpected is what travel is about.

Chapter Thirteen

BRIDGE THAT GAP

My stay at Woody's Top was over and it was time to leave. Andrew and Jenny took details of my blog, fund-raising site and e-mail address. I really hoped they would contact me as I wanted to stay in touch with them and perhaps in the future stay at a hostel where they were on 'warden-duty' and spend a few days with them. Some early morning rain had passed over and the day looked promising as I packed my kit on to my bicycle. I wasn't allowed to leave before Andrew had taken a photograph of me with my bike in front of the hostel, and then I pedalled away with a wave over my shoulder.

Leaving Woody's Top hostel

'Good luck, Enid,' they called after me. They planned on driving over to the coast and among other things put the chips in Skegness to a taste test.

I stayed high for as long as I could along the top of the Wolds then free-wheeled down the steep escarpment into Binbrook. Coming to a halt at a T-junction, a car drew up alongside me, the window was wound down and a young woman looked out and said, 'What a wonderful thing you're doing. Cycling all the way to Dundee. You really are an inspiration to us, we take our hats off to you.'

It was always a pleasurable moment when a total stranger on seeing my intentions on the back of my hi-viz vest made a favourable comment to me. It sent me on my way with a renewed glow and reminded me why I was doing what I was. I rejoined NCN Route No. 1 at Beelsby and followed country lanes to Great Limber where I noticed a village pond. As it was time for a bite to eat I took my bike round the far side to sit down on the bench there. Then an amazing thing happened.

While I was sitting there enjoying my sandwich *the sun came out.* This was the first time since leaving Corfe Mullen two weeks ago that I had sat in the sunshine and felt its warmth infuse through me. It actually brought tears to my eyes – caused both by the gratitude I felt for the sunshine, but at the same time by the grievance I couldn't help feeling because of the appalling and unseasonal June weather I had encountered so far.

I watched as coots and moorhens skimmed along the surface of the water and scuttled amongst the reeds at the pond edge. There was no way I wanted to leave this idyllic little spot and it was only when the clouds hid the sun and I could see it wasn't coming back out that I continued on my way.

I steadfastly followed the signed cycle route which avoided the busy A18 and took a detour through Hendale Wood and several Tops which were named on the map. What a mistake! The lane soon melded into a track and then a bit further on into a narrow path. This was another occasion where I had to dismount and push my bicycle, weighted down with bags, off-road through puddles and waterlogged ground, getting stuck in mud and then just when I thought it couldn't get any worse I turned the corner of the wood and saw that the route ahead was uphill. Okay, Enid, get on with it and push harder. Maybe taking my chances alongside the juggernauts on the A18 would have been preferable to this?

After huffing and puffing my way though the sloppy mire, eventually I emerged down the other side and on to a metalled lane once more. I looked forward to glimpsing my first view of the River Humber. But first I had to negotiate several miles of ups and downs which I was pleased to notice I was coping well with, although saddle-soreness began to bother me here and didn't really completely disappear for the rest of my journey.

Off to my right I noticed a sign-post to Immingham Docks. The name was familiar. It came back to me; forty six years ago, on a July evening I was in an Austin 1800 with my Mum and Dad and younger brother, speeding along these very twisty roads anxiously watching the clock, as we had a ferry to catch at midnight. This was to be my first 'foreign' holiday and I couldn't bear the thought of missing the boat and not heading towards Sweden later that night – the land of the midnight sun, a country which had taken a lead in the new sexual freedom of the 60s and also where Kerstin, my pen pal, lived.

My parents, along with every other family in our street at the time, shopped at the Dundee Co-operative or 'the sosh' as it was known locally. Same as now, a dividend was paid for every pound spent; it used to be recorded in a special *'divie'* notebook. Dundonians are fond of adding the suffix 'ie' to many words and often prefixing it with 'the', as in 'the Fifie' (the old ferry over the Tay at Dundee), 'the wifie' (the wife), 'the mannie' (the husband), 'the chairie' (the highest diving board at the baths [swimming pool]), 'the Conshie' (Constitution Road).

By allowing 'the divie' to accumulate over many years my parents made the decision to withdraw all of it to fund this holiday to Scandinavia. Now, some of my older brothers and sisters were not best pleased by this 'indulgence' of my parents to their youngest offspring, as *they* had never been taken on a foreign holiday. However, I was on cloud nine that summer as I saved up my earnings from the berry fields (picking raspberries in the Carse of Gowrie) to exchange it later for Swedish kroner.

After leaving Dundee on that July morning, before we'd even gone twenty miles we were unfortunately beset by a puncture which put us behind schedule. Spare tyre substituted and back on the road again, we crossed the Forth Road Bridge, then Dad made the decision to avoid the primary A1 road and take smaller roads which he thought would be less busy. But our progress was slow as this seemed to be the route preferred by lorry drivers. At some point on the journey Dad passed my brother and me a small wodge of ten pound notes each and asked us to put them in with our money until we were in Sweden when he would ask for them back. I believe the reason for this was the limit on the amount of sterling that an individual could take out of the country at that time was only fifty pounds.

As the hours ticked by, it seemed forever until we saw the sign-post to Immingham Docks, but we literally only had minutes to spare. There was total silence in the car as we all inwardly prayed we would reach the wharf in time. At five minutes to midnight we arrived at passport control, were quickly waved through, and straight up the *MV Tor Anglia's* ramp into the vehicle deck. Whew!

Breathing a huge sigh of relief, I followed my Dad up to the deck to watch the intricate process of leaving the dock before heading north east to Gothenburg, where we were due to arrive in 36 hours time. We were on our way!

Dad soon got speaking to Swedes on board who were returning home and all seemed to have gorgeous blonde hair– of course, their English was of a high standard. I only picked up a handful of Swedish words during our holiday, e.g. *smørrebrød* (open sandwich), *tack* (thank you). Later on we retired to our cabin which I described in my diary as:

> *...luxurious in every way, even air-conditioned. I slept perfectly on both nights.*

Standing in the long queue the following morning to get breakfast in the café was too much for my adolescent body, low in blood sugar at this early hour, and I fainted. I was led out on to the deck for fresh air and soon recovered. My brother and I spent the day exploring every nook and cranny we were allowed into on the ship and even places where we were not supposed to go such as the casino; watching the ball spin in the wheel of fortune and the piles of chips being pushed over the green baize table was an eye-opener to a young lass from Dundee.

I rose at 5 o'clock on the morning of disembarkation, keen not to miss my first sighting of foreign soil. Up on deck, sailing between dozens of rocky skerries I caught sight of a huge yellow flame burning from a tall thin chimney which appeared to guide the captain towards our berth. After driving off the ship and through customs we waited for a Swedish chap whom my Dad had befriended onboard; he had offered to lead us through the confusion of streets which made up Gothenburg, or *Göteborg* as I now tried to remember to call it.

The next couple of weeks were spent exploring the coasts and towns of western Sweden enjoying the heat wave temperatures and vivid blue skies which apparently were normal here (unlike Dundee's short summers at a similar latitude), before we crossed a high bridge over a deep fjord which marked the border to Norway (diary entry ...*stopped at far end and walked back - marvellous!*)

We made our way to Frognor Park in Oslo to meet my sister, Diana, who was working there for the summer as a chambermaid in a hotel. Having checked on her well-being, we went with her to view Thor Heyerdahl's *Kon-tiki* raft, then the *Fram* (Nansen's polar ice-breaker ship); both were exhibits of great explorations and kept me wholly absorbed for a few hours.

Our next destination was Stockholm where we stayed at Vaxholm Youth Hostel. Now my parents had taken us to hostels in Scotland on several previous holidays but they did not come even close to the standard of a Swedish youth hostel. For a start we were accommodated in a family room, lit by an oil lamp, which perhaps limited reading in bed but piled on the Viking atmosphere.

To complete our triangular route back to Göteborg we crossed through an area of many lakes. Just a short distance from our route was the town of Kungsör where Kerstin, my pen pal, lived with her family. My Dad, never one to miss an opportunity to meet the locals, was insistent about calling in to see them. My Mum (English and more reserved), on the other hand, said 'We can't call on them unexpectedly. What would they think?'

Overruling my Mum and finding our way to the Hedenström house we parked outside – my Mum stayed in the car and my Dad and I went up to the front door. It was opened by a young blonde man who greeted us: '*Hej*!' [Hello]

We explained who we were and asked if Kerstin was at home. Hans, her brother, replied, 'She's out with our parents but will be back soon. Come inside while you wait for them to return.' Fortunately Hans' English was very good and we easily conversed for ten minutes until we heard the door open and in came Kerstin with her parents. She and I had written to each other, in English, for about a year and had exchanged passport-size photographs so I was expecting to see an attractive girl with long blonde hair, but like mine her hair was now chin length, though still blonde. She was shy when trying to speak English in front of her family so she invited me into her bedroom where we could be more relaxed.

Relayed through Hans, who acted as an interpreter for his parents, as they spoke no English, we were invited to stay for lunch. No prizes for guessing what was on the menu – yes, meatballs, potato and gravy (just like Ikea would serve many years later) followed by freshly picked raspberries and strawberries. Extending their hospitality still further, we were invited to spend the night. My Mum stuttered 'Oh no, we couldn't possibly....' while my Dad intervened with, 'Oh that's very kind of you. We'd love to spend more time with you.' So it was with pleasure that we accepted their kind invitation.

Kerstin and I again retired to her room to play Beatles' records; although she hadn't been learning English for very long we did a lot of talking, eager to find out about each other and the differences and similarities between us. After tea we all went to have a look at the church, after which Kerstin generously gave me a cast-iron pendant depicting Kungsör's coat of arms and a man spearing the last bear in Sweden – I still have and wear it today. She also gave me a small brown sitting bear with a thin red ribbon around its neck which became my good-luck mascot and accompanied me into every exam I took throughout school and university.

Klaus, a friend of Hans, popped in later (was summoned?) and took over from Hans as interpreter between our parents who were getting on like a house on fire. Then it really took off when a *press photographer* (who summoned *him*?) arrived and took all our photographs. Who needs a common spoken language? Kalle, Kerstin's Dad, brought out his guitar and the remainder of the evening was spent singing Swedish and Scottish songs to each other, recording them on tape and then playing them back to much clapping and laughter. Kalle

With the Hedenström family in Kungsör in 1966.
I am next to Kerstin who is on the far right.

was undoubtedly the pro amongst us and kept us entertained with his performances and jokes.

Next morning while enjoying a yummy breakfast in the garden someone let the cat out of the bag about it being my Mum's birthday (also called Enid) and she was honoured with a rendering of 'Happy Birthday' sung in Swedish!

Ja må hon leva, ja må hon leva.
Ja må hon leva uti hundrade år!
Ja visst ska hon leva, ja visst ska hon leva, Ja visst ska hon leva uti
  hundrade år.
Ett fyrfaldig leve för Enid.
Hon lever! Hurra! Hurra! Hurra! Hurra!

[Yes, may she live! Yes, may she live!
Yes, may she live for a hundred years
Of course, she shall live! Of course, she shall live!
Four cheers for Enid
She lives! Hurra Hurra etc]

It was time to leave but I had felt very much at home in Scandinavia and loved it from the moment I touched its soil. For me it started a love affair with the Nordic countries, and many years later I would get to know them more intimately.

🚲 🚲 🚲 🚲 🚲 🚲 🚲 🚲

So there I was standing on the southern shore of the Humber estuary at the start of the bridge. It was to be my first time across this great suspension bridge and pedalling over it would be special.

I grew up a time when many of our estuaries were being bridged with longer and grander structures than ever before; the increase in car ownership and modern engineering meant that it had become a feasible undertaking to build new bridges. On my own doorstep in Dundee was the Tay Estuary, scene of the Tay Bridge Rail Disaster in 1879 when, during a violent storm, a section of the bridge collapsed and all lives on board that night perished. It is best remembered from the words in the famous poem written by the worst poet in history, Dundee's very own William McGonagall:

'Beautiful railway bridge of the silv'ry Tay
Alas! I am very sorry to say
That ninety lives have been taken away
On the last sabbath day of 1879
Which will be remember'd for a very long time.'

A stronger replacement bridge was built and opened within eight years: at that time it was the longest in the world; a further excuse for another ode from McGonagall:

'BEAUTIFUL new railway bridge of the Silvery Tay,
With your strong brick piers and buttresses in so grand array,
And your thirteen central girders, which seem to my eye
Strong enough all windy storms to defy.'

However it was another 84 years before a road bridge over the Tay was to be built. I was just ten at the time and remember the great excitement in the city during the three years it took to build. My Dad often used to take us down to the riverside to watch its progress and introduced us to 'cofferdams'. He explained to us the purpose of a cofferdam – a temporary enclosure built of corrugated metal in the water out of which the water was pumped, thus creating a dry area for the concrete piers to be constructed.

Before the road bridge was in place any vehicles wanting to cross the river to Fife did so by a ferry affectionately known as the 'Fifie'. Now, as already mentioned my Dad's favourite weekend pursuit was to take the family out in the car to various spots in the countryside where we could walk, have a picnic or as he used to say have a 'kickaboot' (a game of football). As children we used to beg him to take us over on the 'Fifie' but he rarely indulged us – probably the cost was a factor in his reluctance. I had been as a foot passenger several times, for example, when our Sunday School Picnic was held over in Newport which was on the other side of the water from Dundee.

However, during the construction of the Road Bridge my Dad did take us over in the 'Fifie' so that we could get a closer look at the cofferdams and he could point out to us the water being pumped out of them. Not a very thrilling experience for an 11 year old girl you might think, but my Dad made it sound interesting and I was as caught up in it as he was. Fortunately we were not on the 'Fifie' that wild winter's night in 1966 when it got caught by the wind and dragged over to the new bridge (not yet open) and collided with one of the pillars. The passengers were somehow lifted up on to the road bridge and I remember the photograph in the newspaper the following day which

The Fifie

showed the rescued folk marching four abreast, holding on to their coats, hats and to each other for protection from the howling gale, all the way back along the new bridge to Dundee.

During this bridge-building period, there was a certain amount of rivalry between the Dundonians and the fine people of Edinburgh, whose own Forth Road Bridge was also under construction. Actually there wasn't any real competition because *their* bridge was a grand

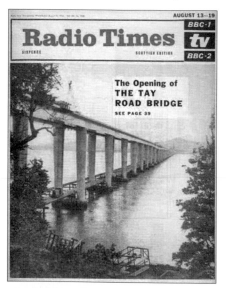

Special edition of the Radio Times to mark the opening of the Tay Road Bridge in 1966

suspension bridge, was to be completed *before* ours and opened by *The Queen*, whereas we were *only* getting the Queen Mother (who had close ties with Dundee as she was born not far away in Glamis Castle).

As a keen member of my local Girl Guide Company I was chosen along with many others to form a guard of honour at the Opening Ceremony on August 18th, my Dad's birthday as it so happened, and the day after mine. We had the day off school and cheered our hearts out as we waved flags to celebrate the opening of 'oor bridge'.

BRIDGE THAT GAP

🚲 🚲 🚲 🚲 🚲 🚲 🚲 🚲

I cycled up the ramp and on to the Humber Bridge with its two tall towers linked by long swooping wires, taking my fond memories of the Tay and Forth bridges with me, as I pedalled slowly high across the water savouring every moment of this ride between 'air and water'. It was another milestone for me on my journey which would end many miles further north on the far side of *my* bridge. I crossed over this one in good spirits.

Chapter Fourteen

SMILE YOU'RE ON CAMERA

I cycled into the centre of Hull and easily found the Ibis Hotel where I had booked a relatively cheap room for the night. I had my usual shower and change of clothes; fortunately I was on the bedroom side of the bathroom door when it jammed and wouldn't open. I called reception and soon a competent young techie chap appeared and quickly fixed it. His comment was, 'Happens quite often – it's the kind of fittings they use – they often get stuck.'

I took the opportunity to wash the clothes I had been wearing for cycling, took down a couple of pictures on the walls, strung a piece of string I carried for such purposes between the hooks and hung my clothes up to dry.

2012 was the year of the London Olympics, and more specifically, the Olympic Torch was being relayed around the UK prior to the Games. On that very evening it was due in Hull and a quick search online showed me that it was passing along the street next to the hotel very shortly.

I left the hotel and joined the throngs of people lining both sides of the street; they were being warmed up by pre-procession entertainment and chatting up the police on duty. Then we heard the drone of the overhead helicopters and into sight came a bus proceeded by the torch bearer, in this case, Sam Neale, flanked by six grey track-suited security people running alongside. He was given a massive cheer – no doubt the people of Hull were trying to outdo Middlesbrough where the torch had started its day. As the torch moved around the country the crowds and the cheers excelled anything anyone had ever guessed would result from this tour. Sam was chosen because he is a mountain-climbing fundraiser and charity cycle-ride organiser, which I found out when I checked my computer later. In less than a minute the show was over and the crowd quickly dispersed.

I walked into the nearby mall and bought some rations in a supermarket to keep me going until the next day. It suited me to eat in my room rather than finding a café/restaurant. It meant I could choose nourishing food and have my meal feeling relaxed. Eating out on my own is usually a pet hate – even hiding behind a newspaper or a book doesn't do it for me – for some reason I feel everyone is looking at me and thinking, 'What a sad person eating there all on her own. Has she not got any friends?' However, I know that says far more about me than them. So maybe in future I'll say it's not the embarrassment of eating alone that I find difficult, but it's the resentment at handing over some vast sum of money for a meal and drink which I can get at the supermarket for a fraction of the cost.

My personal involvement with the Olympic Games was to come after I had finished this trip in August. I had applied for and been successful in being appointed as a 'Games Maker' for the Sailing events in Weymouth; this was a volunteer post, in my case, as one of the transport team. I'd already been to an 'orientation' session back in March held in the Weymouth Pavilion, the only building in town with a large enough capacity for over two hundred Games Makers. The meeting's main function was to show us a film featuring (Sir) Sebastian Coe encouraging us all to do our best, followed by a young couple who modelled the uniforms we would wear, and for an exciting finale they employed a clever trick to get us to read about our role as a volunteer from the fat instruction manual issued to each of us– a quiz based on its contents.

On the day I returned home to Dorset from Scotland after finishing my cycle trip, I drove over to Weymouth to attend my second and final training. At this all-day session we learned more specific details about the venue and what our roles would entail. I met some others members of the transport team and was issued with my uniform – I think we were all a bit gobsmacked by how much kit the sponsors had supplied for each of us, all adorned with the 2012 Olympic logo and in the purple/red colour scheme chosen for the Games Makers: two pairs of trousers, two shirts with a silky feel to them, a shower-proof jacket, a pair of trainers, two pairs of socks, a cap, shoulder bag, umbrella, watch (for good timekeeping?), water bottle, notebook and pen.

My shifts started a week before any of the sailing events took place, and in fact when I reported for duty on my first morning I was surprised to find I was the only transport volunteer working that day. I was assigned to a small core of paid team leaders-cum-administrators who were organising the buses which were to be laid on for the athletes, their officials and all the staff and volunteers – by the way the latter greatly outnumbered the visiting competitors and their minders. My tasks on that first day involved printing and laminating numerous signs and then going out and about in the venue, which covered quite a large area, to put the signs on display. I felt useful and it was a pleasure to get to know the paid team and their various reasons for taking on the temporary work. The 'top' team leader was obviously chosen for her previous experience in the Athens and Beijing Games. Some of the others were keen sailors and some saw it as a springboard for getting to Rio in 2016.

I went back the next day, joined now by a second volunteer, and together we continued my task of the day before, thus halving my workload. But that was okay as I had a pal to chat to and I learnt that Anne ran her own business selling sports equipment to schools.

On my third day we were joined by a further volunteer and a full-time paid Games Maker (official title 'Transport Team Leader'). The bus service, put on specifically for athletes and their squads, was to make its debut today, so it was 'bus' duty for us all. This involved the simple task of directing authorised people on to the bus after checking they had the correct passes, counting the number getting on, counting the number getting off and then relaying precise numbers via walkie-talkie to the team leader standing at the bus stop at the other end of the route. It was obviously important we didn't 'lose' anyone en route, or maybe more important that no 'extra bodies' boarded who might gain entry to the strictly controlled areas. However, the weather decided not to play ball and it was decidedly chilly and wet standing at a bus stop all day in the biting cold wind that was blowing in off the Atlantic, familiar to all Portland residents.

We were in a good position to watch the approach road as a few of the teams rolled up with their boats and huge amounts of gear which provided some entertainment for us. But we had few takers for our buses, which they could board if they wanted to get from the accommodation village to the sailing venue. As it was a long way round by road, once they realised that they could walk a short distance along the sea front to get themselves to the same place, they didn't see much need to board a bus – they were, after all, athletes. Although there wasn't a huge number of passengers it was interesting and good fun chatting to the various people coming and going, especially to the athletes, who on that day were from Argentina, Australia, Denmark and by herself, Helema, the sole sailing competitor from the Cook Islands. A beautiful young woman who, I noticed on the television later, carried the flag for her country at the opening ceremony.

My next shift was not until the following week when the sailing events had begun. Further dedicated bus routes were put on both for competitors and staff to enable them to travel between the various venues, car-parks, hotels and railway station. I deliberately hadn't volunteered for many days as I didn't want it to be a full-time assignment. Immediately on clocking in and after picking up my meal passes for the day (again all supplied by sponsors), I joined the other half dozen or so of us about to begin our shift around a table awaiting the arrival of Helen, our team leader who would allocate tasks and positions for the day. When she saw me there she turned to me and asked, 'Enid, would you be happy to help out in the office today as I have something I want you to do and I know you are familiar with our computers?'

'Perfect,' I replied, thinking of the cold and wet weather that still reigned supreme outdoors. Once ensconced in the warm and dry little office, Helen explained my task for the day, 'Basically, Enid, we've realised we have too many volunteers doing too many shifts, for the amount of work that needs done. Over the past couple of days we've had up to six volunteers plus paid staff [a further tranche of full-time paid transport members wearing black uniforms had joined the staff force] standing at each bus-stop at any one time, often outnumbering the number of passengers on the bus. In other words too many people with not enough to do. I'd like you to telephone everyone on the list of volunteers and ask them if they would be willing to lose any of their shifts. Obviously you'll need to keep in mind that we will need to have a minimum number for each shift.' She then went into more detail about what I would need to do.

'Mmm,' I thought, 'better start with myself then,' and deleted a couple more of my shifts from the spreadsheet. By the end of the day I'd managed to contact most of the team, and the resulting schedule of names and shifts was more to Helen's liking.

Over the remaining couple of weeks of competition I was allocated a place at one of the bus-stops along with two or three others and in between the infrequent buses, the day was spent mainly chatting among ourselves, deciding whose turn it was to have a meal break or a wander around the sailing venue. We were allowed to go into the area directly in front of the jetty where the press, officials and VIPs boarded their boats, and there was usually a rumour going around about which member of royalty or Olympic pedigree was expected that day. I wasn't on duty the day that the Duchess of Cambridge, 'Kate', paid us a visit, or various other 'celebrities' but I did see Princess Anne and her husband disembark from a rather splendid viewing vessel and they even started up a conversation with me as well: 'Do you get the opportunity to watch any of the sailing?'

'Only on the big screen in that building over there, ma'am'.

On the day that Ben Ainslie (Team GB) was to be presented with his gold medal for winning the Finn class, the rumours started early that there were to be some tickets available to volunteers for attendance at the medal ceremony. The excitement built up as we wondered what the process for allocating tickets would be, but in the event, there was standing room for all of us who wanted to be there. It was quite a stirring and patriotic moment to be part of the audience cheering and clapping as Ben was presented with his gold medal by Princess Anne, and the Union Jack raised and the National Anthem sung. The waters of Portland harbour sparkled behind them in the sunshine on this occasion.

And so a few days later, with warm and sunny days prevailing at last, and Weymouth Bay looking beautiful, a stunning backdrop to the Olympic events, my volunteering came to an end. I had been glad to be a part of it, albeit a small part. The nation had got completely behind the Games and Team GB in particular, and there was a real buzz going about the country and everything Olympic. As a Games Maker I was invited up to London to watch the Athlete's Parade along the Mall which culminated in a ceremony outside Buckingham Palace. I'd never previously taken my place amongst the crowds there to watch any of the numerous processions, but it felt good to honour everyone who had competed for Team GB. When I saw the fly past of aircraft I was quite captivated by the dramatic display, as never before had I seen them so directly overhead as they flew along above The Mall.

As well as the uniform which was ours to keep, we were each given a 'silver' replica baton embellished with the Olympic logo. It stands proudly on my dresser as a reminder of that summer.

🚲 🚲 🚲 🚲 🚲 🚲 🚲 🚲

I returned to the Ibis Hotel to eat my pasta salad and cherry tomatoes, followed by a dessert of strawberries topped with lemon yogurt, washed down by some fresh orange juice. There would be plenty left to give me a generous serving for my breakfast the following morning, to go with the Danish pastry already purchased.

I switched the television on to watch the news but nothing happened – after checking that everything that was supposed to be plugged in was and there was nothing obviously wrong I made a further call to reception. The blurb in the Ibis information folder quotes: *A 24-hour reception and service; nothing is too much trouble to ensure you have a good night's sleep.*

My call was shortly answered, 'Our electrician has just left but I'll give him a call and he'll come up to your room shortly.'

I busied myself with the usual writing of my blog, downloading photos from my phone and writing my diary. The electrician soon turned up and I won't bore you with all the details but three quarters of an hour later, a substitute control box in place, new cables tried and the TV about to be exchanged for a different one, as he was pulling out the plug he noticed a drop of water on his hand and looked up – my cycling shorts directly above were dripping on to the electrics – oh dear!

'Em, sorry about that, I'll take them down,' I said quietly, rather embarrassed.

Now that the source of the problem was identified he quickly got the television working again. I thanked him and apologised once more for keeping him from returning home. Lesson learnt – be more careful where I hang my wet stuff.

Later on that evening I reflected on the day's cycling and realised how much I had enjoyed it. This was the kind of day I had been hoping for – time to enjoy the countryside with a ray or two of sunshine to show it off at its best. This is where my relaxation, peace and serenity comes from. Tomorrow would be a shorter day, only 39 miles instead of the 54 I did today, and only 340 metres of ascent as opposed to the 890 climbed today.

🚲 🚲 🚲 🚲 🚲 🚲 🚲 🚲

The lemon yogurt made a tasty start the following morning and I soon packed up and headed down to the waterfront. Just like my Dad would have done; he could never resist an opportunity to watch boats or just look at the sea. Driving back from Broughty Ferry, the 'beach resort' of Dundee, he would often divert through the wharves and along the dockside – surprisingly this area was open to the public in the 1950s and 60s. Here, he would pull over beside a cargo ship and we would have a closer look at the huge cranes which could move along rail tracks. His father before him had worked, as a caulker in the Caledon shipyard in Dundee, so the fascination with dockyards and ships was in his blood as it was with me this morning on Hull's waterfront promenade.

I was able to cycle alongside the estuary and watch boats coming and going, and at the far end where a river entered which prevented me going any further, I dismounted to have a closer look at the marina, statues and new developments. It had a slight continental feel to it. There was a Japanese tourist who was also taking photographs of an appealing statue of a fisherman and his family, but his camera was the proper job and he was taking numerous pictures from all angles, including from a prostrate position on the ground. It was a grey old morning and with any brightness there was coming from behind the statue, the camera on my mobile phone was inadequate to do it justice.

It took me a while to make my way north and then west out of the city and suburbs of Hull, but eventually I saw green fields again and a sign-post for Beverley. There is a youth hostel here and originally when planning my itinerary I'd wanted to stay here but it would have meant too long a run the previous day and a very short run today. As I entered the town I came past the Minster, an enormous but graceful-looking building, so I pulled over, padlocked my bike to the railings and entered.

The Minster is of Gothic style, renowned as one of the finest in Europe, and has been a religious site for over 1300 years. Taking my time strolling around its interior I took in the towering arches and vaulted roof forming the nave, the prominent stone font, the exquisite stained-glassed window's and the eye-catching organ with its 4000 pipes soaring up to the ceiling. There is something about organs which always draws me to have a closer look – perhaps it's because I learnt to play the piano as a young girl.

All my siblings, including myself, were sent to weekly piano lessons with Mrs Matwin after school. My Mum was an accomplished pianist and accompanied the singing at some of our Sunday School concerts and pantomimes. However, anyone who has learnt a musical instrument will know that daily practice is required to attain any sort of competence at all. Our piano was situated in an alcove in the 'front room', a room only used by the family at Christmas and when visitors came (which wasn't often), and no heating was put on for our piano practice sessions. I remember my cold fingers in the winter, rubbing them together in between playing short pieces and watching the clock for my half hour to be over and the next person to take my place. Don't get me wrong, I didn't dislike piano-playing but the cold wasn't conducive to enjoying it during the winter months. I continued my lessons for several years and am glad to this day that I learnt to read and play music.

Beverley's town square was a surprise and a delight – I hadn't been expecting anything half as charming in this little market town. I'd come along narrow cobbled medieval streets to reach the centre and chosen a café with tables set outside for my morning coffee. The cost of the coffee must have reflected its superior central position but it was worth it for the good vantage point it gave me of the bustling streets and for some people-watching.

My laden bicycle attracted the eye of a local Yorkshire chap who came over for a chat, 'Hello there, couldn't help noticing you'd arrived on your bicycle. Where are you heading?' he asked in a friendly Yorkshire manner. I talked about my trip to him and he told me he was a cyclist too, a long-distance cyclist in his younger days, when he would go off 'up t' Moors and cover 100 miles in a day'. It's always a joy to meet a fellow cyclist and instantly have a common language and subjects to chat about.

I continued on my way along the main street heading north-west out of Beverley and passed many interesting old medieval buildings; I added it to the list of places I wanted to revisit in the future. Still following the North Sea Cycle Route I found myself going along small lanes and through little villages; the route criss-crossed the Wilberforce Way several times – a long distance walking trail. William Wilberforce was the politician who introduced an Act of Parliament in 1807 to abolish the slave trade; East Riding was honouring one of its own – the trail starts in Hull where he was born, continues through Pocklington where he went to school and finishes in York where he was an MP.

A bit further on I noticed another cyclist up ahead. As I was travelling slightly faster the gap narrowed and I could see panniers, then closer still I recognised those sandals strapped on to the back – it was Peter! 'Hello, we meet once again,' I greeted him as I went alongside. He seemed pleased to have a mate to chat to and we began to swap stories of the intervening four days since we'd gone our separate ways the other side of Boston. We compared tales of mud and rain in Lincolnshire – he'd taken the A18 to avoid that very squelchy route of mine through the woods and over the hill. We both agreed that Beverley was a charming town and he filled me in on more details because he'd stayed two nights in the youth hostel which he highly recommended.

The hostel was housed in a 600 year old Dominican Friary mentioned in the Canterbury Tales and happily the recent refurbishment has retained many of the building's original features, including beamed ceilings, stone fireplaces and medieval and Tudor wall paintings which can be viewed on the some of the hostel's walls. Definitely the place to stay when I come back for a visit I noted.

The town of Driffield was just up ahead and we both agreed a cup of tea was needed so we found a café with a suitable place to padlock the bikes together and went through to a courtyard out the back and found a table. Peter talked more about his present trip which had started in Denmark and taken him down the North Sea coast through Germany and the Netherlands. He had been plagued by cold, wet weather for much of the trip and didn't seem to be much enjoying it. He was at present living and working for himself in the States which meant he could take a few months off for a long bike ride. He originated from North Yorkshire and was hoping to catch up with some friends when he reached there.

He was continuing on to the hostel at Bridlington that evening, whereas I was booked into a small bunkhouse in Nafferton, just a mile or so east of Driffield. This time before parting company we exchanged mobile telephone numbers so that if either of us needed any support of any kind on our journey we could contact the other. There was a possibility of meeting up again at Scarborough Youth Hostel as we both intended staying there the following night.

Nafferton was easy to find as the No. 1 route went through the middle of it, but I found myself cycling to and fro before I manage to locate Nether Lane Bunk Barn, eventually finding it in the front garden of a detached house. The door was answered by a smiling lady who introduced herself: 'Hi, you must be Enid. I'm Annette. Welcome to our bunk barn.'

Nether Lane Bunk Barn

She was eager to show it to me and we walked over towards an outbuilding, saying, 'I haven't had it open long and I hope you won't mind if you don't unpack your belongings into it quite yet. You see I have two local councillors and a press photographer coming to interview me in an hour about my new enterprise. You will have it to yourself tonight. I don't like to mix people who don't know each other.'

When we entered, I could see immediately why she didn't want my muddy kit spread around. It was immaculate. Annette explained the background of her project to me. She lived with her husband Paul, a businessman, in the house which stood on a small piece of land with a tumble-down outbuilding which they used just as a shed. She felt there was a gap in the market for well-priced accommodation in East Riding for cyclists, walkers, fishing parties and wildlife enthusiasts, because tourism was growing, especially following a large influx of cyclists the previous year. So with advice and support from the local council's business service team she decided to convert their outbuilding into a small bunk barn.

Today was the day when the councillors were coming to visit (and assess its business potential?) and she wanted it to look its best. I hesitatingly asked if it would be okay if I made myself a cup of tea before the 'inspectors' arrived. She replied, 'Of course, and you'll find some cake and biscuits in a tin by the kettle. Oh, and it's totally up to you but I've told them I have a cyclist staying tonight, and if you're agreeable they would like to include you in the interview too?' I could see that my presence could add a touch of authenticity to Annette's bunk barn so agreed to her request.

Looking over at my bicycle and realising the layers of mud on caked to it would not enhance any photographs they might want to take, I inquired as to whether she had a bucket and a brush I could borrow to spruce it up. Even better she showed me where I could use a hose. She left me to it while I had a further look around inside the bunk barn.

There were three bunks made up with clean bedding and duvets, a shower room and a kitchen area up one end. It had been kitted out to a high standard and everything was brand new. No wonder Annette was so proud of her new 'baby'. There was even a vase of flowers sitting on the shelf beside a rack of 'country-style' magazines and a small television fixed to a bracket above.

After a quick cup of tea and slice of home-made fruit cake taken sitting at a table and chairs on the wooden balcony along the front of the bunk barn, I set to with the hose on my bicycle. There was a lot of mud to remove and with the aid of a brush I was able to smarten it up ready for its public viewing.

There wasn't time to also clean or groom myself before they arrived, so apart from brushing my hair I had my usual unkempt after-cycling look about me. Annette led them over and introduced me. After scrutinising the bunk barn carefully, opening and shutting every cupboard door, peering out of the windows, they congratulated her on her splendid addition to East Riding's affordable accommodation for tourists.

Then turning to me, one of the councillors asked how I had found out about this place. I replied, 'It came up on a search on the Internet and Annette was very good at communicating with me by e-mail.' They were curious about my trip and then asked us to line up for some photographs. I stood behind my shiny bike in the hope of deflecting the attention away from my own unwashed appearance. Their final comments to Annette were very encouraging as they applauded her initiative in developing this facility for active tourists and wished her every success. Annette was beaming as they left. I added, 'That seemed to go well – you have every right to be very satisfied with what you have here – the facilities you have provided are excellent. Can you send me a copy of the article if it appears anywhere please?'

'Yes, of course, I expect it will be in next week's Driffield Times, and thank you for agreeing to speak with them. It was good that you were here. Enjoy the rest of the evening.'

I went inside and heated up my ready-meal of lasagne in the microwave and served it up with a bag of salad I'd bought earlier in Driffield. I took it outside to eat as I had no intention of hiding from the sun which was making its first appearance of the day. By moving a chair round the corner I was able to sit in a patch of sunshine and soak up its warmth. I watched as swallows swooped around me, and smaller hedgerow birds took tasty morsels to feed their chicks, but the vegetation was very thick and as I didn't want to disturb it I couldn't see the actual nest. Once the sun disappeared behind the buildings across the road it cooled off quickly so I went back inside and sorted my things out.

I wrote my blog and then watched a bit of television, but I soon began to feel quite chilly. There was a convector heater which I switched on – it had to work hard to warm the room up. Before I went to bed I noticed a hot water bottle in one of the cupboards and filled it and put it in the bed to warm it up. However, even with the warm bottle I still spent my coldest night so far. As this was close to Midsummer's Day I would have to add as a caveat to my unreserved recommendations for this bunk barn that going there out of the summer period might require the occupants to take with them and wear a few extra layers.

Chapter Fifteen

THE BLUE POOL INCIDENT

After breakfast in my little one-person bunk barn, I packed everything into its usual place on my bike, said goodbye and wished Annette good luck with her venture then set off towards Bridlington. It was the first morning of my trip that I wasn't wearing long trousers over my shorts – it felt a touch warmer and I thought I might get a bit of colour on my legs. But that would have to wait until later in the day because for the moment although it was reasonably bright the sky was overcast. I had a pleasant run into Bridlington, about fifteen miles; it was a new place for me to visit and I was in good time for morning coffee on the promenade.

I found a sea-front café and ordered a cappuccino – normally I'm more of a 'black coffee with cold milk' person but it must have been the appearance of the sun which encouraged me to break out of my usual habit. I sat down at a table, leaned back in my chair and soaked up the sun for a few minutes. Perry Como, Matt Munro and the likes were crooning away on the sound system and the ladies behind the counter, doing brisk business, informed me that they played these songs 'because it's what our customers like.' There were plenty of people, presumably both locals and tourists, strolling along the promenade 'taking the sea air'. It reminded me of Bournemouth in Dorset, where I frequently do the same myself. Bridlington had a nice feel about it and I liked it.

I enjoyed the rest of my cycle run along the prom before turning inland to avoid the long coastline around Flamborough Head. A few miles later when I reached Bempton I took a right turn sign-posted *Bempton Cliffs RSPB Site*; it would add about three miles on to my route but I wanted to take the opportunity to see the nesting sea birds on the cliff. I padlocked my bike on to a rack by the visitor centre, had a quick chat to the RSPB ranger on duty about the best spots to visit and then walked down to the cliff edge.

I was quite surprised to see so many other people doing the same as me and as I made my way along the clifftop path it was easy to spot where the birds could be seen by where the small crowds gathered. Joining them, with my binoculars and camera, I watched as gannets, kittiwakes and guillemots brought the cliff to life with their wheeling and calling as they fetched in a constant supply of food for their chicks waiting noisily in nests on tiny cliff ledges.

Of course, everyone wanted to see the star of the show, the puffin, and we weren't disappointed – they were there but not in huge numbers. It appears they have declined by about two thirds across the whole country, although counting puffins is notoriously difficult because they nest in burrows, cracks and crevices. The reason for their decline is not known and more research is needed to fully understand why this iconic little bird is disappearing from our shores. However, on a brighter note, the gannet colony at Bempton is increasing and now numbers an astonishing 7800 pairs.

These statistics mirrored my sightings in Shetland the previous summer when I'd visited these islands as a participant in a wildlife holiday. It's a fantastic place to go to see not only a large variety of sea birds, but also to see them in huge numbers. The spectacle of tens of thousands of gannets there was a sight to remember, as well as the overpowering smell never to be forgotten. There was no shortage of puffins either and they were astonishingly tame allowing us to observe them from just a few feet.

However, I couldn't hang around bird-watching all day, I still had at least thirty miles to go to reach Scarborough and so I got back on my bike and rejoined my route which went due west for a few miles. I must have been enjoying my surroundings too much, lost in another world, because I missed my right turn and went sailing on. Once I realised, I stopped and had a look at the map and instead of retracing my route I saw an alternative right turn further on which would do me fine, only adding on a mile or so. In fact, it was a fortuitous decision because I spotted a farm shop outside Burton Fleming and went inside to buy something for my lunch.

The choice was not an easy one because there was an aroma of warm home-baking and tasty-looking fare laid out in the display. I opted for a sausage roll, heated up, and a slice of ham. Together with the half-full bag of salad I was carrying it would make an appetizing picnic. There was a pond and a grassy area across the road so I went over and sat down to enjoy my break. However, within seconds, I heard a loud 'BRMM, BRMM' noise starting up – the chap across the road had decided that now would be a good time to cut his lawn on a sit-on mower. As a bike is quickly transportable I decided to move on and find a quieter lunch stop, which I did a bit further on – I love to hear the natural sounds of the countryside around me so the minor inconvenience of the upheaval was worthwhile.

It was turning out to be my warmest day so far by a long shot, and I stripped down to T-shirt and shorts. This would be my normal cycling gear in June but the past couple of weeks had not been normal – I wanted to make the most of it as I had, perhaps unwisely, looked at the weather forecast for the few days ahead and didn't like what I saw. Apart from a brief stop for a breather in a recreation ground in Cayton I continued into Scarborough, a town I'd visited before but didn't know very well.

My route took me along the cliff edge above the bay. Seeing the town's beautiful situation made it obvious why Scarborough has become a popular seaside resort – in fact it was Britain's first. Similar to Woodhall Spa, in Lincolnshire, it was a spa which first attracted visitors to Scarborough, way back in the first part of the 17th century. The addition of a railway link from York in 1845 and the opening of the Grand Hotel, the largest in Europe, and one of the largest in the world at that time, sealed its prominence as a resort. My guidebook added a bit of interesting numerological information, interesting that is if you have the kind of mind that I do: the Grand Hotel was built with four towers to represent the seasons, 12 floors to represent the months, 52 chimneys to represent the weeks and originally 365 bedrooms which represented the days of the year – oh, how I love that kind of stuff.

An impressive bridge over a deep valley came into view and I purposefully detoured so as to cross it. A plaque told me an iron bridge was erected here because there was quite a steep descent to the sea front at this break in the cliff. When it opened in 1827 crowds flocked to see a mail coach and horses gallop at full speed across the bridge. It has not changed from the 19th through to the 21st century in that the bridge still provides great views and is a fashionable promenade for Scarborians (official term, not mine) and visitors alike.

After crossing the bridge I pushed my bike down the steep descent, too much of a scaredy-cat to freewheel, and found myself at the South Sands. With summer having descended upon Scarborough this afternoon, the beach was a popular place to be, and I decided to join them, well not exactly on the sand as it's not ideal for the bike, but I sat on a jetty which was being used as a handy ramp for parents with pushchairs to get on and off the beach. I stayed there for a while and it was truly wonderful to get a good dose of summer sun. I watched as children built sandcastles and ran back and forth to the sea for bucketfuls of water to pour into their little moats. The ice-cream vendor was doing swift business. Fathers were joining in the fun. This was Scarborough as I wanted it to be on a late June afternoon. It reminded me of an afternoon in Dorset fifty years ago…

My parents had taken the four youngest children, that was me and three of my brothers, to stay in a rented caravan just outside Weymouth in Dorset. Just to set the scene I'll quote some bits from my diary which I wrote at the time:

> Went into Dorchester… looked into the museum but it charged so we didn't go in…then to Maiden's (sic) Castle but could not see anything because it was all in ruins. Had dinner [picnic] in a big field…started our first test match… Alan and Enid won three, Colin and Bryan won one…one test match still to go. Went on to Blue Pool District.

It's significant here that I don't mention any further details about the Blue Pool, protecting my Dad partly, but his shame was also transmitted to me, and by not recording the incident perhaps it would be as if it hadn't happened. However, that's not the case – I don't need it written down on paper to remember – it's indelibly printed in my mind.

The Blue Pool is a Dorset tourist attraction, a flooded disused clay pit, containing very fine particles that diffract light in different ways, sometimes so that it looks green, sometimes turquoise. Surrounding the

Pool is heath, woodland and gorse inhabited by squirrels, rabbits, badgers and deer, and criss-crossed with sandy paths. So far, so good – sounds an interesting place to take the family for the afternoon – that's obviously what my parents thought.

We drove into the car-park and strolled over to the entrance, where my parents examined the entrance fees, and didn't like what they saw. At today's price a family ticket would cost fifteen pounds but, not surprisingly, I don't remember what the price we saw displayed was in 1963. If my father was alive today it wouldn't surprise me though if *he* could recollect the price, and the reason why is revealed in the following story.

A short, quiet huddle (or was it a loud, noticeable debate?) then took place amongst us and the next thing I knew I was following the others over to the far side of the car-park and down a path which ran alongside a high-interlocking wire fence (to keep intruders out of The Pool). The heath vegetation was too dense to see anything on the other side but we simply were out for an enjoyable walk, or so I thought. However, we came to a point in the fence where there was a large gap and I followed the others through it and started heading towards The Pool. Suddenly, emerging from the undergrowth was a 'security guard' (or the 1963 equivalent), 'Hello there, may I see your tickets please?'

'Ah, well you see sir, we just came through a gap in the fence over there, have we done something wrong?' came my father's reply.

'I'm afraid so, you have entered the Blue Pool and you need a ticket for that. Now let's see there are five of you so that will be *[1963 price]* pounds.'

So my (poor) Dad stumped up and we were then allowed to proceed over to the Blue Pool, but I don't think any of us got much enjoyment out of the rest of the afternoon. I remember my Dad being additionally irritated because he realized afterwards that he'd been overcharged (either he'd paid the price of five adults or he hadn't been given a family ticket – my memory doesn't serve me well enough to remember the detail). My over-riding recollection of the occasion is just the intense embarrassment felt by my father at being humiliated in front of his children – he was, after all, a staunch Church of Scotland elder and we'd been brought up to always be completely honest about money. In later years we used to sometimes mention 'The Blue Pool Incident' to my Dad when we wanted to get a rise out of him, but never once did he ever laugh or even smile when we goaded him about it.

To end this story on a happier note I also noted in my diary: *Came back to Weymouth to go to the carnival. I went on the Wild Mouse and Helter Scelter* [sic] *... on to Bertram Mills Circus ... great ... lady went up ladder with a tray of glasses balanced on a sword in her mouth ... she dropped it so had to start again ... great fun.* [Next day] *Finished 5th test match ... we won.*

🚲 🚲 🚲 🚲 🚲 🚲 🚲 🚲

Back to Scarborough and it was time to head for the Youth Hostel which was on the northern outskirts of the town. I hugged the shore to go beside the harbour – I took the opportunity to cycle out to the far end of the pier where I watched the fisherman messing about in their boats and yachts returning from their day out. Actually I was just putting off the time I had to go inside to the hostel because it was such a beautiful evening, but eventually I did and signed in at the reception. The warden greeted me, 'Hello, I have something for you,' and handed over a small package in a brown envelope.

'Oh, how wonderful. That'll be my camera,' I grinned at him.

I took my things up to the dormitory assigned to me and found I had the room to myself. Then I took my teabags downstairs and put the kettle on, when in walked Peter. So over a cup of tea we chatted about the last couple of days. He'd met up with another hosteller at Bridlington YH who cycled out to the end of Flamborough Head with him which he had enjoyed.

Scarborough YH is situated in a dark (and rather dismal) valley in which I was unable to get a mobile wi-fi signal which would allow me to check my e-mails. As I had no food either I decided to cycle up to a carvery-type restaurant I'd noticed when I passed earlier while looking for the hostel. I thought I'd get a quick bite to eat there and as it was on a hill I would probably get a signal and could do my e-mails.

I was right about the second bit but wrong about the speed with which it took to get a roast dinner – I had to stand in a queue for a good half-an-hour – but it was tasty and filling when at last I did get to eat it.

Back at the hostel Peter and I made ourselves comfortable in armchairs in the television room and chatted some more. I noticed Peter just had socks on his feet. 'Why no sandals?' I asked.

Back came the reply, 'One of them must have fallen off the back of my bike without me noticing it, so I threw the other one away.' He seemed unconcerned by his loss. We watched the weather forecast which issued severe weather warnings for the north-east for the next few days, with specific reference to heavy rainfall and expected floods. With that unwelcome news I went off to bed.

I had really enjoyed the last three days, stopping off at interesting places for a break or to have a look around, made possible because the weather had been clement. This was what it was all about for me. Tomorrow's ride to Whitby sounded a doddle – it was only 20 miles along an old railway track – that couldn't be too difficult could it?

Chapter Sixteen

STRUGGLE THROUGH PUDDLES

I came down to the kitchen the following morning and took my milk, pot of yogurt and bread roll out of the 'refrigerator', only to find they were frozen solid – it wasn't a 'fridge, it was a freezer! Fortunately there was a microwave and I set about defrosting my breakfast before I could eat it. Peter popped his head round the door, 'Good morning, Enid. Are you having breakfast?' I told him of my silly mistake as he put the kettle on.

It wasn't too long before I joined him in the dining room with my breakfast; he was tucking into a 'full English' cooked by the warden. Peter suggested we cycle together to Whitby if I was agreeable, which I was. I told him that on arriving at Whitby, hopefully by late morning, I wanted to visit the Captain Cook Museum, which was sited in the 17th century house by the harbour where the young James Cook lodged as an apprentice. Peter said he'd like to see it too. Looking out of the window we could see that the rain was already with us. I thought, 'Best to get out there and get our short cycle ride over with for the day.'

Our bicycles were in a locked shed across from the hostel's entrance so, trying to stay as dry as possible, we carried our gear over to the shed and packed it onto our bikes (securely, hopefully?) Then set off along the driveway, out on to the road and immediately up a fairly steep hill.

When I reached the top of the hill I noticed that my GPS was telling me that I needed to take the next left turn, and sure enough I saw that it was sign-posted as the cycle route. A bit further along was another sign-post to the right but I thought I'd wait for Peter as he was behind me. After several minutes there was no so sign of him, but not wanting to hang about in the rain I continued.

About a mile further on I crossed the main road and I realised what Peter must have done. He'd stayed on the main road all the way from the hostel and had only joined the cycle path here. By now he would be in front of me and by waiting for him I had let him increase that lead; this was soon confirmed when a bit further on I could clearly see his tyre marks in the mud. He, of course, thought I was ahead of him!

More about this route: it doesn't seem to matter which guide book or website I consulted as they are all in agreement that it is:

Probably North Yorkshire's best cycling trail along an old railway line. With glimpses of the North Sea and several old stations to pass through it is a most picturesque and nostalgic trip back to the era of the steam train.

Needless to say, on this wet morning, the idyllic scene above was not the one I encountered – the cinder path was already waterlogged. The rain turned into a torrential downpour and as well as deep puddles, one after the other, there were also numerous rocks on the path. After trying to dodge these obstacles over and over again I realised that I would have to dismount because I never knew when I was going to hit a submerged rock. Progress was painfully slow. The path was a running torrent coming down the hill towards me and I was soon soaked, mud-splattered and cold.

Although, I believe, I passed quite close to the edge of the cliff in places, I could see nothing because visibility in the rain was next to nothing. When I saw a yellow rain cover lying on the path ahead I realised Peter was dropping more of his belongings. I tucked it into my pack to return to him next time our paths crossed.

Much of the next bit was through woods where the track was washed away; I plodded my way upwards to the highest point on the route, through the squelchy mud and pushed my bike as best I could. I saw a couple of workmen up ahead, in fluorescent waterproof gear – they were wielding spades. I nodded and attempted a smile. One of them spoke to me, 'It's a right mess this, isn't it? We've found the cause though. It's these farmers – they don't put no drainage in their fields and all this water just runs straight on t' track and washes it away. Sorry for the inconvenience.'

I could see from my map that the watershed on this route was at Ravenscar and I hoped that over the other side the water might drain away somewhere else other than down the cycle path. I came out on to a road just before the old station at Ravenscar, described in the guide as:

A former station at 631 feet above sea level. It can be quite a bleak and windy spot.

No truer words were ever spoken – I was freezing – too cold to stop. The route followed a metalled road around the old station before climbing back to join the old track – the streets were deserted. There was quite an eerie gloom about the place – the mist was thick and I could only see a few yards in front of me – there was an uncanny stillness in the air.

I checked my map to see if there was an alternative route by road but the only way would have been up on to the moor (even bleaker and scarier?), then by following minor lanes up hill, down dale and weaving backwards and forwards across a large area I *might* have been able to navigate my way through it on a clear day but I knew I would get hopelessly lost if I left the railway trail in these conditions. So there was nothing for it but to battle on along the mucky and sodden track.

The good news going down the other side was that the path was intact, but the puddles were so large they more or less merged into one long lake. In other circumstances I could have yelled, 'Whee!' lifted my feet off the pedals and gone charging through, but I didn't – I pedalled carefully and slowly through each small lake not quite sure what was lying in wait for me under the surface.

The next time my path crossed a road I had another look at the map and decided that if I turned off on to this road it would go through the village of Fylingthorpe and with a bit of luck I could make my way to a B road and then on to an A road and so on to Whitby. I was so fed up of the state of this atrocious cycle path that I thankfully swung on to the metalled road and free-wheeled down a steep hill into the village. But what goes down must go up, and in the case of the North York Moors this meant *steeply*. After a wrong exit from the village on my first attempt, I then tried a different road but halfway up the hill I was struggling so much that I gave up. My energy levels were low and my dejected spirit wasn't helping.

I could see from the map that all the roads had black arrows on them (meaning steep hills) and in the present conditions I couldn't face the uphill struggles followed by heavy traffic on the A road I would need to take later. I decided I'd rather take on the puddles and lakes on the cycle path – I was soaking wet through anyway – so I retraced my steps back to the railway track.

If my younger brother Colin had been with me, he probably would have made some comment along the lines of, 'I thought you would have felt at home in the puddles, little sis. You seemed to like sitting in one at the bottom of the slide at that place outside Dundee – what was its name?'

'Spitalfield,' I would have obligingly spat out in reply. It's funny how brothers have a habit of remembering these incidents. This one took place on the second day of a summer holiday to the Scottish Highlands when I was 8¾ years old.

We had all piled into the old jalopy on the Friday evening after Dad finished work, with our outstandingly-unstylish caravan in tow, to make a start on our long journey to the Highlands for our annual summer holiday. After Coupar Angus, not much more than 12 miles from home, car-trouble ensued and we had to get out and push the car and caravan into a lay-by, where the decision was made to spend the night.

The following morning it was necessary for my Dad to go back to Dundee to get the car clutch fixed. Just by chance our lay-by was in the small village of Spitalfield adjacent to the playing field where there were swings, a roundabout and a chute.

'Ooh, look a chute,' I cried and ran over to the steps, up them, down the slide and straight into a large puddle at the bottom. 'Splash!' A wet and muddy bottom was my reward and I was never allowed to forget that day. Brothers!

🚲 🚲 🚲 🚲 🚲 🚲 🚲 🚲

Back in the North Yorkshire Moors, I was a lot wetter, muddier and colder than I had been in the Spitalfield puddle but I soldiered on and four hours after leaving the hostel in Scarborough I arrived in Whitby. An average speed of five miles per hour – very slow but not bad in the circumstances really. Being in a cold state did not make for clear thinking and I took a couple of wrong turns in Whitby before I finally found the Backpacker's Hostel which I was booked into.

When I rang the doorbell I wasn't very hopeful of finding anyone in, so was pleased when I saw the door opening in front of me and a lady

Bike dripping in hall, shoes stuffed with newspaper and waterproofs hanging up

standing there, 'Oh, come on in out of the rain. Isn't this weather we're having just awful? Are you Enid? I wasn't sure what time you'd arrive.'

I was so pleased to be greeted warmly by name, but having been encouraged to bring my bike into the wide hallway I was acutely aware of how much water and mud I was bringing in with me. Fortunately the flooring was terracotta tiles. At that moment I resembled a drowned rat and I was very grateful to Birgitta, who later told me she was Swedish-born, and could see that I was in a fairly helpless state.

She encouraged me to take off my dripping outer layers and one by one I hung them up on the hooks along the wall. The filth was getting splattered everywhere but I couldn't avoid it – I could clean it up later. Birgitta explained I was the only booked overnight guest so I would get the room to myself – I was getting used to this, but thankful because it would mean I could spread my gear around the room to dry.

She showed me around the rest of the hostel, consisting of a modern kitchen, large dining area and cosy sitting area with TV. I knew it was going to make a comfortable base for me for the night. As an unexpected and wonderful kindness to me, Birgitta insisted on taking away a bundle of my wet clothes to her apartment upstairs to put in the washing machine and she even dried it for me. What a wonderful guardian angel to appear just when I needed one!

Once I'd showered and changed into warm dry clothes I began to feel more human again; a cup of tea to wash down the sandwich I'd transported through the rain from Scarborough completed the job and then I was ready to go out and explore the town of Whitby. I picked up a town guide leaflet from the dresser. Miraculously it had almost stopped raining, but Birgitta wasn't yet done with her kindness – she even pressed an umbrella into my hand as I went out.

It was difficult to imagine what the town would have looked like in different weather – I was seeing it through a grey mist, with glimpses of dark sea between drab buildings. This road led down to a narrow lane and the Captain Cook Museum. I stopped to read the sign outside – it was mid-afternoon by now and I wavered on the pavement – was it just that my enthusiasm for finding out more about Captain Cook had waned or was it the five pounds admission ('Blue Pool syndrome')? I walked on.

A bridge took me across the River Esk. I stopped halfway over and looked up and down the river – boats, small and large, commercial and private, several deep lined both banks. It was obviously still a thriving port. The bridge itself was a splendid structure – made of steel and able to swing open to allow shipping traffic to pass through. It opened in 1881, to replace an earlier wooden bridge which was creating problems for the larger steel ships being built upstream.

I consulted my guide and was attracted by the Art Gallery and Museum, a short walk up the hill. It was housed in a fine brick building dominating Pannett Park. I walked up to the front desk to gain entry but the gentleman said, 'I'm sorry madam, we are closed. Last entry was at 4 o'clock and we close in thirty minutes.'

Was it really that time already? I looked down at my watch – 4.02pm – I had just missed it. I saw a sign to a tearoom and pointed to it, 'Is there still time to get a cup of tea?' The attendant was reluctant to allow me through because to get to the tearoom in the basement I would need to go past some of the exhibits. Noticing his hesitation, I added with a half-smile, 'I promise I won't look at any of the displays. I'll go straight to the tearoom.'

'If you're quick they might still be serving,' he replied with a deadpan face.

I was in luck, and ordered a pot of Earl Grey tea and a generous slice of homemade fruit cake. There were some newspapers on a stand so I took the opportunity to see what was happening in the world – actually, nothing that I needed to know about there and then.

I ascended the stairs after my refreshments and was able to dawdle for a few minutes in front of a glass cabinet displaying some jet jewellery – a black shiny mineral mined in Whitby in the 19th C – made popular by Queen Victoria when she went into mourning after the death of Price Albert. But not for long, 'We're closed now. Can you please make your way out,' warned the attendant, glaring at me.

However, I wasn't finished with the building yet as the Art Collection was housed in rooms either side of the front entrance and they were open for a bit longer due to a committee meeting or something taking place. I made the most of the short time and enjoyed looking at paintings of old Whitby by local artists.

But there was no escaping the miserable drizzle outside and eventually I went out into the park. Looking about me I thought, 'This looks interesting'; I could see various structures and individual gardens, so I went to have a closer look at the nearest one. It was a series of huge wooden arches – they were made from oak and they led into a commemorative garden – a sandstone rock featured the inscription: *We will remember them.*

I took out my camera and offered up a swift prayer to it for finding its way back to me. Then I amused myself for quite a while taking shots of the wonderful array of trees and plants arranged around ponds and providing framed views of the harbour down below. By using black/white and sepia colours I felt I could capture the atmosphere of what were almost timeless surroundings. I was transported back a hundred years or so as I looked for interesting angles to take shots.

Now in the mood for photography and finding something to usefully occupy me on this dreary afternoon I walked on down to the harbour and past the Fish Quay where I took some pictures of fishing boats. Then I walked out to West Pier and round to a bleak cove – it was a desolate place that afternoon – deserted, a cold spray coming straight off the North Sea. The time-worn iron seats lined up above the sandy cove, empty of people, seemed to sum up this resort on this cold and dismal afternoon.

I couldn't leave Whitby without sampling its fish and chips so I stopped off on the way back to the hostel and bought some. Verdict? Absolutely delicious. They almost allowed me to forget the appalling weather from earlier in the day. I had seen no sign of Peter and wondered where he was staying.

Whitby Cove on a damp and dreary June afternoon

I sat down in the hostel lounge to relax, write my blog and sort out my route for the next few days, and soon Birgitta joined me for a chat. She related her story to me of how she had come over from Sweden, married a local Yorkshire man and taken on the hostel to run.

Andy, my son, rang for a chat and we consoled each other over the dreadful cycling conditions. He was heading to Herefordshire the following day to take part in the Mountain Mayhem 24-hour mountain bike challenge. If the forecast was accurate then he and the rest of his team were in for a mud bath – all great fun when you're young.

This was literally half a world apart from when I cycled with Andy and his elder brother, James, in Africa. They were 9½ and 12 years old respectively when the three of went to live in Botswana. Why did we go there? The simplest answer is because I applied for a job advertised by the British Council for teachers to work for the Botswana Government. The deeper reasons lie within my character and emerge from many of the experiences I have already talked about in this book. My contract was for two years which would tie in neatly with James starting his GCSE course on our return.

Our baggage allowance seemed massive because we were entitled to one each, so not knowing what bicycles might be available to buy there I decided we'd take three with us. That was in addition to the refrigerator, tent, television, computer (our first laptop) and three huge suitcases of personal belongings.

I was allocated to a school in Francestown in the north east of Botswana, because there was a suitable private school there that the boys could attend. I would be teaching mathematics (in English) in a large state secondary school which selected its pupils by an entrance exam; most of whom came from outlying villages and boarded. The local primary schools taught all their subjects in Setswana so wouldn't be suitable for my sons to attend.

Although it was August when we arrived and not the hottest season, we took a while to acclimatise and found it very hot to walk very far, even just along the main street, during the day. Later on I bought a car – but our bikes were our main means of transport for getting to and from school when we first arrived, and they were the coolest way (in more than one sense?) of moving around Francestown. We always attracted a lot of attention wherever we went, a white mother and two young sons, one of whom had blond hair, were an unusual sight – so early on we had to get used to lots of staring and waving.

One Saturday afternoon a couple of weeks after we'd arrived, we decided to venture out of the town on our bicycles along a back road. We didn't get very far before both James and I got punctures in *both* our front and back tyres; then we had to pull two 8cm long thorns out of Andy's tyres. This obviously wasn't going to work.

After asking around we discovered that everybody had solid tyres and so we had them fitted on all three bikes. They sound uncomfortable but they are made of rubber and were just perfect for our purpose. In fact, when I returned my bike to the UK at the end of my contract I kept the solid tyres on for several months – no punctures, no brainer!

After about a month I purchased an *Isuzu* single cab *bakkie* into which we could put the three bikes – under the canopy in the back. One morning we headed out to Shashe Dam – the local reservoir where we could cycle around its shore and along country roads. Early morning runs were the best, as it was coolest, and then we could breakfast under the shade of a thorn tree. There was plenty of birdlife to watch and if our friends, Ray and Val, were with us then they would identify the species we saw.

The bikes made it possible for us to get out outdoors and exercise in a climate which wasn't conducive to walking, as well as giving us a lot of fun.

Andy with our Isuzu at Shashe Dam near Francestown, Botswana

All three of us still have fun cycling but it's a lot more enjoyable when it's not cold and wet as it was throughout England this June of 2012.

But back to the present, and I had some decisions to make over just how I was going to get to Tyneside over the next couple of days. The forecast was for more rain later on tomorrow and the following day, accompanied by strong winds on the moors. Tomorrow was due to be the toughest so far, an ascent of 1232 metres up to the highest point of the day at 250 metres on the moors, and a total distance of 45 miles. My feeling was that if I made an early start I could reach the highest and bleakest point of the day before the worst of the weather set in; the descent down to Middlesbrough on the northern side of the moors would be manageable, but not pleasurable, in the rain and wind. The dreadful storms forecast for the following two days might mean I would look at getting a train for one of these sections if there was a suitable one.

I had been looking forward to cycling on the North Yorkshire Moors, a beautiful scenic area, and wanted to make the most of my opportunity when I was on its doorstep. I wasn't for giving up at this stage, so I got off to bed intending to get a good night's sleep.

Chapter Seventeen

'CAULD WINTER WAS HOWLIN', O'ER MOOR AND O'ER MOUNTAIN'[1]

In the morning I gathered together my belongings (now dry) which were spread out all over the dormitory and got them packed on to my bicycle. As it was parked in the hall I didn't have to brave the weather outside yet. Breakfast consisted of fruit and yogurt, a roll with cheese and a cup of coffee. Birgitta had said she wouldn't be there to see me off so I slipped away quietly.

Well, so much for the morning forecast which was for a dry spell – the drizzle was already quite steady. I crossed the bridge over the river and stopped at the Co-op supermarket to buy some sandwiches and snacks for sustenance during the day. Before I got back on the bike I put on my full wet-weather gear and made sure my panniers had their waterproof covers over them.

I never quite trusted these waterproof covers so everything inside was also in separate polythene bags. My front handlebar bag had been new at the beginning of my trip and seemed rather an expensive indulgence at the time – an *Ortlieb Ultimate* fully-waterproof storage bag, with a magnetic lid and lock to attach it to the handlebars. With it I purchased the optional map case which fastened on the top of the bag with Velcro and was again fully waterproof. In the event, they proved to be terrific buys and kept everything at the front completely dry – both items are highly recommended by me.

I then found my route out of town, a busy road up a steep hill, which soon turned on to the extension of the railway track from yesterday. On consulting my map I decided not to go off-road and to stick to metalled

---

[1] From 'THE ROAD AND THE MILES TO DUNDEE'

roads – this turned out to be reasonably straightforward. To rejoin the No. 1 route in the Esk valley I had to cross a main road and come down a long hill into the village of Ruswarp. Once back on my signed route I enjoyed cycling close to the northern bank of the river – it was very pretty even in the wet conditions on this particular morning.

However, this didn't last for more than a couple of miles, when my route swung off on to a path which all too soon turned uphill. Straight away I knew I wasn't going to be able to cycle up it, it must have been a 1 in 3 slope in parts and it was on a loose surface. It was very hard work even pushing the bike up to the top and I had to take plenty of stops to get my breath back. From looking at the map, it became all too obvious to me I had made a big mistake in going all the way down the road to the River Esk. If I had stayed up high coming out of Whitby I could have joined this route at the small hamlet of Aislaby and saved myself the huge effort of getting up this hill.

By the time I reached Aislaby I was already tired, damp and somewhat irritated by my digression – not an auspicious start to my big ride over the Moor ahead. I noticed a bench so sat down and took a short break here in an attempt to rehydrate, eat a banana and regain my composure before I set off again.

My route now stayed up on the valley side and passed through very pleasant countryside, but because it had strenuous ups and downs for mile upon mile, I found it hard to fully appreciate the scenery. It didn't help that the wind was continuously blowing the fine rain into my face. I wasn't coping well with the hills and found myself having to get off and push over and over again.

I climbed higher on to Lealholm Moor, heather-covered and vast, leading up to various summits hidden in the mist. I saw few cars and was surprised to come up behind two cyclists – why would anyone else want to be putting themselves through this purgatory? They seemed to be struggling even more than me. 'Hello,' we croaked amiably to each other but no one in their right minds wanted to hang around for any longer than necessary in these desolate conditions, so head down, I went on past them. How wild it was.

The road descended down to the Esk valley again and I arrived in the village of Danby. There was a sign-post to the railway station and I thought there might be a waiting room where I could sit and have my sandwiches. This small rural station was unmanned and I found a small waiting room on the platform. Inside I was out of the wind and rain and enjoyed tucking into my lunch. The posters on the wall advertised the Esk Valley Railway:

> *A 35 mile route between Whitby, a seaside resort, and Middlesbrough, a lively city; a stress-free way to view and explore the North York Moors; let the train take the strain as it chugs from village to village forming a link between these communities.*

'Mmm…Middlesbrough, that's where I need to get to,' I thought, 'let's have a look at the timetable. Next train arrives in Danby at 13.19.'

To be honest, I really didn't fancy my chances up on the moor all afternoon; I was less than halfway and the heavy rain and strong winds were due to sweep in from the west any time now. Further on the route left the valley bottom and climbed up and across the moor again. I had to remember I was on my own and if any accident, minor or major, befell me or my bicycle I reckoned that hypothermia could set in pretty quickly in the low temperatures today and I could all too soon find myself in a grim situation. I felt vulnerable being alone in such a wild place. I decided I did not want to take the risk of being out on the moor by myself in these conditions – it would be irresponsible of me.

I looked at my watch – it was 12:28, so 51 minutes until the train was due – too long to sit in the waiting room when it was as cold as this. The next couple of miles were on the road along the valley bottom and even although I knew it would be undulating I knew I could easily reach the next station at Castleton Moor before the train was due at 13:22 and I wanted to be out on the road cycling for as long as possible today.

Not long later I reached Castleton Moor station and I could see from the map that I would still have time to continue to Commondale, one stop further along the line. The cycle track didn't follow the road which went up and across the moor along this next two-mile section – my route kept close to the railway and river. It made use of an off-road track but I reckoned that if I didn't like the look of it I would still have plenty of time to return to Castleton Moor.

In fact, this track turned out to be okay – I think I dismounted once or twice, but on the whole I found it rather pleasurable as it passed through meadows, across small bridges, finally emerging at a farm named *Foul Green* – fortunately it didn't live up to its name as I passed through it.

I noticed a gate leading off my track with a signpost to the station at Commondale and made my way down it and on to the platform. There was another small waiting room where I had about 20 minutes wait before my train was due. I wasn't tempted to cycle on any more at this stage as the route from here would be much tougher and the rain and wind were both picking up. It was a great pity that the conditions today had forced me to curtail my route – I had been looking forward to cycling over the moors – mountains were special to me – they had been part of my life for as long as I could remember.

My parents loved taking the family to the hills whenever they could – that meant either a couple of hours on a weekend afternoon to the Sidlaws or Angus Glens or further into the Highlands in summer holidays. I soon took to running and skipping over the heather-clad slopes and loved arriving at a 'trig' point, the concrete block signifying a triangulation point, and adding my stone to the cairn on the summit.

Our forays further north meant Dad could lead us up higher mountains and few in Scotland come higher than the Cairngorm massif, a favourite of his, with a suitable caravan site at its base, next to Loch Morlich. You may recall my story about falling into the puddle at the foot of the Spitalfield chute? Later on the same day that Dad returned with a new clutch we hitched on the caravan and motored on, spending the night at a site in Newtonmore, on the main A9 'Great North Road'. The following day we arrived at the Loch Morlich site by lunchtime.

The idea of developing a ski-resort on the high slopes of Cairngorm was in its infancy and development of the infrastructure was only beginning. My parents were keen to try out a new road which snaked its way up to a car-park at a height of 1800 feet, above which the first chairlift for skiers was being constructed.

We parked the car and I followed the rest of my family up the steep hill keeping to the line of the new chairlift. After a long ascent of more than 2000 feet we arrived at the summit of Cairngorm, 4084 feet, the sixth highest mountain in the UK. I don't remember the views from the top – maybe they weren't the sort of thing to impress a 8¾ year old or perhaps I was so conditioned to views from hilltops that at times I took them for granted?

The next piece is a quote from my diary:

> *We took the wrong path coming down and got lost. We saw the site from a hill. We got on to the road. Daddy went to get the car and we walked down. Daddy picked us up ¾ way down we were all soaking.*

That was my introduction to hill walking in the Cairngorms with my Mum and Dad. Perhaps there were lessons to be learnt?

Fast-forward one year and one day to 15th July 1962: Our next annual summer holiday to the Highlands.

Place: Loch Morlich caravan site.

Objective: The summit of Ben Macdui, 4296 feet, second highest mountain in Britain.

Members of summit party: Daddy, Mummy, Donald (17), Diana (15), Alan (13), Bryan (11), Enid (9), Colin (8)

Attire: Light trousers or shorts and tops, anoraks, gloves and hats optional, boots for the lucky few, shoes or wellingtons for the rest

Equipment: Map, compass (emm….sadly no)

Food carried: Picnic lunch

Starting Point: Car-park at the foot of the chairlift which had opened the previous December)

Time: 1pm (methinks in retrospect maybe a bit late?)

1st Sensible move: Left a note in a police box at the car-park outlining our route and expected time of return, i.e. 5pm

2nd Sensible move: Rode by chairlift to within a few hundred feet of the Cairngorm summit saving us more than 2000 feet of climbing.

We reached the top of Cairngorm with ease and from there we headed across the 4000 feet high plateau toward Ben Macdui, a distance of around four miles, but more than that when the rise and fall of the hills in-between is taken into account. By late afternoon we conquered our second summit and main objective, Ben Macdui. This time I do remember admiring the views – Dad reckoned he could pick out Ben Nevis which was 63 miles to the west as the crow flies. While we sat in the shelter of the stone cairn and ate the rest of our picnic the mist descended quite suddenly.

> There has long been talk of a Big Grey Man on the summit of Ben Macdui. Many people have reported a strange presence sometimes accompanied by an eerie noise, a crunch, then another crunch as if someone was walking slowly across the stones. Level-headed men have been known to take to their heels, full of terror, and sworn they will never return by themselves.

As the mist swirled around us I could imagine a Big Grey Man lurking close by. When we stood up to start our long descent it must have been like a shot in the dark which direction to take without a compass, with only the 'spectre' to point the way – but was he to be a benevolent guide?

After about an hour and a half, it was soon obvious even to little ol' me that we were lost and wandering about with no clue as to which way to go to reach the top of the chairlift that would take us safely back down to our caravan. It was summer so at least there was no danger of darkness overcoming us at this stage, but there must have come a point when Dad realised he wasn't going to get us off the mountain that night and so what was the best option for spending a night at 4000 feet? He knew of the *Shelter Stone*, either from his days as a Scoutmaster or from seeing it marked on the map. It is a huge boulder which has come to rest at the base of a crag in such a position that it forms a roomy cave underneath. In the 1960s, I believe members of the Cairngorm Club (for hill-walkers) kept some emergency supplies there for lost walkers who needed to seek overnight shelter.

It was to this Shelter Stone that Dad now wanted to lead us. We caught a glimpse of Loch Avon through the mist, 1100 feet below us, and he knew that at its southern end was the Stone. We made our way carefully down the boulder-strewn steep mountainside to the bank of the River Avon, across which we needed to be to find the Stone. I remember my Dad carrying my little brother over the fast-flowing channel of water, and then returning to carry me over. We headed up through the thick mist to locate our shelter for the night but much to

Dad's frustration he couldn't find the Stone he was looking for. Looking at photographs of it now I can see how huge it is and the comparative comfort it would have provided us by having 'a roof over our heads'. But it wasn't to be and reluctantly we made our way back over the river the same way as we had come.

I suppose it was obvious to my parents how tired we all were and couldn't keep walking all night. We went over to a sandy beach on the shore of Loch Avon and huddled down together to get some rest. Me? I just zonked out although I did note that: *it was freezing*. Mum? I guess she didn't get much sleep.

I awoke just as it was beginning to get light and the first thing I saw was Bryan's face close to mine. 'Oh my goodness, he's got measles,' was the first thought that ran through my mind. On waking up properly and having another look I realised it was gravel stuck to his face.

Well, we knew exactly where we were, so it would be straightforward getting out of this mess wouldn't it? We climbed slowly back up the steep mountainside we had descended the previous evening; the mist was just as thick. At the top we were no better off and we still couldn't find the right direction. *We wandered about again,* I noted.

Then Bryan exclaimed, 'Quiet, listen, I can hear something.' We all listened.

'Rompy pompy pompy... Rompy pompy pompy,' we heard faintly.

We yelled in answer, 'We're here, we're here!' And so it was that we were found by a search party. I found out from them later that they yell the words *Rompy pompy pompy* because they contain sounds which travel well.

This group of about half a dozen rescuers soon located us and miraculously produced hot cocoa for each of us within minutes– I watched fascinated as one of the men pulled a catch on a can which instantaneously heated it up. This was quickly followed by *Mars Bars, chocolate and chewing gum* all round. They were an RAF search and rescue team from Kinloss who had been out all night looking for us. However, they told us there were at least 50 searchers in total out through the night scouring a large area of mountains for us; they included members of Gordonstoun School and a group of police and gillies[1] from Braemar.

These courageous and compassionate men, many of them volunteers, willingly gave up their time to look for us. Writing this now I feel very humbled and grateful. There had even been a helicopter out searching for us – I remember thinking how thrilling it would have been to be airlifted to safety by chopper! What a story to have told my class mates.

This magnificent band of men led us to the top of the chairlift; they offered to carry my Mum on a stretcher – she must have looked exhausted, poor thing – but she declined and walked on her own two feet. There were more hot drinks in the Ptarmigan Restaurant before we said goodbye to our rescuers and left them with an enormous 'heartfelt vote of thanks'. Finally after a ride down in the chairlift we limped wearily back to our car and then into our caravan at 10.15am. *We had dinner then went to bed*, was the simple phrase I wrote at the time.

This was 1962, not the present day, but even so within a couple of hours, the media had identified our caravan. 'Knock, knock, Mr Moir can you come outside and talk to us please? We're from the Daily Express/Inverness Press and Journal/Dundee Courier, etc.'

My Dad went over to his car and sat in there with them one at a time as he answered their questions as best he could or was willing to. The rest of the family was then called out by each press man to line up in front of our caravan and have our photograph taken, except Alan who refused to take part in the parade (bolshy and embarrassed teenager?). We are (nearly) all smiling in the published photographs: headlines such as *Family's night ordeal in the hills*, *Father tells of lost night in Cairngorms*. Smiling showed loyalty, I think, to our parents even thought we had gone through a dreadful ordeal at their hands, but we weren't going to breathe a word of what we might have been truly feeling to the media guys.

Last sentence recorded in my diary for that day:

My head was sore so I went to bed. Slept on bunk, got to sleep very quickly.

---

[1] A professional fishing or hunting guide in Scotland

MONDAY

PRESS AND JOURNAL

Family's night ordeal in hills

S... after an anxious night in the Cairngorms—Mr and Mrs Ralph Moir, Dundee, with their eldest son, Donald, and daughter, Diane, and (in front) Brian, Colin and Enid.

A DUNDEE father and mother and their six children told yesterday of a night they spent tired, cold and wet wandering around lost in the wild Cairngorm mountains.

They spoke of how they eventually became so tired they fell asleep on a sandy beach high up in the hills and sheltered behind rocks to try to keep warm.

The family are Dundee accountant, forty-eight-year-old Mr Ralph Moir, 307 Clepington Road, his wife Enid and their six children — Donald (17), Diana (16), Allan (14), Brian (11), Enid (10) and Colin (8).

They were on the first day of a two-week tour of the Highlands, staying in a caravan at Glenmore, when the incident happened.

They set off on Sunday in their car and motored to the car park on Cairngorm, where they left a note in a police box saying they would be returning again at 5 p.m.

The family took the chairlift farther up the mountain and then walked to the summit of Cairngorm.

The mist

From there they walked in fine weather to Ben Macdhui and it was when they set off to return to Glenmore that they ran into trouble.

Said Mr Moir, a scoutmaster in Dundee: "Suddenly the mist came down and we completely lost our way.

"We wandered around and eventually reached Loch Avon. We were wet and cold and tried to find the shelter stone nearby where we could get cover.

"But we lost all sense of direction and eventually decided to spend the night on the sandy beach at Loch Avon.

We sat down and tried to shelter as much as possible behind rocks and boulders.

"In the morning, conditions had cleared up considerably. We set off for our caravan and had only been walking a short while when we were met by an R.A.F. rescue team." he said.

Mr Moir, an experienced climber, said he had a map with him but no compass.

He said his compass had broken and he had intended to get another.

The mountain rescue team gave the family hot drinks and sweaters and took them down the chairlift to the lift station.

Mrs Moir said: "We are all fine now. We are glad to have got back safely."

More than 100 searchers from various centres, including Gordonstoun and Elgin schoolboys, took part in the search for the Moirs.

Press and Journal newspaper cutting telling the story of our ordeal in the Cairngorms.
I am on the right in the front row.

I do wonder what the media would have made of that story if it happened today. Who knows how long it would have run and run for, ending in a government inquiry no doubt questioning whether parents should be allowed to take their children into the mountains without some sort of qualification?

We all lived to tell the tale, although I am acutely aware that we did involve a large number of other people in our rescue. It was all part of forming the person I am today, just as everything else I have experienced has formed my character.

Post script to above: most fathers you would think would have learnt their lesson by now – not my Dad. A few years later there was a further incident, this time on Ben Loyal (in the far north of Scotland) involving the three youngest children and Dad. Near the top there are rocky buttresses leading to five different tops and we got separated from each other in different gullies. I was in tears – I didn't know where my Dad was. He wasn't answering my yells. Then I saw Alan, who appeared, full of terror crying out, 'Dad's using that thin bit of rope he took with him to climb up the rocks.' He then went haring off down the mountain to report this to my Mum, who was waiting patiently in the car at the foot of the mountain.

Poor Mum was incapacitated with painful varicose veins, and looking after my younger brother who had injured his ankle under a moving roundabout (it wasn't just chutes that came to bite us!). Her reply must have been something along the lines of, 'Why does that not surprise me about your father?'

Once again, we did all get back down safely, but goodness knows how. Perhaps Ben Loyal has its own *Old Grey Benevolent Man*?

🚲 🚲 🚲 🚲 🚲 🚲 🚲 🚲

The two-coach rural train chuntered into Commondale Station on time at 13.26. I opened the door and went to lift my bicycle on board when who should appear in front of me but Peter! He took the bike from me but had a struggle to find a place for it as there were already four bikes propped up in the entranceway. Bike stowed, I then joined Peter in the carriage where three Yorkshire lads were lounging.

Peter introduced me to his new friends. They had all got on the train at Whitby. It was obvious that none of us thought this was a day suitable for cycling over the moor. They were good fun and it was fortuitous that I was on the same train and able to share in the banter and laughter. The train rolled into Middlesbrough Station forty-five minutes later and many hands made light work of lifting my bike on to the platform for me. One of the lads asked where I was heading. 'A guest house in Clairville Road,' I replied showing him my map.

'Oh right, I know where that is. Turn right when you come out of here and you'll see a sign-post for a cycle route. Follow that and you'll be fine.'

They wished me well with the rest of my journey to Scotland and waved good bye. Peter was catching another train which would take him to stay with some friends for a few days in another part of Yorkshire. I think he had given up on his idea of travelling to Berwick-upon-Tweed; the wet weather had dampened his spirit for further adventure for the time being.

I found my guest house; my instructions were to telephone the landlord fifteen minutes before my arrival, but I had forgotten to do this so I phoned him from the front door step and waited for him to arrive by car. He was an Italian who owned several business properties and was very helpful when I asked him where I could safely leave my bike. 'Put it in my office on the ground floor. I'll give you the key for the morning.' He also showed me the dining room where breakfast was to be taken; there was a table already stacked with cereal packets. He pointed to a 'fridge and said, 'There will be milk, orange juice and butter in here in the morning, and fresh bread and rolls on the table. Just come in and help yourself. Coffee and tea bags are over here.' It was a 'do-it-yourself' breakfast but seemed well-organised.

I was given a room upstairs; it was quite small which I was glad of, because I put the heater on full blast (so what if it was Midsummer Day?) and soon heated it up. As it was the middle of the afternoon, the guest house was quiet and I took advantage of the bathroom along the corridor to have a long soak in the bath, also making good use of the warm soapy water to wash out a few clothes.

Feeling much better and carefully arranging my wet clothes around the room, *not* above the TV, I decided to go out and find a shop where I could buy some food for my evening meal. I ended up walking a couple of miles there and back but found an Aldi supermarket where I purchased what I needed. The rain was back on as I returned along the streets to my room.

The evening was spent as usual catching up on e-mails, my blog and watching a bit of television. I wasn't tempted to venture back out as I could hear the rain hammering against my window and the news reported 35mph winds in Middlesbrough. In addition there was the frequent sound of emergency-vehicle sirens looking after the residents of Middlesbrough on a Friday evening.

I knew I had made the right decision in getting on the train for part of my journey today. Lizzy's words came back to me, 'This is your journey, Enid, and you can do it in whatever way you want to.' I was safe and warm, and at that particular moment that was what mattered. I would do this one day at a time, not taking on more than I could chew on each section. This way it would be within my grasp to complete what I had set out to do. I was glad I wasn't stranded somewhere on the North Yorkshire Moors waiting for the sound of sirens as they tried to reach me.

Chapter Eighteen

DOWN, IN AND ACROSS RIVERS

I partook of the 'do-it-yourself' breakfast in the dining room which, true to my landlord's word consisted of a copious spread. I ate alone – as it was Saturday the other guests, who were probably long-stay guests, would have either gone away for the weekend or were having a lie-in. I wheeled my bike out from the office and was on the road by 9 o'clock.

My route took me on a cycle path along the southern bank of the River Tees which I crossed at the Tees Barrage, consisting of a dam, bridges, lock and fish pass. When it was constructed in 1991 it was the largest civil engineering project in the country. I got somewhat confused with the various cycle ramps looping on and off the bridges and it took me a few circuits before I found the correct direction heading north. On the north side of the river is a White Water Rafting Centre described as *'International class with four huge Archimedes screws'* – sounds like it could be painful if you navigated wrongly at these features. It promised *'adrenaline junkies and thrill seekers an exhilarating experience'*. I was ready for my first pause for the day so what could be better than to watch a couple of kayakers paddling the raging waters – not an activity for the faint-hearted though.

During my more-intrepid years I had tried both white-water kayaking and white-water rafting. As a young teacher in Glasgow I helped to run a hill-walking club for pupils in the school and was offered the opportunity to do a Mountain Leadership Training course at Faskally Outdoor Centre, near Pitlochry. I leapt at the chance, as I expect my father would have too if this course had been available to him as a Scoutmaster forty years earlier.

One thing led to another at Faskally and for a couple of years it became my 'home from home' at weekends as I grappled with navigation on all sorts of terrain, camping expeditions, river crossings, the finer features of weather and lightning, mountain rescue and learning about exposure – its causes, avoidance, recognition and treatment. How lucky I was to spend time building up my outdoor knowledge with a great bunch of instructors and with a lively group of other would-be leaders.

Friends I made there encouraged me to join a kayaking course which was spread over a few months. As well as practising various strokes we each had to carry out an Eskimo roll in front of the group. I admit, prior to our 'public demo', I went along to a swimming pool in Glasgow on 'kayak night' where we practised rolling over in diminutive-sized kayaks – I didn't find that so scary as on a proper river. The final day of the Faskally kayak course was a long run down the River Tay where there were several white-water rapids to negotiate. By the end of the day I had completed it and found it to be great fun; under the watchful eye of our experienced instructors I felt safe.

With the skills I had learned I was able to take my kayaking further afield: one trip was with a school group across Loch Morlich then paddling up a fast-flowing stream with white water; another was sea kayaking with a friend in Loch Broom at Ullapool; and I also explored the sunken city of Kekova, in Turkey, which was ruined by an earthquake in the 2nd century.

My first outing in a Canadian-style canoe was coincidentally enough in Canada, across Clearwater Lake in British Columbia to be precise. It was part of a trekking holiday I did in the Rockies when I was in my late forties. Our instructor's name was Ian and he told me his mother was born on the Island of Skye. This led us into an interesting chat with each other about Scotland and his previous jobs, one of which was as the Operations Manager for Mountain Wilderness Guiding in Nepal. He informed us that Clearwater is so called because the lake system is completely within the National Park area where there is zero tolerance to pollution and thus the water is 100 per cent pure; he demonstrated his trust by taking a drink straight from the lake. I found I liked the sitting position in an open canoe which allowed me to relax and enjoy the beautiful surroundings.

While living in Botswana we made a few visits to the Victoria Falls just over the border in Zimbabwe – an absolutely spell-bounding sight, especially when the Zambezi River was in spate and the flood waters gushed over the top at a rate of up to 3000 cubic metres a second. Bungee jumping off the Victoria Falls Bridge has to be one of the most challenging, terrifying, craziest things to do. We stood on the bridge a couple of metres away from the jumpers and watched them as they jumped – most did a forward-head dive, but a few did a backward flip. They dropped down into the water 111 metres below, not called the Mighty Zambezi for nothing, where a rescue boat was waiting to pick them up. We once gave a lift to a young couple on the far side of the bridge back to Victoria – they had both just done the jump – the tell-tale sign was their eyeballs on stalks popping out of the sockets. Only kidding... but definitely an activity I have never been tempted to do and never will.

I'm not quite sure why I was keen to go white-water rafting down the Zambezi; it was my choice entirely. It was advertised as:

'The best one-day white-water rafting experience in the world'.
Nearly half of the rapids are graded as *'Grade 5'* [grade 6 is unrunnable] – *'extremely difficult, long and violent rapids, steep gradients, big drops and pressure areas.'*

I opted for the half-day trip, because it conveniently fitted in with a morning's guided canoeing trip on the tamer waters *above* the Falls for my two sons.

The safety briefing beforehand was thorough – one piece of information which stuck in my mind was: 'If your raft capsizes and you fall in, you will float to the surface, but may immediately sink back down. Be patient because you will come back up again.' We were also related a scare story, which was fair enough: 'Last season one lady didn't have her lifejacket zipped up properly and she didn't survive...'

There would be ten rapids to negotiate throughout the morning – some of their names say it all:

Against the wall
The Boiling Pot
Morning Glory
Stairway to Heaven
Devil's Toilet Bowl

Commercial Suicide
Gnashing Jaws of Death

Strangely, when I got into the raft with the other four riders, our lifejackets all zipped up securely, I didn't feel particularly fearful – maybe I just thought it would be like my white-water kayaking and I managed that okay, didn't I? Well no … it wasn't at all like that.

Wedzi, our rower, sat in the middle higher up than us and from there gave us our instructions: 'Just do exactly as I say. When I shout 'move to the right' you all shift your weight over to the right....' and also, 'remember to do it at the exact moment I say it.'

'Okay Wedzi,' I thought, 'I've got that, sounds easy enough.'

We went down the first two rapids like clockwork obeying Wedzi's every word and I can honestly say I loved the thrill of it. On rapid number three, or was it four, we presumably weren't quick enough to shift our weight because the whole raft upended, went flying through the air and flipped over upside down in the water.

I remember realising I was underwater and rapidly moving downstream not having any idea whether I was upside down or not in the water – I didn't know which way was up and which was down. Fortunately, nature does though, and eventually I popped up out of the water, only to sink straight back down again. Ah, but I remembered being told this might happen so I allowed myself to go down and when I popped up again I was next to the raft. My time under the water had seemed like several minutes, although in reality I suppose it was only a minute or two. Wedzi hauled me back on board and soon the others were all accounted for too.

That spill and underwater experience had unnerved me so much that I was determined I would not fall out of the raft again. I reckoned if I clung on to the rope at the back of the raft even if we flipped again I would at least stay with the raft.

The rest of the trip down Batoka Gorge fortunately didn't provide any more spills. However, my knuckles were stiff for the following three days due to my clinging on to the rope for dear life for so long. If I had been able to relax I could have enjoyed the beautiful scenery of the narrow ravine we passed through. When we pulled the rafts out of the water for lunch on the beach I was relieved to be going no further and did not mind the steep climb out of the gorge to the Land Rover that returned us to Victoria. Once reunited with James and Andy they excitedly told me about their canoeing trip which they had thoroughly enjoyed; a part of me secretly wished I had opted for their milder trip.

Rafting on the Zambezi river. I am on the right desperately clinging on

As it turned out, our next canoe trip was a joint venture, joined by Will who came to Botswana to spend some time with us. We drove via Victoria Falls, then embarked on a twenty-four hour ferry trip down the full length of Lake Kariba, which took us to where the River Zambezi flows out and continues on its way through Zimbabwe. There we met with our guides for a four-day canoeing trip down the river to Mana Pools National Park They were Shay and Vitalis, a white and a black Zimbabwean respectively. Our companions on the trip were an Australian gent and two ladies, one Danish and the other Dutch.

We were put two to a canoe, except for James and Andrew who were paddled and guided by Vitalis. I hadn't imagined the river would be so wide; at times the far side was barely visible. We didn't always stay close to the bank as the crocodiles, sometimes huge (up to five metres?), basked there with wide-open mouths baring ferocious teeth – their way of cooling down Vitalis informed us. As we passed them, they usually slipped silently into the water, not to attack us I hasten to add, but because they felt safer there.

We had to watch out for hippopotamuses as we rounded bends; the guides knew where they were likely to be and were always very careful while approaching them, telling us to knock on our canoe with a paddle to give the hippos time to submerge before we passed. The message being, 'Do not spook a hippo.'

Hippos cause more deaths than any other animals in Africa, even although they are herbivorous. On this trip, the danger was that a hippo could tip our canoe over, and a crocodile could then make a meal of us. Shay carried a gun by her side at all times.

On our second day, I asked Shay whether they often took children on this trip. Her answer gave Will and I quite a shock.

'No. I was surprised when I saw that my boss had booked your two sons on this trip. I can only think that he was eager for clients, it being close to the end of the season.' We probed Shay a bit further on why children were not usually included. 'Well, you see, if an adult is attacked by a crocodile or a hippo I might have time to grab my gun and get in a shot as the beast seizes its prey. However, with a child, it would all be over too quickly and I wouldn't have time to do anything.' Silence.

Oh, oh and ouch... We didn't repeat Shay's utterings to the boys, at least, not until after the trip.

As we were travelling downstream we went with the current, but the headwind could be quite strong and it was tough work paddling all day and managing the steering as well – Will and I had a few differences of opinion about the direction our canoe was taking at times as we headed towards *another* island or bank.

Ablutions in the Zambezi river with Andy and James

Before setting up camp for the night on an island (less likely to receive a visit from lions there), we would stop on a shallow part of the river for our ablutions, where hopefully a crocodile couldn't make a grab for our legs. The evenings were spent relaxing over a huge meal cooked by Vitalis and washed down by beer and wine (all transported in our canoes). A special treat was a neck and shoulder massage from Shay, to ease aching muscles. During the night, safe in our tents (we hoped), we could hear hippos grunting as they grazed not far from us (they come out of the water at night to feed – more about this in a later chapter). In the morning we would spot animal tracks around our tents and, with Vitalis' help, identify the species – he assured us they were made by small mammals.

Enid and Will paddling on the Zambezi river

Actually, it was simply amazing to paddle down the Zambezi. We spotted elephant, buffalo, impala, kudu, baboon, waterbuck, wildebeest and warthog from our canoes. Apart from the splash of our paddles in the water, the silence was immense. It was almost too much to take in. I had come so far from my birthplace – the exploration books about Africa I devoured so eagerly as a child were actually part of my life at this minute. I was living my dream. The excitement as well as the fear was real. I could feel it in every fibre in my body. Africa had got to me just as they said it would.

Four days after starting we hauled our canoes on to the beach at Mana Pools. I breathed a sigh of relief and said a silent prayer of thanks for delivering us all safely back on to dry land. Although it had been a tense time, once it was over I could fully appreciate the wonderful experience it had been. I can understand it's not the way for every parent, but for me in this instance, I can concur with Ruth P. Freedman when she said, 'Only those who dare, truly live.'

🚲 🚲 🚲 🚲 🚲 🚲 🚲 🚲

Back on Teesside; it was time to move on from the rafting centre, and continue through Stockton-upon-Tees and the urban jungle which seemed to go on forever. Eventually I got clear of buildings but that meant I also lost the shelter they had been providing; the rain and wind coming from the west stung the left side of my face as I cycled north.

I entered Wynyard Woodland Park on the old Stockton to Wellfield railway line, now the No. 1 cycle route. The old station made a welcome coffee break, not only for me, but also for a local cycling group, who tucked into bacon butty rolls. But there was no getting away from the steady rain and once refuelled, I continued head down, for several miles along the old railway track. I rested again ten kilometres further on by Hurworth Burn Reservoir to watch great-crested grebes swim gracefully across the water.

Cycling through towns and villages in Teesside I couldn't help noticing a tethered pony or two or three on every available green space. Can it really be true as I heard that they sell for as low as one pound?

It wasn't until I approached the coast at Sunderland that brighter weather took over from grey and wet skies. I was keen to see the sea properly so deviated from my route through Hendon where I succeeded in finding a track which led to a stony beach. I ate my sandwiches on a cliff overlooking it, buffeted by a strong wind, and watched a solitary Dad and his kids combing the shoreline looking for washed-up treasure. It was a joy to see the sea again and hear the waves crashing up the beach.

Today's mileage was a longish one, 55 miles, including nearly 1000m of ascent, so it was imperative I kept going. Sunderland was about halfway but at least the bulk of the climbing was over. From here to Whitley Bay, tonight's destination, the route followed the coast closely and if I was lucky the sea would be visible most of the time. The rain had stopped and the sun peeped out from its hat every now and again – this afternoon's ride promised to be good.

Another river to cross, this time the Wear – a steel arch bridge built by the same firm as the Forth Rail Bridge and Tower Bridge in London. I passed a café on the clifftop above the estuary mouth where several tables outside were occupied with people enjoying a pot of tea or an ice-cream. The sun was out and it looked a good idea so I joined them.

The section between the Wear and the Tyne was some of the most enjoyable cycling I had done over the last two and a half weeks. It was warm and I wanted to take my time and linger. I arrived in South Shields and found my way through town streets to the Shields Ferry, the only means of crossing the Tyne this far down, and only for pedestrians and bicycles – one pound and fifty pence for a seven minute crossing (bike no extra charge)– not bad. Motorised vehicles wanting to cross have to drive a further couple of miles upstream to the Tyne Tunnel.

Crossing the Tyne was another milestone in my journey for me. As mentioned previously, ferries have fond memories for me and being onboard the *Spirit of the Tyne* was no exception. I left my bike downstairs and went up on deck to view the river and the tall cranes on the bank. A Geordie man obliged by taking my photograph as we approached North Shields; the smile on my face is a broad one – I was proud and pleased with the distance I had come so far. It was a moment to savour.

Crossing the Tyne

Chapter Nineteen

Vikings and a Celt with

a Broken Bone

As I crossed the River Tyne by ferry I looked downstream and encountered a scene well-known to me. When I lived in Norway my point of departure with my car from the UK was North Shields. Once I had parked the car on the vehicle deck of the North Sea ferry and deposited my bags in my cabin I would go up on deck and watch with interest as the wharves, ships in dry dock, new business developments, and upmarket riverside apartments with private marinas slipped past on either side. The river mouth was sheltered by long breakwaters extending into the open sea and once clear of them the ship pointed north-east and headed for Kristiansand or Stavanger in southern Norway. James or Andy often accompanied me on the voyage as they could help out with the driving and help me settle back into my Norwegian home, a two-bedroom rented house in Sandefjord, located on the coast about 75 miles south of Oslo.

I had been appointed to an International School to set up and manage a learning support department and teach geography to all students in the year prior to the start of their International Baccalaureate Diploma course. The senior school consisted of a couple of hundred students in just three year groups, the majority of whom were Norwegian but also a significant number from international backgrounds. For all the students, or at least their parents, their reason for enrolling at the school was to gain the IB diploma *in English*, which would give them an advantage in securing places in the finest universities worldwide and to access the best opportunities for employment.

The staff were an interesting mix of Norwegians and other nationalities; during my three years there were teachers from the United

States, Panama, Japan, Germany, Sweden and of course the United Kingdom.

I had seen the job advertised in the Times Educational Supplement and as my job at that time in mid-Dorset turned out not to be the one I wanted to stay in until my retirement, I started scanning the job ads. As well as sending my *curriculum vitae* off to Norway, a copy also went to a school in Prague and to the Education Department responsible for teaching children about nature on Brownsea Island. After a hastily arranged interview for the Norwegian post with the principal and his deputy in a London hotel I was offered the job and readily accepted. Later I was contacted about both the other jobs to arrange an interview but my mind was made up by then.

I knew that Norway would be right for me in so many ways: the job would be demanding and interesting, the country is without doubt one of the most beautiful in the world, my love affair with Scandinavia had kicked in as a teenager, and last but not least was my younger son's situation.

Andy was in his final year at university in Cambridge and I still wanted to provide a home for him during his vacations. By renting out a room in my house to a mature woman who would take care of it (and my cat) during term-times, I could return there in each of my holidays (slightly more generous than school holidays in Britain) and so could Andy. In addition, there was a flight between Sandefjord and Stansted (not far from Cambridge) which only took an hour and a half, less than the time it takes to drive from Dorset to Cambridge, so I didn't feel I was abandoning him!

Andy came to stay with me many times during my time in Norway. Within six months of my moving there, James, my other son, transferred with his Civil Engineering firm in Swindon to take up a post in Dubai. He also visited me several times and I travelled to Dubai from Norway as well. By this time, personal laptops were common, and so talking over the Internet was straightforward (well, most of the time!). During my final winter they both came over for a Norwegian Christmas with me which was great fun.

As the Learning Support Co-ordinator I was given my own office, where I could assess and coach students. The school is situated on the waterfront and my window overlooked the town harbour at the end of a fjord (Norwegian word for an inlet from the sea). It's a wonder I got any work done – the large car ferry to Sweden passed by twice a day, eider ducks wintered on the water of the fjord and in summer, a Viking ship sailed up and down. No, it wasn't a group of seafaring raiders getting ready to invade and pillage some foreign land; it was a bunch of harmless school children learning about the invaders and pillagers of their past and how they sailed their ships. They were aboard the *Gaia*, an exact replica of the *Gokstad*, which was found buried in a mound outside Sandefjord in 1880.

The Gaia, a Viking ship, photographed from my office

Every morning I walked down a steep hill from my house to the seafront past where the *Gaia* was housed in a huge shed, purpose-built while I was there. The school was just a few minutes further along the waterfront. It was the most marvellous commute to and from work I've ever had, and in addition to the view, on many mornings the sky was the clearest blue it is possible to imagine. When there was snow lying it was like a winter wonderland. Of course, from November to February my morning walk to school was in the breaking dawn of sunrise and then the sky could be a kaleidoscope of shades from pink through to gold.

I enjoyed supporting the students with their learning and teaching geography. On the whole they were a keen and enthusiastic troop, and treated the staff with respect and politeness. I wasn't there long before my qualifications as a mathematics teacher were also put to good use, and during my last two years I taught the IB maths course as well.

What I especially enjoyed about being part of this school was the variety and challenge of the activities in which I was expected to engage. I was a willing participant and volunteered for extra beyond the responsibilities of my post.

An innovative part of the IB diploma is the extended essay (4000 words) which asks students to engage in a personal exploration of their chosen topic and to communicate ideas and develop arguments. Each student is given a supervisor, chosen from the teaching staff, to offer advice and guidance. My first student chose a question related to the novel *Of Mice and Men* by John Steinbeck. As I hadn't read the novel, my first task was to purchase a copy and read it; it was quick to read and I soon became familiar with the main characters – George, Lennie and Candy. My second task was to discuss with one of English teachers what top tips she could offer me about the question my student had posed. I was then ready to meet, let's call her Ingrid, and my monthly sessions with her kicked off; it was interesting reading Ingrid's interpretations of George and Lennie's shared dream of owning their own ranch and the problems they encountered along the way. Then with advice and suggestions from me on how she might improve her essay, Ingrid would go away and make changes and so the process went on until she was ready to submit her finished essay. Remember she was writing this in her second language, but it would be assessed equally alongside those of native English speakers. It was satisfying to see later on that she attained a decent grade which helped towards her achieving the diploma.

At the heart of the IB diploma is the Creativity, Action and Service (CAS) programme which involves students in a range of activities that take place alongside their academic studies throughout the programme. At our school the latter part of Wednesday afternoons was put aside for CAS activities and each teacher had to put on a course which would fit the requirements. I found out during my first week in the job that a subject matter was already pencilled in opposite my name. Lars, my principal, said, 'Enid, what are your cooking skills like? John, who left last year, ran a very popular cooking class and we thought you might continue it?'

So, that solved that question for me. We didn't have a suitable kitchen in our school but I scouted around the nearby buildings and found one which the owner was willing to let us use for a small payment. Thus, Wednesday afternoons became cooking sessions; I encouraged my budding chefs to form themselves into small groups and take it in turns to prepare a menu which everyone would cook. They were responsible for producing a list of ingredients and to divide the shopping list amongst themselves. My office on a Wednesday became a storage area for supermarket carrier bags full of food. Keeping in mind our curriculum, we tried recipes from all over the world; one of the girls was from Ghana and she introduced us to a traditional recipe for a one-pot dish of chicken, ham, rice and vegetables cooked in a tomato-based sauce with chillies. Of course, once the food was cooked, the table set, a delicious meal was served up and enjoyed by all.

At Christmas, one group of Norwegian girls was keen to prepare a traditional Norwegian festive meal. They decided they wanted to make it into a big affair by inviting friends and teachers too. I was pleasantly surprised by their joint ability to organise and hold such an enjoyable and delicious feast. Needless to say, it became an annual event which grew year on year, and the limited number of tickets for it became highly sought after.

The school also ran several Global Awareness Projects to allow the students opportunities to fulfil the Action and Service components of their CAS programme. These included:

> a Habitat for Humanity project which I described in chapter six.
> a project in Tanzania to build facilities for local primary schools.
> a link with a school in Leh, a town in Ladakh (western end of the Himalayas) to give support to a secondary school there (described in chapter 22)
> MUN (Model United Nations) – a worldwide initiative involving thousands of students who engage in research in order to simulate the work of the United Nations in the role of delegates from specific countries. We hosted the European conference at

our school one year and I assisted by accommodating three French delegates at my house.

Every winter a ski-day was an integral date on the calendar although, perhaps surprisingly for a Nordic school, not everyone chose to get involved. Our nearest downhill ski resort was at Kongsberg and a number of coaches were laid on to transport us there, a journey taking a couple of hours. It was on these slopes that the experts among us, mainly but not exclusively home-grown, were able to demonstrate their talents on skis and snowboards. I was definitely not one of them but felt it was an opportunity not to be sniffed at, so my first year there I arranged to have a lesson. Oh, how incompetent I felt amongst all those young people who looked as if they were born on skis.

By the second year, I had decided downhill skiing was not for me; I felt I was too old to learn, and in any case cross-country skiing was the national sport and I thought with my hiking background it might be more my cup of tea. I had done a week of it in Switzerland a few years before so knew the basics.

In Kongsburg I hired the necessary skis and boots and headed off on a prepared track into the forests. As the others were all involved in downhill activities I went alone, which secretly I was grateful for, because it meant I could go at my own speed (slow), as being rushed could only spell disaster for me. I hadn't learnt the art of controlling my speed on the descents and fell over often. Getting back on my feet after a fall was an ungainly process and one which I was happier to take my time with, preferably unwatched.

What I enjoyed most as I skied along were the beautiful snowscapes unfolding around every twist in the track; the snow lay thick on the ground, weighing down the branches of the fir trees with a backdrop of a clear blue sky. There were a number of Norwegian adults also on the trail and as they overtook me they greeted me with a friendly '*Hei*'; if I was in a heap on the ground they invariably stopped to help me up, automatically speaking in English because what respectable Norwegian would be floundering around in the snow?

It took me a few hours to complete the course and some of my fellow teachers were beginning to get a little bit anxious for me but I arrived back to the warm and inviting cafe in time to sip a hot cup of chocolate before the coach was due to leave. I had enjoyed the day and went back for another helping the following year.

After which my friend Jean came to stay with me in the March – by then I felt brave enough to put my mediocre skiing skills to good use by taking Jean for a skiing weekend. She had done a fair bit of downhill skiing previously so thought that her skills would be somewhat transferable. There wasn't a lot of snow at ground level when we left but further heavy snowfalls were forecast so I borrowed snow chains from a kind friend who demonstrated how to put them on my car. I had a go too, and he seemed satisfied that I knew what I was doing.

I drove Jean and myself to Rjukan in the Telemark region where we were booked into a picturesque wooden lodge for a couple of nights. In the morning we located the prepared cross-country track and set off. Quite soon I realised I had left Jean behind, which surprised me, because I thought she would be the faster skier. However, it soon became obvious that she was struggling with the different technique needed and was playing safe by gliding slowly. I was not too bad on the flattish sections and was able to pick up a bit of speed (by my standards, not a Norwegian's), but I still didn't have as much control as I would have liked on descents. So it was that on one longer downhill section which had a bend at the bottom I tumbled over and hurt my shoulder. More or less at the same time Jean did a similar thing. However, we

The snow at Rjukan, Telemark

152

both got back on our skis and completed the trail a few hours later.

By that evening we were both feeling pain in our shoulders and resorted to painkillers. There was no enthusiasm from either of us the following morning for a further bout of skiing and we chose to go for a walk instead. Overnight a couple of feet of snow had fallen and we had a wonderful morning's walk looking at the spectacular winter scenes and taking many photographs. After lunch it was time to head home as we had a longish drive ahead. Our lodge was a couple of thousand feet above the deep U-shaped valley below and to get down it we had to negotiate a series of steep hairpin bends. Coming up had been no problem because there was little snow, but I realised I would need the snow chains on to descend so set about fixing them on to the car tyres.

Immediately on starting driving we both could hear a loud 'clunk, clunk' so I stopped to check and tightened the chains before continuing. Unfortunately so did the 'clunk, clunk'. I checked again but couldn't find anything wrong with the way I'd attached them so carried on driving but I wasn't able to go more than 10-15mph down the whole mountain because of the clunking sound and the worry of damaging my wheels. In this instance two women and a set of snow chains just did not gel. We got to the bottom, removed them and drove on. My shoulder was hurting badly, but as Jean wasn't confident enough to drive on the right, I carried on with the help of painkillers. We arrived back in Sandefjord in one piece, but not any the wiser about dealing with snow.

I flew back to the UK for a few days soon after Jean departed and as my shoulder was no better I visited my doctor who pulled and prodded then stated confidently, 'You've strained some muscles in the shoulder. You might benefit from some physiotherapy. There's a bit of a wait though, you'll probably not get your first appointment for at least four weeks.'

I explained I was flying back to Norway the following afternoon so he added, 'You could see a physiotherapist privately – they should be able to give you an appointment.' So the next morning I found myself in a physiotherapist's consulting room. After some more prodding and pulling, he too stated with confidence, 'You've strained it. I'll give you some exercises. If it hasn't started to improve in a month come back and see me again.'

I flew back to Sandefjord where more snow had fallen. I was due to teach the following day but my shoulder was so bad in the morning it was making me feel quite ill and I knew I had to see a doctor. I was able to get an appointment for a couple of hours later but didn't want to further aggravate my shoulder by digging my car out of the snow so walked the kilometre to get to the surgery. I used my walking pole to steady me as there was a risk of slipping and causing more injury.

Within minutes of examining my shoulder the doctor was on the telephone to the hospital to book me in for a scan. She covered the mouthpiece to speak to me, 'If you can drive to Porsgrunn, about half an hour away, they have an appointment tomorrow. Would you like it?' As that was better than waiting a few days to be seen at the local hospital I accepted.

The efficiency at Porsgrunn scanning unit was unbelievable. There was *no* waiting time; I was scanned straight away and out of the building in less than ten minutes! It cost me the equivalent of about fifteen pounds. The Norwegian health scheme is partly contributory – so that each visit to the doctor costs about five pounds, hospital appointments a bit more, and so on. Subsequently there is a cap of approximately one hundred pounds per annum on the total amount an individual is expected to pay for treatment and after that is reached any further care is free. With prompt and efficient care such as I received I was happy to pay this relatively small amount.

Two days later I had a telephone message from my doctor asking me to call her urgently. 'Enid, the scan shows you have broken a bone in your shoulder. Actually you could say this is fortunate because it means you will get free physiotherapy. If you had only strained it you would have to pay for the physiotherapy. I'll make the necessary arrangements and you'll get a call asking when you would like an appointment. Oh and also make an appointment to see the nurse here and she'll put a sling on your arm.'

It was a sensible idea to have a sling because it prevented me from using that arm and also signalled to others that I had an injury. This elicited lots of sympathy from pupils and teachers alike. Fortunately it was my left shoulder so I could soon carry on pretty much as before.

Within a couple of days I had my first session with the physiotherapist and he showed me a series of exercises using a long thin piece of elastic attached to a chair. A couple of months later I was all better and healed. On the other hand, Jean, who was treated solely by the NHS, took more than a year before she felt her shoulder was completely healed.

Throughout my time in Norway, I had a succession of family and friends to stay. There's something about the word 'Norway' that gets people booking flights and eager to visit. It was great for me as I loved the company and exploring different parts of the country with my visitors. I travelled up to the very far north to Kirkenes on the Russian border, to the Lofoten Islands, to Bergen and, of course, to Oslo several times. If it hadn't been for the stream of visitors it would have been a much less exciting career deployment.

After three years, I was ready to return home, even although I was in the best job I had ever had. I missed my home, my cat and having family and friends close by. My house and garden were beginning to suffer from lack of care and attention. I'd enjoyed myself. It was time to come home.

🚲 🚲 🚲 🚲 🚲 🚲 🚲 🚲

With my bicycle I disembarked from the ferry on the north side of the River Tyne. I only had seven miles further to reach my day's destination at Whitley Bay and I wanted to make the most of the clement weather and being next to the coast. Pedalling slowly and stopping frequently to take photographs I enjoyed the views.

I pushed the pedals up to Tynemouth Castle which is located on a rocky headland high above the sea below. There were few people about, partly because it was early evening by now, but mainly I suspect because the recent weather hadn't encouraged many people to plan outdoor trips for the weekend. In fact events all over the country had been cancelled because of the weather: the Olympic torch was extinguished by rain in Blackpool and the plan to take it to the top of the Blackpool Tower had to be abandoned, English cricket at Headingly was rained off, the Great North Swim in Windermere was off due to strong gusting winds, the Badminton Horse Trials and cheese-rolling in

Gloucestershire suffered the same fate, the County Show in North Yorkshire was cancelled, festival goers to the Isle of Wight Music Festival spent the night in their cars because the site turned into a mud bath, and so the list went on. Seventy eight flood warnings for northern England were issued by the Environmental Agency on this day.

It was a quiet run along the coast for me. What I noticed as I stopped above each beach to take a photograph was the emptiness. North Shields, Cullercoates, Roker, Whitley Bay – all devoid of human life. It was a strange phenomenon, but then the weather for June had been extraordinary.

An empty beach in the north-east

I overshot my guest house as I sailed with the wind along Whitley Bay's sea front and came to a nature reserve and the lighthouse at the far end, so I had to turn around and come back into the wind. I found my night's accommodation opposite the esplanade; Mariea, the proprietor, showed me the backyard where I could securely leave my bicycle. She added, 'There are some take-away menus in the hallway. They will all deliver here.'

My room looked out over the sea – I put on the kettle and sat down by the window with a refreshing cup of tea or two. Then I fetched the take-away menus from downstairs and had a choice of Chinese, Indian or Italian. I plumped for Indian, made the phone call, and was informed, 'It will be with you in half an hour.'

Time for a shower, wash out a few clothes and change into something a bit fresher. Then I sat looking out of the window on to the road below with my phone next to me – I didn't want to miss the arrival of my food. The only problem was, it didn't arrive, well, not for an hour and that was after two more phone calls. There was something about the driver going to Blyth, and then the food had gone cold so he had to return to the restaurant for a replacement meal before finally turning up on my doorstep with it. What can I say? Let's settle for, 'I was more than ready for it. It was tasty and filled me up.'

Actually I haven't mentioned the other guests staying. I really couldn't have missed them, because of the hubbub that was coming from rooms both above and around me. When I saw a couple of youths standing outside the front door, cigarette in one hand, beer can in the other, it didn't take me long to figure out they were on a stag weekend. The intoxicating aroma of hair gel and aftershave in the shared bathroom down the corridor and emanating from their open bedroom doors confirmed this. Soon a convoy of taxis arrived to whisk them away to give the bridegroom a night to remember.

After my little feast I felt the need to stretch my legs and see Whitley Bay on a Saturday night for myself. Actually, from the little I did see happening I don't think I was in the centre of the nightlife on offer in this area. The stag boys, no doubt, were in Newcastle, the party town of the north-east. What time and what state would they arrive back to their rooms?

The answer came at 03.45 hours, with a lot of thumping feet and banging of doors, until finally all I could hear were voices in the room above, but it was either me that rolled over and fell asleep first or it was them because that's the last I remember before morning.

Chapter Twenty

WIGWAMS AND CASTLES

Needless to say I was the only one taking breakfast early on Sunday morning in the guest house. I had a long ride ahead of me, 59 miles and 850 metres of ascent. The forecast was not good: rain moving in, heavy at times, with a strong north-westerly wind.

I joined the cycle track behind the dunes and encountered more joggers and other cyclists than I've seen anywhere else at that time on a Sunday morning – lots of local people must follow a regular fitness regime. We played out a dance dodging each other and the numerous puddles – there must have been heavy rain during the night.

Somewhere between Seatown Sluice and Blyth any brightness there had been in the sky vanished and the downpours started. Blyth was once a prosperous town and port, relying on coal mining, shipbuilding and fishing amongst other things. As usual for me I sought out the riverside and the old docks. In the first half of the twentieth century the town boasted one of the largest shipbuilding yards on the north-east coast, with five dry docks and four building slipways; HMS Ark Royal was built here for the Royal Navy in 1914. Sadly now that its principal industries have declined, it looked somewhat rundown to me and obviously a shadow of its former self. Much quayside regeneration has taken place including nine wind turbines in place along the pier, but it seems to hark back to its former glories. The award-winning *Spirit of the Staithes* sculpture on the Quayside stands fifty feet high and was created in 2003 to represent the heritage of its coal mining tradition. The sculpture comprises a series of polished stainless steel panels which merge to create an image of a train pulling coal trucks. Staithes were the short piers projecting out into the river to allow the coal to be dropped directly into the colliers (coal ships).

It was interesting following the wide river two miles upstream to the bridge which I could use to cross it. There was evidence all the way of old industrial structures, derelict warehouses and empty tracts of land. How different it must have looked sixty years ago when I was born and the shipbuilding and coal-mining industries were in their prime.

Having crossed the river, my route diverted backwards and forwards from the coast, first crossing the River Blyth, then the Wansbeck and then the Lyne at their lowest bridging points. I wasn't enjoying the ride very much so far. There were some long stretches alongside main roads which were not much fun. However, I could see from my map that I was approaching Druridge Bay, an eight-mile stretch of sand and dunes with a cycle track going through a country park – it promised to be of more interest. I was feeling peckish so would look for a suitable spot to eat my lunch.

As I crossed an open grassy area I was caught by strong gusts of wind so kept my head down. I took a break where it looked like I might get a bit of shelter behind a dune and ate a hurried sandwich before the rain came back on. Seven miles across this windswept bay was quite an ordeal in the circumstances and I wasn't sorry when I reached the end of it and entered Amble. A welcome teashop provided me with a break from the elements. I noticed a small supermarket which was open and went in and bought a few items of food to see me through until the next day. As it was Sunday I wasn't sure whether I would find another one further on.

I followed the side of Warkworth harbour up to the town from where I could see an impressive castle on a hilltop. Then there was another stretch of main road before I turned off it to descend a steep hill down to Alnmouth. I had decided to investigate this little seaside town for two reasons.

Many years ago as an undergraduate in the company of a dozen other geographers studying 'urban planning' we came here on a Saturday field trip from Edinburgh. Our main point of call had been Alnwick, a medieval market town with cobbled streets, butchers' shambles and fish market, where we had gone to look at a fine example of historical town planning. Afterwards we made a detour to the river mouth to take in some further matters of geographical interest, the essence of which completely escapes me now, but if it was worth visiting then, it was surely worth visiting now. My second reason for wanting to take a closer look at Alnmouth was the large sign advertising its Arts Festival this very weekend in 27 different venues around the settlement.

I found and perused several of the collections and thought the standard of artwork to be exceedingly high – wonderful paintings, ceramics, jewellery and much else besides. Between showers I took the opportunity to sit on a bench overlooking the bay, next to a young couple who were also taking a break from viewing and I joined them in having an ice-cream.

The climb back out of Alnmouth was short but steep. I was tiring by this time – pedalling into a north-westerly was taking its toll and my last rest day had been at Woody's Top a week ago. Tomorrow was to be a day off for me and maybe it was psychological but I seemed to struggle most to find the energy I needed when a rest day was almost in reach.

Looking at the map I could see that not only did I have over 20 miles still to do but my route seemed to visit every village along the coast usually at the foot of a steep hill. By cutting out a couple of them I saved myself a few miles and a hundred metres or so of climbing but I was still finding it exceedingly tough. This wasn't helped by the increasingly frequent heavy showers. Every time I saw the telltale looming rain cloud up ahead I would look for a large tree to shelter under. This worked to some extent until nearing the village of Embleton up a hill from where I was.

I'd been keeping my eye on a particularly dark cloud coming my way and when I felt the first drops I halted and pulled my bike under the nearest tree. For the first five minutes the canopy acted as a reasonably proficient umbrella but when the rain turned into a brutal hail storm it served as a colander to drench me. Streams of water were running down the side of the road and I tried to push myself further into the hedge to keep my feet out of the torrent of water flowing past. Eventually it eased off and I extricated myself from the dripping vegetation and pushed my bicycle up the rest of the hill. Guess what? I was feeling a bit sorry for myself at this stage.

After several more miles and probably the same number of showers I tottered wearily into Springhill Farm Caravan Park. Since booking my accommodation I had been looking forward to my two nights here because I was to be in a wigwam! Although called wigwams, the structures were actually constructed of wood, their distinctive shape inspired by the upturned boat sheds at nearby Holy Island. These boats had once been part of the largest herring fleet on the east coast of England. Once the boats became unseaworthy they were turned upside down and used as sheds instead. I couldn't wait to see mine.

At reception, Julie welcomed me warmly, 'Hello, you must be Enid. Sorry about the weather – it's not usually like this.' I was too whacked to respond with more than just a few nods. Julie showed me the kitchen where I could cook and eat, the shower room, and then took me over to my wigwam, named Aiden's House after St Aiden, the first person (whose name is known) to have lived on the holy island of Lindisfarne. It was a soggy walk over to the waterlogged grass to get to my wooden dwelling, but it looked as if the gravel area with a picnic table in front would provide me with a dry place to unpack and get sorted out. Julie left me to get on with it.

I made a pot of tea and brought it inside, sat down on the bed and let myself recover for a while before taking my bags off the bike, getting them inside, showering and cooking a meal. By then I just about felt human again. It was cold, damp and dismal outside so there was no temptation to sit at the picnic table and admire the incredible vista all round – the sea on one side with the Farne Islands visible, Bamburgh Castle over the other way and the Cheviot Hills in the distance. The latter marked the border between England and Scotland – I was getting nearer all the time! I stayed inside, got out my little computer and made use of the wi-fi provided free of charge on the site to watch live television. It was all I had the strength to do that evening.

I reflected on my day. It had been one of my toughest. Not just physically, but even more so mentally – I found it hard to endure all that rain, wind and cold. A day off in the wonderful county of Northumberland was what I needed and even better, the weather forecast was for a dry sunny day tomorrow – it wasn't the first time that my rest day had been dry, falling between wet days on either side. I was glad because I wanted to explore Bamburgh Castle.

The next morning brought a fresh clear sky and after breakfast I got on my bike to pedal one mile there and back into the village of Seahouses to buy my daily rations.

Breakfast outside my wigwam in Northumberland

I had realised that to make the most of my day off in this beautiful part of the country I would need to use my bike to get around – I wouldn't have the luxury of a whole day out of the saddle, as the site was in a rural position. However, by stocking up on picnic food it would mean I could do my own thing during the remainder of the day and give myself maximum opportunity to recharge my batteries.

I packed just a few items into the front bag on my bike – it was a delight to cycle without full panniers – and set off along a back road in a northerly direction to Bamburgh. It was only a couple of miles and the castle was in view most of the time. I located the car park and went over to the attendant in his little box to ask him where I should leave my bike.

He gave me a broad Northumberland smile and replied, 'Padlock it to this fence and give me your helmet and anything else you don't want with you and I'll keep it for you inside here.' It felt warm enough to take off my jacket so I left that in his safe-keeping too and he wished me a pleasant visit.

I walked up to the castle entrance, paid my fee and went under the Postern Gate – fortunately no English defenders were hiding in wait for me to bombard me with burning oil as I passed under. After all I am Scottish and this castle was an important border garrison to withstand attack from the rebellious and raiding neighbours to the north. Henry Percy, or *Harry Hotspur* as he was immortalised by Shakespeare in *Henry 1Vth, Part 1* (one of the plays we read at school), was tasked with protecting the castle in the early 15th century. He was an uncrowned king of the north but gained his 'hot spurs' for his boldness in battle and his quickness to settle any insult with his sword.

I spent the next three hours wandering around the towers, ramparts,

Museum exhibit at Bamburgh Castle.
Ouch! Think of the saddle sores riding this bicycle

courtyards and museums. I was in no hurry and wanted to soak up both the atmosphere of this hotbed of history and take in the spectacular views. They were voted Britain's second favourite view in a recent television poll (Wastwater in the Lake District was in first place). Janet Street Porter, the writer and broadcaster, summed it up with the words: 'As you stand and stare you're not just

On the ramparts of Bamburgh Castle

looking at a view, you're standing in the footsteps of kings, and on one of the most dramatic coastlines nature has to offer.'

I enjoyed recording my tour both inside and out on my camera, found quiet out-of-the-way places to sit and just admired the beauty all around me. I chatted to some young archaeologists who were scraping away at the earth with trowels. They were current students at Edinburgh University spending a few weeks of their holiday on this dig. 'What has been your most exciting find?' I asked one.

'Oh, some Anglo-Saxon coins, that's about it, but it's good fun.'

I reminisced with them about my years at their university and we talked about some of the things that had changed.

The castle and its environs were a serene place to take some time off from the tiring schedule of the past week. When I'd had my fill of history, Henrys and halcyon thoughts I made my way back to the friendly chap at the car park to collect my bicycle. I stopped to pass the time of day with him – it was turning out to be that sort of day for me.

From the castle I made my way via St Aiden's churchyard to see a very brave young lady's memorial stone (her identity will be revealed later) and then on to the beach. The poppies were fully out and their red blooms provided a colourful foreground to my photographs of the castle. Hundreds of early purple orchids stood proud and handsome amongst the grass. It wasn't difficult to find a quiet spot on the beach – there were a few others about but they were just doing the same as me – taking a short stroll while admiring the view. Only a couple of miles off the coast are the Farne Islands, made famous by the Grace Darling story. What follows is a story about a stormy night and its consequences to those who were out in it. This story was related to us in Primary School and it has always stayed with me, perhaps because of its link to Dundee.

The paddle steamer, SS Forfarshire was travelling from Hull to Dundee, when on the night of the 7th September 1838 she hit rocks off the Farne Islands. Unfortunately for 56 of the passengers they died, but fortunately for the remaining four plus five crew members, Grace Darling and her father were the keepers of the Longstone Lighthouse close by. The survivors managed to cling to rocks all night and in the morning Grace and her father came to their rescue by boat. While her father clambered on to the rocks to help them on to the boat one by one,

Grace fought hard to stop the boat from getting smashed against the rocks. They brought them all to safety. Grace was only nine years old, the seventh of nine children, and had to work hard with her father to keep the lighthouse lantern burning all the time. She was awarded an RNLI (Royal National Lifeboat Institution) Silver Medal for Gallantry and fifty pounds from Queen Victoria. Grace died aged 26 from consumption (tuberculosis) and was buried in the churchyard in Bamburgh. The lifeboats in Seahouses have since been called *The Grace Darling* in memory to her. At the request of local seamen her memorial was placed where it could clearly be seen from the sea.

I gazed out over the Farne Islands bathed in sun and spent some time taking photographs, including filming the tide slowly filtering into the rock pools and capturing the wonderful sound as each incoming wave gently caressed the rock. Photographs and videos I took through the water in the pools clearly show anemones and limpets clinging to the rocks, green and brown fronds of seaweed swaying in the tranquil current and small bubbles of air escaping upwards.

The Farne Islands

I wandered slowly up the beach to the dunes and snuggled down into a gap, sheltered as well as I could be from the breeze. There I made the most of the weak warmth reaching me from the sun. I deserved this. I'd worked for it. My eyes closed and all I could hear was the pacifying sound of the sea.

Later, back at the camp site I took advantage of the washing machine and put in all my clothes that I wasn't wearing. In the kitchen I put a pizza in the oven and when the cheese was bubbling and hot I served it up with salad and took it over to my picnic table to eat al fresco while looking out to sea. Pretty good. The evening was spent drying my clothes, writing e-mails and refining my route for the days ahead. Then I watched a weather forecast for the three days ahead which had me scratching my head and wondering if it was going to put the kibosh on my plans.

The forecast for the next day and the one after was generally okay but following that there was a severe weather warning for heavy rain and storms. My biggest cycling day in terms of both distance and hills to climb was to be the day after tomorrow, when my plan was to head inland into the Borders Region of the Southern Uplands to spend a night with Stuart (my nephew) and his wife Natalie. From there I would have to cross the remaining Uplands area and descend to Edinburgh where I had arranged to spend two nights with my friends Jenny & Alastair. Jenny had got tickets for us to see the current star attraction at the Zoo – the recently arrived giant pandas – I was quite excited about seeing them.

I knew I had to rule myself out of crossing the high hills in a storm, so my options were: (1) to take the train from Berwick-upon-Tweed to Edinburgh and miss out on seeing Stuart and Nat, or (2) if I could reach Stuart and Nat's before the worst of the storm, spend an extra night with them to ride out the storm before continuing to Edinburgh which would mean my missing the pandas. Either of these deviations from my original plan would be a big disappointment as I wanted to see Stuart and Natalie and the giant pandas, and not mess Jenny and Alastair around either.

I thought about what doing this trip had come to mean to me and a large part of it was commemorating the memory of my brother Donald. Not going to see his son Stuart was unthinkable for me at this moment.

In the past there have been times in my life when I have had to contend with grief, pain or suffering. Struggling against the weather on this present trip cannot be compared to these past trials. By extending myself I have got through difficult times before and the current bad weather was only a momentary thing – I told myself I would get through this one way or another too. However it does sadden me when I can't enjoy the cycling and the countryside to its full, because I know when the weather is playing ball it's the very best of times.

My decision was made – I would phone Stuart tomorrow evening from Berwick-upon-Tweed and discuss it with him.

Chapter Twenty-one

5000 TOOTHBRUSHES

It was time to leave my wigwam and push on to pastures new. The rest day had done wonders for me and I felt fresh and raring to continue along this north-east coast and my last day's cycling in England. A couple of miles later I met four cyclists going in the opposite direction. I asked them where they were heading, 'We're doing the *Coast and Castles route,*' they told me, which turned out to be a 200 mile trip from Edinburgh to Newcastle mainly following the coast.

'What about you?' they asked.

I explained I was heading to Berwick, and then told them a bit more about my trip. They expressed their respect for what I was doing and we chatted about Berwick and bikes. One of them obligingly added, 'I can recommend *Wilson's Cycles* if you want your bike checked over. Ian is very knowledgeable and fixed my gears for me. It's across from the Youth Hostel.'

'Thanks for the tip. I'm staying at the Youth Hostel and my bike has been through so much mud that I wouldn't mind someone taking a look at it for me.'

We wished each other a safe journey and cycled on in opposite directions. Soon I crossed the main London to Edinburgh railway line over a level crossing, then directly afterwards, the main A1 road between England and Scotland. Then followed an undulating section along the edge of the hills and from that vantage point Holy Island should have come in to sight with its iconic view of Lindisfarne Castle perched on a hilltop. However, there was a sea mist completely obliterating any view I might have had in that direction.

But the island was where I was heading next, mist or no mist. I had visited it once before but was eager to go again because it is a wonderful spiritual place to spend some time. I had checked the tide times and knew that the causeway would open by 11 o'clock which would give me a big enough window to get there and back and not be stranded overnight.

As I came back down to cross the main road and railway again to reach the coast, my track turned east and directly into a very strong wind. I had about four miles of cycling in this direction to do until I reached the shelter of the island. The causeway is completely unprotected and it was the strongest headwind I had to face on my whole trip. At least it was completely flat and the wind was beginning to disperse the thick cloud still hanging over the island.

There was a line of tall posts in the mudflats marking a safe route at low tide for the handful of hardy walkers who were making it on foot to the island. My progress was very slow, only slightly faster than another cyclist who had given up and was pushing. All the time cars were flashing past – it looked as if most of the population had the same plans as me that day. I took a breather halfway and then at last I turned the corner and passed the car park (jammed full) and into the village. It was at this point that the mist lifted completely and the sky cleared to reveal my first view of Lindisfarne Castle.

I couldn't help but feel slightly smug as the car occupants collected all their belongings from their cars and traipsed on foot along the side of the road as I cycled past on my bicycle, although for those who wanted it I later noticed a 'castle shuttle' bus. I explored the village, appropriately called Holy Island, cycling up and along each little road – I wanted to take in the whole picture. I had decided not to go into either the priory or the castle, both of which I'd looked around previously. So I took the lane leading out to the castle at the far end of the island. It was thronged with visitors and fast-food stalls and above a beach I noticed the upturned boats and the similarity to my 'wigwam'.

What an imposing view in front of me – the castle on its craggy outcrop so distinct and picturesque against a clear backdrop of sky. It had been built in the 1550s using stones from the demolished priory after the dissolution of monasteries by Henry VIII.

After taking some photographs I found a quiet spot out of the way on the grass where I could eat my sandwiches and contemplate the view in solitude. The castle balanced on rocks reminded me of the monasteries and palaces I had visited in Ladakh in the Himalayas. Leh Palace stands on a rock promontory high above its surroundings, with similarities to the castle before me now.

Lindisfarne Castle

Our school party of thirty, including some of the dads, had flown from Oslo to Leh via Delhi. Flying over the snow-covered Himalayas for two hours brought home to me just how remote Ladakh is. Leh has the highest commercial airport in the world at 3256 metres. The descent into it is truly incredible – quite the most spellbinding I have ever witnessed. The town sits in the deep U-shaped valley of the River Indus. Our aeroplane descended steeply from several thousand feet until it was below the level of the top of the valley sides and close to its left (or should that be 'port'?) wall, in fact *incredibly* close to the wall, almost as if I could reach out and touch it. This allowed the pilot to make a very tight 180° turn to the other side of the valley to bring the aircraft safely down to land on the runway. The passengers applauded in appreciation and relief.

Lined up on the tarmac to greet us were a small deputation of smartly-uniformed pupils from the school we had come to visit, led by the head boy and girl. I bowed my head in anticipation of the garland of beautiful orange marigold flowers and a silk scarf which were placed around my neck.

It is vital after landing in Leh to take it easy for a few days as everyone who arrives by plane feels the effects of altitude to some degree or another. On our second day I joined in a gentle stroll through the charming ancient alleys of Leh to reach the Old Palace which stands majestically above the town, therefore allowing the king to keep a close eye over his subjects. Many of the householders still keep livestock in their backyards and dry fodder on the roofs.

After lunch we were taken by bus, first to see Thikse Monastery, an impressive sight, situated on top of a craggy hill. A smiling lama showed us around and willingly posed as I stood next to him for a photograph of us together. Then it was back on to the bus and the next stop was Shey Palace which sits in a strategic position on a spur jutting out into the Indus Valley.

Again we were shown around by an informative lama – by now I was getting the hang of some Buddhist terms – *stupa* (monument), *gompa* (monastery), *chorten* (another kind of stupa) and prayer wheels. Unfortunately, many of our group of teenagers were by now flagging – the heat, altitude, tiredness and too much culture were all contributory factors – they were lolling about on the steps, leaning against each other and even closing their eyes when the monk was explaining the significance of yet another particular statue of Buddha. So as soon as we could politely bring our visit to a close we did and before departing, kindly thanked our hosts for a very interesting tour.

The students accompanying Tom (the other teacher) and me were all sixth formers from our International School in Norway. They had opted to come to beautiful and remote Ladakh as part of a Global Awareness Project and in particular, to visit Lamdon School with which we had established a link and actively raised funds for throughout the year. A large number of the pupils in this school board in hostels, only returning home from November to February when their school is closed. The areas served by the school are so remote that the families living in these outlying valleys are virtually cut off by snow during these months. Children making their way back to their families can be faced with many days of walking in harsh conditions.

In previous years our school had raised enough money to build a new hostel for the girls and we had heard it was now functional so were looking forward to seeing it. It had also come to our attention that pairs of skates would be appreciated – it may at first seem a strange request, but skating is an activity which can be enjoyed by the children whenever it is cold enough for ice to form on their flooded playing fields. Asking Norwegians if they have any skates they don't need is like asking British families for football boots their children have grown out of. They sit hiding in corners of houses all over the country gathering dust.

A further intriguing story which involves Lamdon School is this. Soldiers of the Indian Army are posted to the high-altitude areas of Ladakh to defend its borders with Pakistan over the disputed region of Kashmir. The army has brought many significant advantages to this area including roads and airports which have opened Ladakh up to the rest of the world and introduced many everyday products we in the west take for granted. One of these was the sudden introduction of refined sugar, a totally new commodity to them. Almost immediately the former dental problem of breakages was replaced by epidemic levels of tooth decay, in fact, a staggering 100 per cent impact was noted amongst not just the children but the general population too. The suffering must have been unimaginable.

Two girls from our International School in Norway secured a donation of 5000 toothbrushes and toothpaste from one supplier, others procured dental instruments. All of this plus more was brought to my office and stacked into the store cupboard next door, along with dozens of pairs of skates of all sizes. The sheer amount of extra supplies we needed to transport out with us on top of our own personal luggage was staggering. I contacted the airline to ask for their cooperation and generosity towards our project – their short answer was: 'We can't increase your baggage allowances.'

Tom and I pleaded with our troop to minimise their own kit and persuaded them to collect donated items from me to pack into their own bags. Thanks to a kind-spirited check-in clerk at Oslo airport we got away with taking on board overweight bags.

I looked forward to visiting Lamdon School during our trip as there was to be an assembly to formally acknowledge our donations and we had been invited to attend. However, before we could take up the invitation, we had the little matter of an eleven-day trek in the mountains – along yak trails, through remote settlements and over high passes, the highest being the Gongmaru La at 5100 metres.

I was aware that this trek would be my toughest physical test yet, so I trained as best I could in the months leading up to it. I tramped the hills and valleys up and down in Vestfold (the county around Sandefjord) after school and at weekends, so by the time the trip was upon us I felt reasonably fit (for me anyway), but knew that this was no protection against altitude sickness – even Olympic athletes can suffer. However, I was to be in experienced hands – our Sherpa guides were hand-picked by Bill, who was our host and trek organiser in Leh; our programme allowed for time to acclimatise – before ascending to 5000m we would have been in the region for over a week; and fortunately, Tom was an experienced Alpine guide. Also his father, David, an academic researching cardiovascular health, was accompanying us and would be carrying out a study of the effects of altitude on us.

A couple of days before setting off on our trek David gave each of us a pre-health check and carefully measured the saturation percentage of

David giving a pre-health check to one of our Sherpas

oxygen in our blood with equipment he had brought with him. At this stage mine was one of the lowest. However, one mitigating fact may have been my sex – I was the only adult female amongst us and as there are few studies on women at altitude their responses may differ slightly. Anyway there was nothing I could do about it, except of course, to pace myself slowly and drink plenty of liquid. Because I had been going up and down hills since I was first able to stand on my own two feet I was pretty sure my lung capacity was satisfactory if not more than.

This is not the place to go into detail about the trek so I'll try to sum it up in a couple of paragraphs. It was epic, no doubt about it. No trip in the high Himalayas could be anything but. The jagged mighty peaks soaring upwards against a deep blue sky will be forever with me. Fluttering multi-coloured prayer flags at all the high passes were a moving and unforgettable sight. There were wide rivers to cross by foot, raging torrents to cross by rickety bridge, isolated farms in the remotest of places. Children with brown weather-beaten faces, their enormous eyes following us as we passed; one day three little girls came

Ladakhi children with me at my tent

over from a nearby house to sit with me outside my tent and stayed for nearly an hour – we entertained each other with the artefacts around us – their beads, my books, camera, moisturising cream to rub into their parched and sun-baked skin. They smiled and looked into my eyes – these were wonderful moments and to have them captured on film is a treasured memento for me.

The physical effort required each day was immense, but manageable, and the sense of achievement felt by us all on completion was worth all the breathlessness and exhaustion. The youngsters excelled in their physical, mental and spiritual attitudes throughout and we were all proud of each other. Of course we couldn't have done it without our Nepalese guides – without those cups of tea brought to my tent each morning how would I have begun each day so willingly?

And my blood's reaction to the altitude? Over the course of the trek the amount of oxygen in my blood did not decrease substantially from its low starting point, whereas many of the others' measurements did and actually fell below mine. I found that as long as I paced myself really, really slowly I was fine – something I was quite good at – better than teenagers (and their dads!) at slowing down. As a result of some of them letting their competitive spirit get the better of them they often suffered quite badly from headaches and nausea, but to give them full credit, they battled on through their suffering and on the following days were to be found near the back of the group having learned their lesson.

We arrived back in Leh different people from when we had left – if we had not grown in stature then we had definitely grown in maturity and spirituality. We had worked as a team and to have been accepted into this Norwegian band of lovely people was to me an amazing gift.

Our tour in India was only half over though; we still had a full day's programme at Lamdon School which promised to be a real treat, a homestay with families of pupils in and around Leh, then a flight back to Delhi to visit to join the tourist trail finishing up in Agra at the Taj Mahal.

We were asked to arrive at the school soon after dawn to take part in, or just witness if we preferred, the whole school lined up on their parade ground for morning assembly for their 'Salute to the Sun' – a movement from Buddhist yoga to start off one's day. This was followed by the

'Salute to the Sun' at Lamdon School, Leh

carrying in of our donations to them – I can best describe it as constituting about 15 cubic metres of various articles which I have already itemised. The towering pile on the stage represented many hours of work and generosity by our students and their families. The recognition and appreciation of our efforts was acknowledged by the school principal in a most heartfelt and humbling manner. We felt honoured to be actually in the presence of these uplifting people. Afterwards we were entertained with music from the school percussion band and much joyous, singing and dancing.

Next came a tour of the school and the hostel facilities – extremely interesting and quite an eye-opener to compare the new girls' hostel with the original boys' one which seemed cramped, cold and past its sell-by-date. Lunch was served in a gaily painted dining room, and afterwards we had plenty of time to relax and chat to each other and to the school lama who was dining with us. After school ended for the day our crowd paired up with their homestay partners and parents and were whisked away for several days of traditional Ladakhi culture. Tom, his Dad and I had been invited to stay at the home of the principal.

Eshey Tondrup's English was excellent as was his hospitality and we had a real taste, literally, of the local customs. On one of the days, David and I hired a driver to take us up to the top of the Khardungla Pass, promoted as the 'world's highest motorable road' (the Peruvians might argue with that claim) – anyway this one is 18,380 feet (5602 metres) and it was an incredible sight to look out over the panorama on the other side of the pass – like looking over the roof of the world. There was a large group of Indians on Enfield motorbikes posing for a group photograph – they were on a grand tour to reach this summit from the plain hundreds of miles below. Our drive back down the dozens of hairpin bends (on a gravel surface, because of the need to remake the road after each winter), was frequently halted as we pulled into lay-bys to allow Indian army trucks laden with soldiers to pass.

I was especially looking forward to arriving in Delhi, because James, my son, was flying in from Dubai to join us for the rest of our trip. My side of organising the trip was to take care of all the flights and the touristy bit around Delhi and Agra so I was a bit anxious that it all went okay. Tom's expertise lay in the trekking, equipment and medical side of things and I had left him to take charge of these.

The Taj Mahal, Red Fort, India Gate, more tombs and further forts were all in great contrast to the remote mountainous area where we had spent almost three weeks, but while we were in India it was too good an opportunity to miss not to visit these iconic monuments.

All too soon it was time to go home and for me to say goodbye to James. It had been a remarkable trip enjoyed by all. For me personally I could be satisfied not just with my physical achievement on the trek, but also for the successful preparation with Tom over many months that resulted in a great expedition for everybody.

🚲 🚲 🚲 🚲 🚲 🚲 🚲 🚲

My sandwiches all eaten, it was time to explore more of Holy Island. A signpost to a garden on the other side of the lane beckoned me over to take a look. I opened the gate in the old wall enclosure and entered; the garden had been designed by Gertrude Jekyll for Edward Hudson, owner of the castle in 1911. Actually Hudson's first idea was to make a water garden and tennis court in this marshy spot (atmospherically named *The Stank*); Jekyll instead made a summer flower garden for his employer. Today the elegant purple spikes of the foxgloves were providing vivid colour, framed by bare branches pushed into the ground awaiting the sweet peas to climb and wind their wispy tendrils around the twigs. Attractive crazy paving had green herbs growing between the stones and a sundial positioned in the centre of the garden added a nice touch. It was a charming little oasis on this otherwise windswept and bare end of the island.

From the garden I rode back to the village, ready for a hot drink of something. I avoided the popular cafés heaving with groups of chatting bodies and found the Post Office with just a couple of small tables on the pavement outside. On the counter inside the homemade scones looked tempting and I ordered a large cup of coffee to accompany one. Sitting at the table and enjoying my little snack I watched the world go by for a few minutes. The sun was shining and some shelter was provided by the wall behind me. As before, Holy Island fed not just my stomach but my spiritual self too.

Cycling from Holy Island back across the causeway to the mainland with the wind behind me was effortless – a cyclist's reward for the toil and sweat of the tough bits. The remaining distance to Berwick was only about twelve miles along the coast and the sun was shining so I looked forward to a pleasant ride.

Chapter Twenty-two

BROWNIE POINTS

After coming off the causeway from Holy Island I took a sharp right at the signpost for the cycle route to Berwick – it was a narrow path between fields which soon opened up on to an extensive grassy area with a view of the North Sea beyond. Apart from trying to stay in the tricky narrow sunken earth path between lush green grass, it was beautiful and for a few miles I was adjacent to the coast. There was not another soul to be seen – just me and the black-faced sheep – at times I was cycling just above the wide sandy beach which stretched out to the blue sea merging into one with a blue sky. I enjoyed it all the way to Berwick.

The final stretch into the town was above cliffs and as I got nearer the mouth of the River Tweed the town came into sight: the buildings nestled among trees, the pier with a lighthouse at its far end reaching out into the turquoise-coloured sea, in the middle distance the white-crested waves crashed on to the rocks sending up plumes of spray and in the foreground, tall swathes of golden grass waved in the wind. It was without a doubt the finest view I had come across since I left home – my judgement perhaps being influenced by the bright and sunny weather.

My passage across the Tweed was over a very special bridge; a grade 1 listed sandstone bridge, built in the early 17th century. The previous bridges on this site had all either been washed away in floods or destroyed by the English. It is a handsome structure to look at with its fifteen arches on Doric columns. Fortunately I wasn't a motorised vehicle or I could not have crossed it from west to east – it was one-way only except for pedestrians and bicycles. I'd made good time – it was not quite 3 o'clock and my plan was to explore the town.

But first I made my way through the Georgian streets to Dewar's Lane – home of the Youth Hostel, in a 240 year old restored former granary. Across the yard a bike shop caught my eye, 'What is its name?'

I asked myself. 'Ah, Wilson's – that's the one that was recommended. How handy. I'll just nip inside.'

My approach to Berwick-upon-Tweed

I pushed my bike inside and Ian Wilson came forward to attend me and asked how he could help. I explained I'd been cycling for a couple of weeks through a lot of mud and grit and could he check over my bike to see whether it needed any maintenance. 'Of course, I can do that. Where are you staying?'

'The youth hostel – I'm just about to book in.'

'Fine, well you book in and then come back and see me and by then I'll have had a chance to look at your bike.'

'Super, thanks, see you soon.'

I unfastened my panniers and other bags and carried them into the hostel. It looked very modern with a café-cum-bistro on the ground floor. I was assigned to a dormitory on the third floor, easily reached by a lift. None of the beds were reserved so I chose one next to the window and sorted out a few items to take with me on a walk around the town. Then I went back over to the bike shop.

'Hello,' said Ian when he saw me walk in, 'Your bike needs new brake blocks and a few small adjustments to the brakes and gears.'

I was surprised that I'd worn out another set of brake blocks but I expect it was due to the conditions I'd encountered and my tendency to use the brakes a lot when I'm on rough or pot-holed tracks. I told him to go ahead and replace them, and then asked him if he could recommend a town walk for me.

'The best one is to go round the Walls. It will take about three quarters of an hour by which time I'll have your bike ready.'

I thanked him for his suggestion and checked with him what time he closed and said I'd be back before then, finally adding, 'Where will I find this walk?'

'Easy,' he replied, walking over to the door, 'You see that gap at the end of the hostel building? Just go through there and the wall is in front of you. Enjoy yourself.'

I did as he said and found some steps to climb which took me on to the top of the wall and looking over the river. I decided to go in an anti-clockwise direction and set off towards the river mouth. As I rounded the corner and saw the pier I wasn't prepared for the sudden blast of air which met me head on; the sunshine had been replaced by clouds and a few spots of rain so it wasn't quite so pleasant as earlier.

I stopped by an information board and learned that these are the only intact Elizabethan walls remaining in England. They were the most expensive undertaking of this period, but it was felt necessary because the Scots needed kept out. It's these wretched folk from north of the border again – marauding troublemakers!

Berwick does, of course, stand in a strategic position on the Anglo-Scottish border and for centuries there was almost constant warring between the two countries invoking lawlessness in the countryside. Families on both sides of the border were frequently harassed by passing armies – their homesteads were burnt, crops destroyed, people murdered or displaced. Who could blame them when they took to reiving? (an old word from the Northumbrian and Scots dialect meaning 'to raid')

Their loyalty was not to a distant monarch or to inefficient government or corrupt officials; their allegiance was to their own family, community or clan. They sought security through their own strength and cunning and wanted to improve their livelihood at the expense of their enemies. Within families, the inheritance system declared that land was divided between the sons – good arable land was in short supply because there was mile upon mile of harsh moorland, suitable only for grazing. Cattle and sheep were the main target for the mounted border reiving parties, although anything transportable could be taken, resulting in household goods and valuables also being stolen.

Most raids were within a day's ride and could consist of any number of men from a few dozen up to 3000 for an organised campaign. The main season for reiving was after the harvests were gathered in, the horses well-fed and in their prime, and when the long hours of darkness provided ample cover for their activities. The courts were in recess over a three month period at the end of the year which gave the raiders a good chance of escaping detection or retribution. Reiving was regarded as a profession among the border families and was passed down through the generations – there was no shame in being a reiver and it wasn't confined to any one social class.

The attitudes of both the English and Scottish governments of the time towards the border families was one of indulgence, even encouragement, as these families served as the first line of defence against invasion from the other side of the border. They were the guerrilla fighters of their day. You could say that the history of the border reivers has many similarities to that of the American Wild West – it produced its share of outlaws and broken men, misery for many and a struggle for survival. Some great characters such as Kinmont Willie, Auld Wat of Harden and Little Jock Elliot emerged over the years.

The reiving continued for over 400 years and only began to come to a close with the unification of England and Scotland in 1603 when strong measures were used to enforce the law. Reiving gradually died away, leaving in its place a fine independent people with strong qualities of resilience and resolution. Many of them moved away to other parts of England, overseas to Ireland and to America where their descendents live today.

Only recently there have been calls in the Scottish Parliament for Berwick to become part of Scotland again. It is argued that the border be moved twenty miles south – backed up by a poll in Berwick which saw a majority in favour of redrawing the border. *My* only hope was that a raid wouldn't take place in the next twenty four hours or so. The Walls seemed a good place for a walk to soak up some of the turbulent history this place had seen.

I continued along the line of the wall, not along the top but in its lee out of the gale-force wind, and came to the site of the ruins of Berwick Castle and its ramparts on an open grass-covered area. I'd also noticed some signs marking the Lowry Trail and there was one here, indicating *The Lions*.

L. S Lowry's paintings appeal to me – I'm irresistibly drawn to his 'matchstick men' and unfussy depiction of urban and industrial areas. It turns out that he was especially fond of Berwick and returned here on holiday many times, almost buying a house on the castle walls. And here I was – standing in front of it; *The Lions* is a pair of fine stone sculptures on top of the gateposts. Lowry was advised against purchasing this property because of the rampant damp but there was no doubt that he was attracted to it – the theme of a derelict and decaying house recurs in many of his paintings.

'I'm attracted to decay,' Lowry once said. 'In a way to ugliness too. A derelict house gets me.'

I carried on following the trail in Lowry's footsteps, and realised it was also the walk along the Walls – I was getting 'two for the price of one'. Further display boards identified the site of some of Lowry's paintings – I came across *The Football Match* and *The Town Hall*. The latter depicts the central spire of the town hall which still dominates the town today and which I had first spotted from the other side of the Tweed. Lowry sold this painting in London for thirty guineas (£31.50) which even then was beyond the pocket of the ordinary man in the street (so although he drew the working class man, the market for his work was among the more affluent).

From this corner of the Walls I had a clear view of the Viaduct Bridge and a plaque told me that it was built by Robert Stephenson (son of George Stephenson, the 'Father of Railways'); this is Berwick's other Grade 1 listed bridge, opened by Queen Victoria in 1850. Surely the second finest way to arrive in Berwick from the south must be by train over the viaduct, 121 feet above the River Tweed (the finest being by bike along the coast as I had done).

There was just time to nip into a small supermarket for something to cook for a meal later before collecting my bike. Ian and I had a pleasant chat about bikes; he obviously was a cycling enthusiast and it was a good opportunity for me to get some sound independent advice. He advised me that my bike's transmission was on the way out, but that it would last long enough to see me to the end of my trip.

He surprised me by asking, 'Where was the grey-cinders path you cycled along?'

'Scarborough to Whitby,' I answered. 'Oh, you must have found grey cinders still lodged in the workings – that's amazing after all the miles I've covered since.'

I wished *Wilson's Cycles* had a branch in Dorset. I thanked Ian and pushed my bike over to the shed next to the YH and collected the key to open it. Once back in my dorm I saw a young woman sitting on one of the bunks unpacking her case. We chatted and she told me about her plans for the coming week.

'I'm joining an archaeological dig on Hadrian's Wall and thought I'd spend a couple of days looking around Berwick first. It's my first time here.'

Susan had come up by train from south-east England and had been to a few archaeological digs before. She made it sound very interesting and sociable; perhaps it was an activity I might take part in sometime.

As usual the hostel was quiet and I had the kitchen to myself. It was stocked with every utensil you could want. After eating and clearing away my dirty dishes, thoroughly aware that I had to 'leave it as I would want to find it myself'. I remembered that I wanted to telephone Stuart, so after checking the weather forecast on the TV ('rain moving in from the west later on tomorrow') I went to find my phone.

'Hello Auntie Enid,' answered Stuart in his attractive Highland lilt, 'great to hear from you. How's it going?'

It was very cheering to talk to Stuart and he seemed as keen for me to stay with them as I was to go there, so I knew we'd find a way of accomplishing it. I explained to him that I had a long run the next day, over fifty miles and over 1200 metres of hills to climb. 'To be honest, Stuart, I'm not sure that I will manage it especially if the weather is against me.'

'No problem,' he replied, 'you've got mine and Natalie's numbers. Just ring us if you need to and one of us will come out and give you a lift.'

I knew that my bicycle would not go in their car, but even just taking my luggage and knowing that they were on hand would give me the extra reassurance I needed to get to their house.

'Thanks, Stuart. That will really help. Can't wait to see you all tomorrow, especially my newest great-niece, Emily. Bye.'

I sat in the hostel lounge and checked my route for tomorrow – I wanted to see if I had any options to shorten it or reduce some of the climbing. After Kelso the marked cycle trail appeared to criss-cross an undulating area – the only alternative for me would be to take the main A road – I would need to size it up when I got there.

Tomorrow, all being well, I would cross the border into Scotland. This would be a big moment in my journey. All Scots will identify with the strong emotions invoked in returning to their homeland; I expect people from every country in the world feel the same when they go back to the land of their birth. Obviously I have returned many times since leaving at the age of 27½ to live in London, but I had always made the journey by train, car or plane – cycling over the border having come all the way from where I live now in Dorset would be special.

I took myself out of Scotland all those years ago, but it will never be possible to take Scotland out of me. I love it with a passion. As soon as I cross the border I feel one hundred per cent at home – I truly belong here. The voices, dialects, accents all sound the right note in my ear; the people are warm and friendly, there are so many grand stone buildings to be seen everywhere from the great cities to the smallest croft, and last but not least, the countryside and hills beckon me to tramp their soil once again.

When my eldest son travelled from Dubai with Somayeh, his Iranian fiancée, for their first holiday together to the UK it was to Scotland he brought her. They landed at Edinburgh Airport and motored up to the Isle of Skye to potter about on beaches and walk through pine forests. Notice the significance of this though: James was born in England, with an English father and a Scottish mother, lived twenty four years in the south of England, except for the 1½ yrs in Botswana, before moving to live in Dubai. Yet the love for Scotland that I have, has passed down a generation once more and if it's not in his DNA, then it's definitely in his psyche. It's a similar thing with his younger brother, Andy, who also hightails it off to Scotland, and to the Highlands preferably, when presented with the slightest opportunity.

When I finished my exams at the end of my four year geography degree course in the month of June many years ago, I went directly to Waverley Station in Edinburgh to catch the train through to Glasgow and then transferred to the West Highland line which took me to Mallaig. I stayed a couple of nights in a youth hostel nearby but that wasn't my ultimate destination. The following day I boarded a Caledonian MacBrayne ferry to cross 'over the sea to Skye'; there's something about going to an island which makes it feel more remote (in 1974 Skye had not yet been connected to the mainland by bridge so it still seemed a far-flung place).

On reaching Skye I walked along the little pier and through the village of Armadale until I was out of sight of any buildings, then I made my way down to a deserted pebble beach. I collected some bits of driftwood and a fish box that had washed up on the shore and took them over to a sheltered spot next to some rocks. I laid a fire, lit it and succeeded easily in getting a good blaze going, then placed the upturned box next to it to serve as a table. I opened up my canvas knapsack (an old one of Dad's) and took out a neat little cooking set (consisting of a tiny saucepan and lid with a black removable Bakelite handle, frying pan and a lid which doubled as a plate and a metal cup whose handle I'd bound with thin rope to prevent scalding myself) and set them on my table. Also from my bag I lifted out a tin of baked beans, a small plastic box containing some sliced bread, a metal cutlery set and a bottle of water. I opened the tin and emptied the beans into the little pan and placed it carefully on a solid piece of post at the edge of my fire. Then I put my fork through a slice of bread and toasted it until it was

My 'banquet' on Armadale beach, Skye

golden brown, by which time the beans were bubbling away. The completed savoury ensemble was served up and I sat back against the rock and dined out in my five-star restaurant.

The sun bathed me in its warmth and I looked out over the Sound of Sleet and contemplated the moment. I'd studied hard for four years, loved every minute of it, but my brain now needed a rest. For me this meant solitude in my beloved Highlands and even better to be on one of the Islands. I sat there for a long while – I didn't feel the need to move – everything I wanted at that moment was there. It was my way of recharging my batteries which were depleted. When I lived in Norway I found similar boltholes where I could escape to and were equally picturesque, although not so emotionally charged for me as the country of my birth.

My soft spot for cooking over an open fire stemmed from my days in the Girl Guides, first joining the Brownies at the age of five, before I was even properly eligible. The expectation was always there, because both my elder sisters and my mother and her sister had all been ardent Girl Guides. So Monday night became Brownie night for the next six years; Mum produced an early tea for me so that I could run along to the Church Hall and join the fairy circle, dancing around the red and white painted toadstool. Three of us joined at the same time, but as we were all too young to be in a proper 'Six' we had our own 'Three' and were called the 'Imps'. I thoroughly enjoyed everything about being a Brownie, from working towards my badges, to the games we played every week, the songs we sang and the annual Christmas and Halloween parties.

Well, the last one had its good bits as well as its not-so-good bits: I enjoyed the 'dooking for apples', which meant biting at an apple bobbing around in a basin of water (some schools in Scotland now ban this activity as unhygienic) but wasn't so keen on the fancy-dress aspect.

My sister came up with the idea of dressing me up as 'Return to Sender' – now I was clueless as to what the relevance of this was, but as she was an avid Elvis fan and this record was No. 1 in the charts it was the 'coolest' thing going, so *she* thought. My sisters and mother stuck used and readdressed envelopes all over me, then sent me off to the party looking like, well actually, I can't think of any words to describe the look. Not only did I not know what I was supposed to be but neither did any of my fellow Brownies – perhaps Brown Owl and Tawny Owl knew but they weren't my peers. Since then I have disliked and avoided fancy-dress parties like the plague.

At the age of eleven I gained my 'Wings' and flew up to the Girl Guides where I spent some of the most enjoyable times of my teenage years. As well as the usual badges, I gained proficiency badges in first aid, pathfinder, knots, cooking, navigation, hostess, needlework, camping and so on – I don't think the fact that my sister was the Guide Captain proffered me any preferential treatment. It was with pride that I wore my guide blouse which displayed the badges I had sewn on both sleeves.

I became leader of my patrol, the 'Purple Heather', and during school holidays I would arrange with the half-dozen younger girls under my wing to meet me at the bus station in Dundee's town centre where we could catch the yellow Alexander bus going to Forfar. I'd previously scrutinised my Dad's Ordnance Survey map for a suitable wood near to a bus route and identified Tarbrax as where we needed to ask to be let off. From there it was a short hike into Tealing Woods where we set about gathering firewood. I'd learnt that dead gorse branches caught alight easily and flared for long enough to light the smaller kindling laid on top, so I passed that tip on to the others in my patrol. We were allowed only two matches to get our fire going but if we had gorse then one was sufficient.

Once the fires were going we cooked sausages and made 'dampers' out of flour and water – these were wrapped around a stick and baked over the hot ashes. It was all great fun and very satisfying to fend for ourselves without adults.

I continued on to the senior branch of the Guides, called the Rangers; there was only one group in Dundee so I got the bus into the town centre on a Friday evening to go there – fewer than a dozen of us went to this meeting. I met a new set of like-minded friends and carried on with my badge work. But it was very much a sociable gathering and we indulged in a bit of tomfoolery too.

On occasions we would set up a séance table with an upturned glass in the middle of it, surrounded by a large circle of the letters of the alphabet on pieces of paper plus one each with YES and NO written on them. We then put all but one light off and sat around the table, each with a finger lightly on the edge of the glass, and someone would ask a question, for example: 'Will Molly get married?', 'How many children will Enid have?' and we would watch as the glass skidded around the table answering our questions.

But frivolous as some of the evenings were, in my spare time I undertook the tasks needed to complete my Queen's Guide seriously. For my Commonwealth study I chose New Zealand; I went into the Old People's Home next to my library to carry out community work, but it was the Outdoor Challenge that got me most excited. It was decided that I would do a two-day hike across the Cairngorms from Deeside to Speyside with a woman called Sue who knew the leader of our Ranger group.

The plan was for Sue's husband to drop us off at Glenmore Lodge, beside Loch Morlich, at the start of the walk. When they came to my house to collect me Sue welcomed me and introduced me to her young daughter, 'Karen is going to join us on the walk.'

I was a bit surprised because Karen didn't look a day older than eight years old, but in fact, she was an absolute star throughout. Our route was through a pass known as the *Lairig an Laoigh*, less well-known than the *Lairig Ghru* to the west. We carried everything we needed in our rucsacs for an overnight stop in a bothy – my Dad's ancient canvas Bergen rucsac on a frame sat uncomfortably on my back.

The walk took us through pinewoods and up on to bleak moorland until at the end of the first day we reached the bothy which was in an isolated position high up in the Cairngorms. I remember it being roughly made of stone with a roof of corrugated metal and turf along its edges all securely tied down against the force of the winter storms. It was dark and cramped inside and quite a squash as there were half a dozen other males there too – the smell of sweaty socks and bodies must have been powerful as it has stuck in my memory.

The following morning was misty but Sue, with the aid of her map and compass, knew exactly what she was doing and directed us on the right course south towards Deeside. On the way we had to cross the River Avon, a substantial river which we needed to wade through –

when in spate it is impassable. Later on we crossed another fast-flowing torrent by jumping from rock to rock. My boots, a borrowed pair, were

rubbing my feet constantly by now, and when we reached the last mile or two along a road in Glen Derry, I was in such pain that I took off my boots and walked in my socks. When I examined my feet afterwards I found I had blisters the size of an old penny (3.6cm) on both heels, rubbed red raw. I made it to the gate where Sue's husband was waiting with the car to transport us back to Dundee. It had been a great adventure and I'd really enjoyed Sue and Karen's company.

Me crossing a fast-flowing stream in the Cairngorms

Soon afterwards I achieved the highest award in the Girl Guides, my Queen's Guide badge – there was no special presentation ceremony to mark it – I think it was just handed to me one evening. I recognised its value and never forgot my Aunt Marjorie saying to me, 'The inclusion of the Queen's Guide award on your curriculum vitae will mark you out as a doer and an achiever.'

The memory of my earlier and disastrous Cairngorm and Ben Loyal trips was becoming less significant as I started to tick off some successes in the mountains. These included reaching the summit of Ben Nevis four years earlier with a couple of my brothers, led by my Dad who, I hasten to add, got us down safely in one piece.

On the summit of Ben Nevis next to Dad, Colin and Bryan

Chapter Twenty-three

ACROSS THE BORDER

'Ping ping...ping ping,' I reached out and switched off my phone alarm before its crescendoing sound awoke my room-mate. I needed an early start to give myself the best possible chance of completing what was going to be a demanding day's ride. It didn't take long to gulp down a quick breakfast and go through the now familiar routine of packing my bags and attaching them to my bicycle. I put the waterproof covers over the rear panniers as I could smell the dampness in the air already.

With a grey overcast sky looming above me I cycled due west on a minor road and it wasn't long before I saw the large brown and white sign with a blue thistle up ahead:

SCOTLAND
welcomes you

At exactly 9.15am I crossed the notional painted line on the road. I set up my camera to take a delayed-action shot, positioned myself and my trusty two-wheeled conveyance in front of the sign and recorded for posterity this moment in my journey.

A few miles further on there was a cycle route signpost to the left, which meant almost doubling back on myself but it was a means of descending down to the crossing point over the River Tweed, where a marvellous surprise awaited me.

At the Border

It was a wrought-iron suspension bridge – superlatively strung between two stone towers. I spent a little while observing it and while I was standing mid-deck and peering through the wire cables at the slow-flowing water below I heard 'clickety clack, clickety clack,' as a lady drove her car over the bridge – I squeezed myself and the bike against the side to allow her passage across the narrow thoroughfare as she smiled and waved at me.

I couldn't see a plaque giving me details about this bridge but later on I investigated its history and found out that when it opened in 1820 it was the longest iron suspension bridge in the world with a span of 449 feet (137m). Today it is the oldest suspension bridge still carrying traffic, but only one vehicle is allowed on the bridge at a time – the weight of one car <u>and</u> one bicycle fortunately did not add up to overload.

The Union Suspension Bridge
over the River Tweed

For me it was yet another bridge I crossed which was a Grade 1 listed building in England (Category A listed building in Scotland). Yes, the river formed the border here and took me back over to England! In fact I criss-crossed the border a couple more times that day, but crucially ended up well inside Scotland at the end of the day.

I enjoyed a pleasant ride with occasional views of the river and the partly-ruined Norham Castle, a stronghold of the English against the Scots during the feuding years. The Tweed Valley is an extremely beautiful valley and I was lucky that the rain held off during the morning. Whenever I crossed the river I couldn't stop myself from slowing down to gaze into the deep pools beneath to look for salmon for which the river is famous, but if they were there they kept themselves well-hidden.

I could see from the signposts that this national cycle route was also a local one called the Four Abbeys and it was taking me on long detours up into the foothills in order to avoid the main roads. On one of these loops, I went through first the village of Eccles, then Ednam. The names rang a bell somewhere in my distant memory – then it came back to me what my connection to them was.

Our geography department at Edinburgh University was invited by the Borders Regional Department in 1973 to study various aspects of their region. They purposefully wanted objective views from people not familiar with the region, and so our final-year cohort was chosen to take part and the various topics distributed among us. I and three fellow students were asked to examine the role of the village in the context of changing social and economic conditions.

Our main findings seemed to be that rural depopulation was taking place (no surprises there), and that more and more houses were being bought by outsiders as second homes which was mainly considered to be a disadvantage as it raised houses prices dramatically – example cited was that five thousand pounds was paid for a small cottage with a tin roof.

In our report we listed the population of each village so I thought it would be interesting to compare them with the newest figures available:

	1974	2001	Increase/Decrease
Ednam	124	140	+16
Eccles	84	69	-15

In our summing up we said, 'Villages are not necessarily fated for extinction because of our ageing populations. Housing older people may come to be the principal function of many of the remote villages,' and one of our recommendations was, 'The existing number of bus services should be maintained and any means of improving them considered.'

Using information from then and now, it appears that the frequency of bus services to both villages does not appear to have declined – they both have services on three to four days a week. I was surprised to find that the populations of both villages had not decreased dramatically, in fact Ednam's had increased; without further analysis I cannot be sure, but I would expect the percentage of *older people* in both places to have increased. It looks as though the existence of a bus service and nowadays, a free bus pass for the elderly, help to make it a viable place to live in the first part of the 21st century. I'm glad to see villages in the Borders are thriving and that the rural areas have not become impoverished backwaters.

I can also state that I was finding the hills to get to those villages hard work and was aware of the distance I still had to cover. As Kelso came into sight at the bottom of the hill, I decided not to take the right turn as signposted at the edge of the town. That way went back up to the hills and I wanted to go in to the town and have a break and choose which route to follow for the next section.

The cold and 'dreich'[1] weather was taking its toll on me and I realised that what I wanted more than anything was a hot bowl of soup. It felt too much effort to find a suitable cafe where I could padlock my bicycle securely so it was simpler to buy from a take-away. I purchased a polystyrene cup of thick steaming Scotch broth. I found a bench in the town square to sit on; opposite me was a prominently positioned notice that informed me I was in the largest market square in Scotland. I admired the elegant Georgian and Victorian buildings on all sides of the square as the feeling gradually returned to my cold fingers wrapped around the cup of warm soup.

I perused my map and decided to risk ten miles on the main A669 route between Kelso and St Boswells – it would eliminate the big hill climbs on that section.

I cycled out of Kelso past the Abbey and across the Rennie Bridge over the Tweed – designed by John Rennie over two hundred years ago, reckoned to be his finest and a prototype for his Waterloo Bridge in London.

Almost immediately afterwards I came to the confluence of the River Teviot with the Tweed and after crossing the former a magnificent castle came into view on the north bank of the Tweed – I could see from my map that it was Floors Castle – later on when I checked it out I saw that it is the home of the Duke of Roxburgh.

He is not the only Duke who lives in the Tweed Valley. Several miles further west is Mertoun House, home to the Duke and Duchess of

---

[1] Scot's word meaning bleak or miserable

Sutherland, where one of my nephews worked for over eight years. Grant, second son of my brother Donald and his wife Barbara, is the only one to have followed in his father's footsteps to earn his living as a gardener. When he was eighteen year's old he was interviewed for a job at the Mertoun Estate, but Alfie, the head gardener, felt he was too young. Grant's reply was, 'Thank you for the opportunity to see the wonderful gardens here. I'm very impressed with them and hope that you will consider me for a job here one day. I would love to work on the Mertoun Estate with you.'

Grant got his wish when he was backpacking around Europe a few years later; Alfie contacted him about a vacancy. Grant told me the story: 'The timing was perfect and felt like fate. Working under Alfie who had been there for 50 years, and his father before that, gave me an insight into what working on an estate would have been like 100 years ago.'

I concentrated on the road in front of me listening out for vehicles coming up behind so that I wouldn't be taken by surprise when one whipped past me. It took me slightly less than an hour to reach St Boswell's where I turned on to the even busier A68 to Melrose, but just around the corner I stopped in a recreation ground for a breather from the traffic before continuing.

I was able to rejoin the Four Abbeys' cycle route here and was only on the A road for a mile before turning on to a minor road through Newton St Boswells and an old railway track, now the cycleway, to Melrose. I didn't stop in Melrose, home to another Abbey, but continued along the old railway to Galashiels.

Wow, was I tired though. I knew I would need an extended rest if I was to complete the remainder of the ride from Gala to Stow, about ten miles further on and a hundred metres higher up in the hills. It was mid-afternoon and the rain, apart from a few light showers, was holding off for the time being. I saw a large supermarket which I guessed would have a cafeteria. I padlocked my bike under cover beside the trolleys and trotted upstairs where I ordered a pot of tea and a scone and sat down to recover my strength for the final push of the day.

Over half an hour later and duly revived, having conveniently missed a heavy shower, I emerged ready to continue. I had no option for the first few miles but to take the A7, the main road between Gala and Edinburgh. It was not pleasant. Buses and lorries came too close as they passed me up the winding and gradually-ascending valley of the Gala Water. I pulled over on to the side several times when I felt I might be squeezed too far and tumble over the edge into the ravine below.

I was more than happy when I reached the bridging point which would take me on to a minor road on the other side. The last few miles along this peaceful moorland road were some of the most idyllic I encountered anywhere. Sheep with their lambs next to them looked up at me and 'baa-ed' as they grazed by the side of the road. The fast-flowing streams ran as clear as a bell. This was my sort of countryside – a world away from the noisy heavy traffic on the other side of the valley. A watery sun even made a brief appearance.

My first sight of Stow was the parish church spire rising up 140 feet, in front of which was a field of lush green grass with a herd of brown and white cows lying down. As I crossed the river I caught a glimpse of an ancient packhorse bridge downstream. Stuart and Natalie's house was on the main street and easy to find – I reached it at 4.30pm after cycling 54 miles over quite a hilly route. I was pleased to be ringing the door bell knowing that I had made it here under my own steam.

'Hello Enid. I bet you could do with a cup of tea. What an amazing challenge you've set yourself,' said Natalie as she warmly welcomed me.

'Hi, it's great to have got here. This must be Emily. How old is she?'

'She'll be six months in two day's time.'

After carrying in my bags I sat down in a comfortable armchair and soon was sipping a welcome cup of tea. Emily was a real sweetie, looking around her, playing and gurgling away quite happily. Natalie and I had lots to chat about, not least the plans for their forthcoming wedding in ten day's time at Dryburgh Abbey. 'We're hoping so much for a dry day, but with all this rain we've had we just don't hold out a lot of hope.'

As she spoke we heard a clap of thunder and the cloudburst that had been threatening all day sprung into action and lashed against the windows. My timing had been perfect, thank goodness. There was the sound of a door opening and in walked Stuart.

'Hi, great to see you. This bike ride you're doing is just incredible. When did you arrive?'

I stood up to give Stuart a warm hug and he joined us for more tea, chat and catch-up. They were an easy young couple to speak to, wanting to know all about my journey and how my family were. They were understandably in excellent spirits with their wedding fast approaching; I was glad to know that they, especially Natalie, appeared to have everything under control and nothing left to chance.

While they prepared dinner I had a lovely hot soak in the bath and felt refreshed in a set of clean clothes. They even offered to run a load of my washing through their machine which was a kind and thoughtful gesture and one I gratefully accepted. Dinner sitting round the kitchen table was lasagne and salad, followed by a home-baked cake – just delicious.

Before it was time for Emily to go to bed I said, 'I'd really like to take some photographs of Emily and also of us all together.'

Emily was 'suspended' in one of those baby-walker devices hanging from the door frame in which she could sit and by just touching her toes on the floor propel herself about – she was doing a little dance of her own and obviously loving it – such a bundle of fun. So I started off with some portraits of her then moved on to a few delayed-shutter shots of us all sitting together on the settee. Natalie then asked, 'Would you like your picture taken with Emily – just the two of you?' So the final shots were of Emily sitting on my knee wide-eyed with a big smile.

With Emily, my great-niece

I gave her a kiss and said 'Goodnight, little sweetie, sleep tight.'

I hadn't had the opportunity to chat at length with Stuart for a while so the three of us delved into and discussed all and sundry that evening.

One thing playing on Stuart's mind was his mother's health. Barbara had been through a lot – she'd lost her husband and best friend when still a young mother with four boys to raise. Several years ago she had sold the house and Nursery in Acharacle in the west of Scotland and moved to Kelso in the Borders to be closer to the two of her sons who lived there.

Stuart explained further, 'I got a call from Grant one morning last week while at work to tell me that Mum had fallen and couldn't get up so had called the emergency services for assistance.' He went on to describe how she was struggling to walk even with the aid of two sticks or a walking frame, and that her house had a step between some of the rooms making it quite impractical for her in her present condition. He and Natalie were obviously deeply worried and once the wedding was over vowed to do what they could to alleviate her situation, which would probably mean helping her to move to a more suitable house.

My extended family had over the years expanded greatly. It was rare for many of us to be in the same place at the same time, but when it did happen we tried to capture the gathering on a camera. This year was a special one because not only was my nephew getting married, but a few months later my niece Kat was marrying Alex in Reading, and one month later my son James was marrying Somayeh in Dubai. They would all be opportunities for some of us to get together; not all of us, as my brother and his wife who live in Australia would not be joining us, and not everyone else would be at all three weddings.

Without photographs I wouldn't have any memory of the earliest family weddings I had attended. My eldest sister, Jean was the first in the family to get married and she had asked her two sisters to be bridesmaids. Our dresses were all made at home out of a coral pink satin with shoes to match (my first time in high-ish heels). The morning of the wedding was spent at the hairdresser having my hair curled with rollers, back-combed and sprayed copiously into a beehive style finished off with a humungous pink silk flower. While under the noisy hairdryer, my first-ever experience of a hair salon 'shampoo and set', I spoke to my sister in what I thought was my normal voice. Back came her reply, 'Ssh, there's no need to shout. Everyone in the shop can hear you.'

The resulting black and white snap of the three sisters posing outside the church is my only window back on to that day; if you can picture the Ronette sisters in the 1960s or any similar girl group then that was us. I cannot recognise myself from the image of the girl with the bouffant hair and dress with big bow looking up shyly for the camera; on the other hand my two sisters are instantly recognisable to me.

Jean's wedding day. I am on the left and Diana on the right.

In the space of a few years I made two further appearances as bridesmaid, first at my other sister's and then at Alan, my brother's wedding. By this time I'd grown my hair long and wore it loose over my shoulders.

Family weddings were the only time I ever saw my cousins, there were only four of them, all on my father's side and all older than me, thus I never felt I got to know them well. Our house was so full with the nine of us that I guess the thought of entertaining such a large family was considered too great a burden to undertake. Probably my aunts and uncles shied away from inviting us – who in their right minds would take on catering for an extra nine people?

The exception was a couple, known to me as Agnes and Bert, who had no children of their own; I do not know my relationship to them – perhaps cousin once removed or something like that? They invited us to their house several times and always prepared a scrumptious feast for us followed by a couple of hours of board games – we were less than the full nine, some of my older siblings had left home by then. It seemed to me to be a kind gesture and I enjoyed the visits all the more because they were a rarity.

My first niece, Lorna, was born to Jean and Ian in 1968, and over the next twenty years I gained twelve more nephews and nieces and, of course, two sons. Added to that number are now fourteen great-nephews and nieces. Together with spouses and partners there are at least 53 of us and counting as new ones arrive.

So it's not surprising when two or more of us get together we can talk long into the night catching up on news of our large family. Eventually Stuart, Natalie and I called it a day and went to our beds.

Chapter Twenty-four

BETWEEN A ROCK AND A CANDLE

I opened my eyes, saw it was light and all was quiet. Surely I could not be in the same house as a six-month old child? Emily was a remarkably content little girl and did not utter one cry or whimper all the time I was there. As I walked into the kitchen to join the others for breakfast she turned round in her high chair to have a better look at me and then smiled.

'Good morning,' I said to her parents, 'may I take Emily with me please? She is so adorable. I could sit her up on the top of my panniers and strap her in securely.'

Natalie and Stuart laughed. We talked about my plans for the day which in a nutshell were to cycle to Edinburgh. As usual heavy rain was forecast for later so I wanted an early start. I knew Stuart was driving to Edinburgh where he worked as a civil engineer and he volunteered with, 'I can give you a lift to Edinburgh. I'm sure I can fit your bicycle in somehow.'

It was my turn to smile, 'Thanks, it's very kind of you to offer, but I would like to cycle. But you know what Stuart? If you could take my pannier bags that would make my ride a lot easier and maybe quicker too.'

He was very happy to oblige and we arranged that he would call at my friend, Jenny's house, after work and drop them off then. It didn't take me long to pack and put the bags into his car, then I waved him off. Not long after his departure, I gave little Emily a final hug saying to her, 'Not long until we see each other again. I won't be wearing this cycling gear and you'll not be in a babygro – we'll both be in pretty dresses.' I thanked Natalie and wished her well with all the last-minute planning and told her how much I was looking forward to the wedding.

'Bye Enid. It's been lovely having you. Take care and enjoy your ride to Edinburgh. Rather you than me!'

I cycled back over the Gala Water to take the minor road up the valley in a northerly direction. Once again I enjoyed the rural aspect of this dale, and the sound of bleating lambs looking for their mothers resonated all around me. Although I was cycling along a road, I could see below me the track of the old railway next to the stream.

If I was doing this journey in 2015 then I might have the option of boarding a train at Stow and travelling into Waverley Station in Edinburgh by rail. Stuart had told me of the *Borders Railway Project*, an ambitious scheme to re-open the old Waverley Railway which was closed in 1969. It will be the longest new domestic railway to be constructed in Britain for over 100 years – thirty new miles of rail track will be constructed. I could see that work had already begun on rebuilding the station in Stow.

I was feeling good this morning, with no weight on the back of the bike, it felt like I was flying as I scaled the 220 metres to reach my highest point of the Moorfoot Hills in the Southern Uplands. The eight miles of steady climbing took me just over one hour. I had noticed a big difference in my fitness over the past three weeks when I was cycling up hills – it was less of an effort than it had been before the trip and I was doing it in a higher gear.

The landscape up here on the moorland was bleak, emphasised by the mist shrouding the highest hills; there were few dwellings apart from a few isolated farms. Mainly the vegetation was grass or bracken with some extensive areas of heather on the slopes. Dry-stone walls separated fields from one another but it was too high for cultivated crops – it was all pastoral land for sheep and cattle.

On the other side of the pass the run downhill was exhilarating – the five miles of freewheeling was extended by a mile and half because I was enjoying it so much I forgot to swing off left on to a smaller road and only realised when I met the main road with busy traffic zipping along it. A quick look at my map showed me that I would have to retrace the last mile and a half to get back on to my correct route. What had taken me only three minutes to race down took almost fifteen minutes to go back up – oh well, it would teach me to look at my GPS more often.

The visibility was not very good or I would have been able to see the city of Edinburgh and the Firth of Forth as I was descending the hill. However, I knew what was hiding in the haze and I had a real feeling of entering home ground. I knew this city well, having lived in it for five years.

I had already covered about half of today's mileage and so only had about twenty miles left to go when the sky suddenly darkened and the heavens opened. I pulled up sharply under the nearest tree and waited for the heavy shower to pass over. This happened a couple of times more, but trees alas are not bus shelters and they do tend to drip after a while. My body cooled off rapidly and I put on an extra layer.

As I rode into Bonnyrigg the main thing on my mind was a cup of coffee and so when I spied a suitable cafe on the High Street I parked up, leaned my bicycle close to the window and put an empty carrier bag over the saddle to keep it dry – I would be able to keep an eye on my bike from the empty table I could see just inside.

'What can I get you with your drink?' It was uplifting to hear my own accent reflected back at me from the girl pouring my coffee. As I sat next to the window munching on a substantial piece of homemade shortbread, the feeling of excitement was building up inside me because I was closing in on the capital city. The familiar pitter patter of rain on the window alerted me to another shower of rain. I waited until it had passed over then went back outside to continue on my way.

I had only gone a few yards along the High Street when I saw another cyclist, weighed down with a large rucsac on his back, in a lay-by so I stopped to say hello. He told me his name was Paul and with encouragement from me went on to tell me what he was doing.

'I started off from Land's End twenty-seven days ago with no money and no belongings. My intention is to reach John O'Groats to raise money for a charity which aims to end child poverty in Malawi. I'm entirely dependent on people's generosity for accommodation and food. Walking in all the rain early on gave me terrible blisters so I transferred to a bicycle. A bike shop in Exeter donated it to me, but people have given me so much stuff along the way that I've ended up carrying this 35 pound backpack and it's killing me. However, the good side is the wonderful generosity I've been shown from both individuals and businesses – I've even spent a night in a 5-star hotel.'

'Actually, I remember reading about you in a news article recently,' I put in, 'you're obviously getting some good publicity.'

We exchanged stories for a while longer – it was satisfying to talk with another person who was undertaking a similar challenge and was experiencing some of the same things. He, too, was staying with a friend in Edinburgh for two nights and was looking forward to the rest and company. After that he was hoping to ditch the bike and walk the rest of the way to the top of Scotland. We exchanged blog addresses and wished each other well for the remainder of our journeys.

My story had appeared in the Dundee Courier a few days earlier under the headline 'Enid gets on bike for Wedding.' My friend Mary who for many years worked for D. C. Thomson, the well-known publisher of newspapers and magazines, had submitted the article.

An underpass took me to the other side of the Edinburgh city-bypass road and a couple of minutes later I saw a familiar maroon and white double-decker bus, the striking colour of the city bus fleet – now I really felt I had arrived in the city. I chose to come in on Dalkeith Road because I wanted to pass by Pollock Halls, the university halls of residence where I'd had a room for part of my time as a student there. In 1970 the Commonwealth Games were held in Edinburgh and to house the competitors a village was constructed next to the new Commonwealth Pool. The apartment blocks became student accommodation following the Games.

My room was on the far side overlooking Salisbury Crags, a cliff formed from a basalt intrusion connected to the volcanic vent of Arthur's Seat, a prominent peak providing a panoramic view of the city and surrounding area. Geology was one of the subjects I studied in my first year and I soon learnt that James Hutton, in the18th century, found evidence in Salisbury Crags that it was once molten igneous rock. From this, he surmised that the sedimentary rock underneath was laid down at a different time and so disproved the suggested theory of the time which stated that all rocks had crystallised from a primordial sea. Hutton became known as the 'Father of Modern Geology'.

Many a time my gaze would wander from the books I was studying to the cliff face which filled my window, and I would follow the line of rock silhouetted against the skyline to the summit of Arthur's Seat. I

watched it change with the seasons: in winter the slopes were white with snow, in spring the sheep and lambs grazed the extensive pasture and in autumn the leaves on the trees glinted gold and yellow. It was the ideal room for a country lover like myself, and when I needed a break from studying I could stretch my legs and get a good blast of fresh air just minutes from my door. Fond memories of my student days were

My student room at Pollock Halls, Edinburgh University. Looking out over Arthur's Seat.

rekindled as I passed the 1970s 'shoebox' buildings.

I then followed a well-trodden route of mine to The Meadows, a large grassy area I had crossed many a time by foot to get to the library and other university buildings where my lectures were held. During the winter of 1972, I lived with a couple of friends in a flat overlooking the Meadows. It was the year when the miners went on strike and picketed power stations in an attempt to step up pressure on the government to yield to their pay demands.

As a result of the diminishing stocks of coal for generating electricity, it was necessary to instigate a rota of power cuts. A state of emergency was declared on February 9th. We knew in advance when it would be our turn to be without power for the nine hour stretch. By good fortune our flat and the library, although separated by only a couple of hundred yards, were in different zones for power cuts, thus my evenings were spent in the one which had the lights and heating on. At home when the power was switched off, we sat by candlelight and engaged in conversation, instead of watching television as would be the norm. This was repeated in homes all over the country. I can remember going into shops dimly lit by candles and walking home in total darkness. The country was almost brought to its knees for a fortnight, but once a settlement was reached the power was switched on and everything quickly returned to normal.

Crossing Edinburgh in the 21st century by bicycle was novel to me – trying to negotiate the road closures and diversions around Haymarket caused me a bit of head-scratching, as the main thoroughfares were no-go areas due to the building of the new tramway. Originally started in 2008 to run between the airport and the waterfront, there have been numerous delays in its construction. The final cost is expected to exceed one billion pounds which is hideously over budget, only go as far as the city centre (half the original planned distance) and the latest estimated opening date is now summer 2014. Many Edinburgh folk are sick to the back teeth of the delays, its concrete ugliness and the increase in expenditure of this project 'which will end up costing more than the rocket used in the moon landing.' Their anger and frustration has resulted in comments such as: 'we could have put a Scot on Mars for less than this fiasco,' and 'the most embarrassing public transport project in Europe'.

Weaving my way through back streets I found Corstorphine Road and headed out west to Jenny and Alistair's house. Amongst all my friends and acquaintances I have known Jenny the longest. She grew up in the same road as me in Dundee and we attended the same Brownie pack and Sunday School, same secondary school and same university.

During our second year at university I asked Jenny to go to a party with me which some of my geology friends were holding in their flat. It was there that she and Alastair met for the first time and have been together ever since; as a result she credits me with introducing them to each other. I didn't know him as Alastair then – everybody called him 'Snuff', but if I ever knew why I have long since forgotten the reason. Forty years on it doesn't seem quite right or respectful to call him Snuff so I have reverted to Alastair.

Alastair was out when I arrived but Jenny made me most welcome and we sat in their bright sitting room and chatted nonstop for hours. Jenny has kept up with many more friends from school than me, so she was able to fill me in on what they were all doing now. Through her husband's contacts with his geology set of friends, especially those living locally, she also recounted their life stories to date. There were both happy and sad stories to relate. On hearing the door open she said, 'Oh, there's Snuff coming in now.' That left me in a quandary – should I call him Snuff or Alastair?

After dinner we retired back to the sitting room and were surprised to find the sun providing a very pleasant end to the day – not the rain as forecast. Tomorrow was a rest day and there was no better place to spend it than in Auld Reekie[1] with friends.

---

[1] Edinburgh's nickname – from the days when the smoke from countless fires filled the town

Chapter Twenty-five

HIPPO HIGHWAY

Corstorphine was the home of two relatively new inhabitants and it was our intention to pay them a visit – I hoped they would be awake. Their names were Yang Guang ('sunshine') and Tian Tian ('sweetie') and they were two giant pandas loaned to Edinburgh Zoo from China for ten years, with the hope that together they will produce baby pandas.

We lined up with the rest of the zoo goers who had tickets to see the special guests and after much milling around, the rules of engagement for visiting the bears were read out:

It will take approximately 20 minutes to see the panda experience; due to any unforeseen animal welfare issues viewing sessions may be suspended without notice; during certain points of the day, the pandas will be taken off-show for short periods of time, we will alternate this so there is always one panda on-show; no flash photography is allowed whilst in the panda experience.

When it was our turn to enter the first specially-built enclosure, we could see a very large black and white shape sprawled out on a high shelf with its back to us. 'This is Tian Tian,' we were informed by our guide, 'she is nine years old and has previously given birth to twins. She is quiet and appears quite reserved and eats very slowly and delicately, however this ladylike image hides a mischievous side and she will have a swipe at you if you are not careful. She is also quite fussy with her food and so far we have had to cut fresh bamboo for her daily.'

We watched and photographed Tian Tian for the allotted time slot and then were led next door to see if Yang Guang would be livelier and he did not disappoint. He was sitting in the fork of a tree munching on a large and thick bamboo cane, which we were told is his food of choice.

The guide added, 'He loves to be outdoors even in the heavy rain, and then afterwards he likes to climb into his basket for a snooze.'

It was but a brief glimpse into their lives but a privilege nonetheless to watch these beautiful and serene creatures in our country, without necessitating a long trip to China. As I waved goodbye to TT and YG I murmured a short silent prayer wishing them every success on their holiday in Edinburgh and that they would return home with a leaving present of little baby pandas.

Alastair left us to go to Aberdeen on business while Jenny and I continued on around the zoo. I am ambivalent when it comes to seeing animals caged – if the only reason is so that we can gape at them then I cannot be party to it, but I know that there is more often than not an emphasis on conservation and research. Zoos can play a major role in the ever-increasing need to maintain populations of threatened species.

Near to my home in Dorset is a wonderful example of an animal sanctuary where primates, usually babies or youngsters, are brought to be rehabilitated in natural family groups. Monkey World rescues chimps, orang-utans, gibbons and lemurs from all over the world, from situations in which they were abused or neglected. This worthy centre exists to stop the smuggling of primates around the world; every time I visit I am thrilled to see the large variety of primates living healthy and contented lives in first-class accommodation – undoubtedly their well-being is in expert hands.

Sometimes while travelling in the bush in southern Africa we had encounters with wild animals which were too close for comfort. One example which springs to mind is when James, Andy and I were camping in the Matopos Hills National Park in the south of Zimbabwe – we'd taken our bikes and gone out for a morning ride – cycling was an officially-permitted activity in this particular area as there were no lions or other such predators, except that our guide book did mention that late-afternoon or early-evening visitors may be 'lucky enough to spot leopard'. As far as we were concerned the biggest dangers lurked in the water – crocodiles and bilharzia!

Our cycle ride was going well and we were enjoying the tranquillity and beauty of the park and watching a pair of black eagles circling high above us. We were passing a hill-side of granite *kopjes* (large rocks or crags) when James noticed something in front of him: 'Mum, what do these footprints belong to?' We closed in for a better look and none of us had any doubt what they belonged to – one of the books we carried with us was *Signs of the Wild* and both boys had spent long hours studying the detailed diagrams of spoor on its pages.

Spoor 6,5-9 cm long

'It's leopard isn't it?' The animal had walked along the sandy road for a short way and then gone off into the bush, and the pug marks were *on top of* the most recent tyre tracks on the road. They were fresh!

The photograph of leopard spoor in our identification book

I looked around us, but of course, no self-respecting leopard would allow itself to be seen so easily and there were numerous hiding places on this stretch amongst all the rocky outcrops.

'Stay close together boys – let's cycle on.' It was easy to imagine a leopard watching and following us as we continued along the track, invisible to us but ready to pounce. We pedalled on in silence; the air now had a menacing feel all around us – were we being stalked by the leopard? It was a while until we relaxed and felt safe once more.

However, that wasn't the closest encounter with a dangerous animal we experienced – it came on a camping trip in the Okavango Delta of Botswana, when it was more than just footprints in the sand we saw.

My *Isuzu* truck was not suitable for driving in the Delta area so we hired a four-wheel drive *Toyota Hilux* to enable us to tackle the sandy and/or muddy areas we would pass through. We'd started off this part of our trip with another family from Maun and were enjoying watching wildlife from the safety of our vehicles. We arrived at Xakanaxa campsite (unfenced), a beautiful spot close to lagoons and lakes, where we were to spend our second night, but unfortunately the other family felt they had to return home because one of their members had fallen ill.

We stayed and pitched our two tents under the shade of some trees from where we could see the edge of a reed-covered lake. Before cooking dinner we went for an early evening drive to view the animals at dusk and were lucky to see lion cubs (part of a tribe known as the Xakanaxa tribe), in addition to zebra and many impala.

Back at camp, James lit our braii (an open fireplace), for us to cook on – he had acquired expert fire-laying and lighting skills on our previous camping trips in the African bush – while Andy and I gathered wood. I had even purchased a braai fan for James, described as 'a convenient and essential accessory for the professional braai maker,' which helped him get a good fire going quickly. Having eaten our dinner and cleared up most of our dishes, we left a couple of pots soaking on the ground, retired to our tents and went off to sleep to the sound of crickets chirping in the long grass...

...our dreams were abruptly interrupted by a loud clattering sound close to our ears. 'Something' had obviously got a hold of our pots, so I yelled, 'Go away!' and heard 'the something' run away. I saw through the mesh of my tent door that the pot had been dropped. James called over, 'What was that Mum?'

'A baboon,' I answered, not needing to add that the baboon has sharper teeth than a lion. From a distance the sound of a roaring lion could be heard. 'The Xakanaxa lions don't like the baboons on their patch – they're roaring at them to scare them away.'

I lay down to try to get some more sleep, then...

'Thump...   thump...   thump...'

The steady thudding noise was getting nearer – I then realised it was a hippopotamus approaching – I sat up and listened as it got closer and closer. I could not see it because it was coming up behind the boys' tent. The ground began to tremble with each footstep and I stayed sitting bolt upright, rigid with fear – the only other sound was the hammering of my heartbeat. Was it going to trample over our tents? I waited soundlessly, just listening intently...

... at the very last second it deviated from its straight line, and through the canvas I could just about make out a large shape manoeuvre its huge bulk around the side of the other tent...

... now it was coming straight for my tent – I held my breath not wanting to make a sound – then the inside of the tent went into shadow as the hippo obscured the mesh door and my nostrils became aware of a strong pungent odour. The hippo's halitosis had penetrated the whole tent! It plodded slowly and steadily on past, but still I didn't move or utter a sound. I thought it might come back.

I waited until its dull footsteps receded into the distance. Then, without hesitation, I gathered up my sleeping bag, rushed out of the door and over to the other tent, 'James, are you okay in there? It's gone. Bring your sleeping bag and we'll get into the truck.'

'Andy's sleeping – shall I wake him up?'

'Yes, and tell him to bring his sleeping bag too.'

I helped a dozy Andy out of the tent and into the back of the vehicle where he promptly went straight back to sleep.

'Mum, I was petrified the hippo was going to walk right over the tent,' James confessed.

'Me too, James. I was scared stiff – it came far too close.' Neither of us got much sleep for the remainder of that night but, most importantly, we felt secure in the truck.

In the morning we talked to some other people around the campsite and learned that the hippopotamus regularly came out of the water at night and walked along a path by the edge of the water – we could now see that our tents were directly in the track of his nocturnal ramble! 'However,' we were told, 'it hasn't ever been known to trample anyone's tent.' We filled Andy in on the details of the terror of the night before – James and I were amazed that he had slept through it all.

We were taking no chances – we had no intentions of becoming 'Henry the Hippo's' first victims. We unpegged our tents, lifted them on to the roof of the *Toyota* and moved

Moving our tent to a safe position

them 20 yards beyond the hippo's path behind a tall termite mound, where we felt safe. The following night there was no repeat encounter with Henry but James did call over to me in the middle of the night, 'Mum, I've just seen a hyena looking though our tent door.'

'Stay inside your tent – you'll be fine in there,' I reassured him. I didn't open my eyes – if there were two eyes peering through my mesh window I definitely did not want to see them.

We left Xakanaxa as planned the next day and continued our game drives through the striking scenery of the Delta. I was surprised when we came to a river called the Kwai and delighted to find that we needed to cross the *Bridge over the River Kwai* –a wooden pole construction wholly in keeping with its surroundings and more picturesque than the famous iron railway bridge in Thailand. Without doubt, the Okavango Delta is one of the most incredible places I have had the good fortune to visit.

Our last trip before we left Botswana in the mid-1990s was an extended journey lasting several weeks through Namibia and the northern part of South Africa. Our expedition and camping skills in the African bush were well-honed by then and I felt confident enough to go away with the boys by myself – most of our earlier trips were in the company of others. We used the experience we had gained, often after some tough lessons, to have a successful and memorable trip, and carry through our plans on our own initiative.

The wildlife we saw in Etosha topped every other National Park we had visited, and the boys had the statistics to back it up – they kept lists and drew graphs to illustrate what they had seen (an interesting way to learn maths). But Namibia was more than just a tick list for game. The landscape was equally awesome – from the Atlantic coastline, through the 'moonscape' of the Namib Desert and to Fish River Canyon there was always something jaw-dropping to see.

We loved the morning when we got up early to see the sunrise over the highest dunes in the world; unfortunately the sun hid behind large clouds, so instead we climbed Dune 45 – James reached the top but for every two steps I was going up I slid back one and eventually my tired calf muscles screamed at me to give up.

I took away with me from Africa the knowledge that I was able not just to survive life on a daily basis with my two boys there, which was no mean feat, given the dangers that lurked around every corner – malaria, robberies particularly from expat houses, vehicle collisions with cattle or drunken drivers, wild animals, heatstroke, disease and I could go on – but, it all added a richness and a quality to our beings which we could not have gained in any other way or anywhere else. Memories may fade but they never leave us entirely.

More recently James has lived in Dubai, and when I visit him there he drives me out into the desert or over the high passes of the Hajar Mountains in Oman. We go in his four-wheel drive *Mitsubishi* and I can't help thinking how the tables have turned. When he suggests going to a remote place at dusk to light a fire and cook our dinner over it (before returning to our hotel!) I remember the African savannah with the same million stars above us, guiding each of us on our individual path through life.

With James on one of our adventurous forays into the Hajar Mountains. Oman

🚲 🚲 🚲 🚲 🚲 🚲 🚲 🚲

The lonely leopard and the rather scruffy-looking tiger in Edinburgh Zoo did not quite match up to my aspirations for these beautiful animals in the wild, although I'm sure their needs were catered for as well as possible. I sense that one day I shall return to the savannah of Africa and recall the sounds, sights and smells I have never quite forgotten.

My time in Edinburgh was almost over, just one more evening of reminiscing with Jenny, then the next morning I would be on the penultimate day of my trip and heading to St Andrews.

Chapter Twenty-six

'ON THE ROAD TO DUNDEE'[1]

It was dry and sunny as I cycled out of Edinburgh alongside the A90 through Dalmeny and on to the Forth Road Bridge. Many years ago I had walked over this bridge but it was my first time crossing it by bike – it's always a thrill to cross an estuary by bridge and the view from here is not only an iconic one but very familiar to me.

The Forth Rail Bridge opened in 1890 and still has the second longest single cantilever bridge span in the world (Quebec Bridge has the longest). It took seven years to build (by the same builders as the Wear Bridge I had crossed earlier on my trip) and cost the lives of 63 men – perhaps the current health and safety regulations that we often moan about for being applied too rigorously are not such a bad idea after all? The steel design was deliberately chosen to look strong, due to the public anxiety following the collapse of the first Tay Rail Bridge just four years earlier.

The sun had disappeared for the day as I entered the Kingdom of Fife, known by this grand title because it still retains boundaries from when it was a Pictish realm. I was looking forward to cycling along part of the Fife Coastal cycle route; the names of the places were all well-known to me – Inverkeithing, Dalgety Bay, Aberdour, Burntisland, Kinghorn and lastly Kirkcaldy where I would turn inland to cross to St Andrews.

At times the track was adjacent to the sea and there were fine views along the coast and back over to the city of Edinburgh. But this coastal path was not as easy as I was expecting it to be – there were many 'ups and downs' over quite high headlands, and just as many 'in and outs' to get past certain no-go areas on the coast (mainly industrial areas).

---

[1] From 'THE ROAD AND THE MILES TO DUNDEE'

Cycle path adjacent to the south Fife coast

Aberdour's *Silver Sands* provided me with a pleasant stop and welcome cup of coffee in the cafe; I remembered coming here as a teenager on the train with a boyfriend from Dunfermline to meet up with his friends.

After several more tiring uphill sections I cycled down into Kirkcaldy just as the first shower of the day enveloped me. I needed to refuel before continuing but didn't want to stop for long so bought a hot bridie (a meat and onion-filled pastry case whose origins are in Forfar) from a chip shop and found a covered shelter along the promenade. It was awfully cold and bleak and I soon got back on my bike.

If things had turned out differently I might have spent some of my growing-up years in Kirkcaldy . . .

When I was still in primary school my Dad, an accountant, took a job in Dysart near Kirkcaldy and travelled by train, a commute of over an hour door to door. He obviously settled into the job okay because our house was put up for sale and Mum and Dad found a house to buy in Kirkcaldy. I don't remember thinking too much about it except that it was quite exciting to consider a move to another town, although when I heard this little rhyme being recited around the house over this period I was less sure it would be a good move:

> *For I ken mysel' by the queer-like smell*
> *That the next stop's Kirkcaddy[1]!*
> *(*Two famous lines from *The Boy in Train* by MC Smith)

---

[1] *ken* = know, *Kirkcaddy* = Kirkcaldy

Kirkcaldy was the world's main centre for the production of linoleum, a floor covering backed with jute; this industry coincided with the production of jute in Dundee's mills. One of the other key ingredients of lino is linseed oil and this is what gave off the 'queer-like smell'.

However, our move was quickly forgotten when Dad found out that his Kirkcaldy boss expected him 'to cook the books'; he found a new job in Forfar and commuted there instead – this journey he did by car. Thus, Dundee continued to be my home.

My Dad started off life in a Dundee tenement with one brother and three sisters in just a couple of rooms with a shared toilet on the stairs. He left school at 14 to work as a junior clerk in an office, and in his twenties decided to go to 'night school' to study for his accountancy exams, which after a number of years of toil he successfully passed.

On the other hand my Mum was born to a middle-class family and lived in a pleasant house in Paddington in London; she and her older sister enjoyed a privileged upbringing with a live-in housekeeper and a private education. Mum became a shorthand typist and one of her holidays was with the Ramblers' Club to the Lake District where she met my Dad.

The war intervened and my Mum joined the WRENS ('Women's Royal Naval Service'), thought of by some at the time as the glamorous service for women. She was posted to Dundee and was billeted to HMS Unicorn; the coincidence is not what it seems – Mum presumably knew there was a fair chance she would be posted to Dundee if she joined the Wrens, and she wanted to be closer to my Dad.

HMS Unicorn is a fascinating wooden ship and is preserved as a historic ship as part of Dundee's *City of Discovery* visitor attractions. The Unicorn was one of the ships always pointed out to us by Dad on our drives around the dockyards. 'That's the ship which your mother trained on when she was a Wren,' he would always say.

She was built as a 150 foot long sailing frigate with three masts in Chatham dockyard during the transitional period between traditional wooden ships and the advent of iron ships. But before she was launched in 1824, an unexpected decision was taken to roof over her hull and she became one of the most successful warships of the age – fast and powerful. Due to the decks being protected she has survived intact and

My parents' wedding in London in 1943

is now one of the six oldest ships in the world and considered to be the best preserved from the great age of sail.

My parents were married during the war and Mum came to live in Dundee and went on to have seven children. Dad never lived anywhere other than in Dundee – he knew every nook and cranny of it and was always interested in any new buildings or housing estates under construction. He was a true Dundonian who loved his city and he made the most of living there. He died at the age of 78 from a sudden heart attack brought on in all probability by the rheumatoid arthritis he had suffered from in his latter years.

It was very sad to see the strong and active man that my Dad had been all his life and of course, also an ardent country lover, succumb to the pain and disability of his disease. He fought its progression and when his consultant asked him if he would opt to be a guinea pig for any new treatment for his arthritis my Dad always jumped at the chance – I remember one treatment involved injections of gold.

After his death Mum moved to Dunbar to be closer to one of my sisters and lived out the rest of her life in an apartment overlooking the Firth of Forth. When I visited she would always tell me how much enjoyment she got from looking out of the window at passing ships, birds on the rocks below, or looking over to the Isle of May just visible at the mouth of the estuary – a pair of binoculars lay on her windowsill. Although born a Londoner, she fell in love with Scotland which was her home for most of her life – she died just short of her 85th birthday.

🚲 🚲 🚲 🚲 🚲 🚲 🚲 🚲

Today's ride to St Andrews was 49 miles so there was no time to dawdle and I cycled on through various villages and towns in Fife. The afternoon was punctuated by sudden and heavy showers: I had to make do with sheltering under a tree on the outskirts of Glenrothes; in a doorway in Markinch; then the gaps between showers lessened so much that I had no choice but to keep cycling through them.

As I entered the village of Ceres I heard the faint sound of bagpipes, and as I approached it got louder and I saw crowds of people gathered on the street up ahead so I pulled over to have a look. Their annual Highland Games was in full swing in the field next to me. Even under a dark and ominous-looking sky it was a colourful event: I could see there was caber-tossing, wrestling, Scottish Country dancing, cycle racing and children's running races all taking place simultaneously. The gentleman next to me, noticing my bike, turned to me and inquired, 'Are you taking part in the ladies' cycling race?'

I laughed and replied, 'You obviously haven't seen me cycling.' I didn't wait to see the end of the men's race because the heavens opened at that minute and all the spectators not holding umbrellas ran for cover – in my case it was to another doorway with no room for my bicycle – so it got a soaking. I consoled myself with the thought that it was only about 10 miles to the campsite where I was staying that night – perhaps in just over an hour I'd be there?

However, not only did the showers continue to have me dashing for the nearest tree or bus shelter but I missed my turning for the campsite. Once I realised my mistake, I was already in the outskirts of St Andrews and rather than go back I decided to continue into the town because then I could find a shop where I could buy food for dinner and breakfast the next morning, and not have to leave the campsite later on to go shopping.

The next couple of hours before I eventually found the campsite went from bad to worse and I found myself once more really struggling and digging deep in myself to keep going. It was caused by a combination of rain turning to hail, a cold wind, a hilly route and an inability to find the correct way to the campsite which resulted in a state of exhaustion on my part.

When, at last, I saw the sign for Cairnswell campsite up the hill ahead I was ready to drop. I struggled up to the reception, booked in, had the bunkhouse pointed out to me, made my way across a couple of fields of caravans, found the little room assigned to me, went inside and collapsed on the bottom bunk and didn't move a muscle for over half an hour.

Once I had gained my second wind I showered, changed and cooked myself a stir-fry in the communal kitchen. Both the caravan site and the bunkhouse were full as the Scottish school holidays had begun and, despite the awful weather, families had come to East Fife to enjoy themselves. I spent the remainder of the evening quietly in my room reading, writing my blog and checking my route for the following day – my final run into Dundee, a short one of 25 miles.

The bunkhouse was quiet when I got up the following morning and had breakfast in the kitchen – holidaymakers often like a Sunday lie-in. I went back to my room and inserted my keycard into the lock – nothing! In, out, try again – no response to the key card each time I inserted it. I heard someone in the kitchen so went back to see if they could be of any assistance to me. 'Good morning. I'm locked out of my room – my keycard isn't working. Do you think you could try it for me – maybe I'm doing something wrong?'

The gentleman camper tried it, 'No, I can't get it to work either. I tell you what I'll do – I'll phone the reception for you and ask them to send someone over.'

I thanked him kindly and went outside to look into my room from there – I had left a small window open which might just be big enough for me to climb in but it was quite a bit off the ground. I was grateful my keycard had opened the door for me earlier when I'd gone to the bathroom in my pyjamas on first waking – at least I was dressed now!

After waiting for a while a groundsman arrived, but his universal keycard didn't work either and he had no other solution. 'Perhaps I can climb in the window if we take a chair outside?' I suggested.

So he held the chair firmly while I got on to it and managed to fully open the window, climb over and drop down inside. I was glad he was standing outside to give some authority to my climbing through a window into a room! 'Try the door,' he shouted through to me.

Fortunately I was able to open it from the inside. I wedged a shoe under it to stop it from closing, 'That's okay now, I replied. Thanks for your help.'

I got my belongings packed and on to the bike with no further mishap and left the site. I enjoyed the long freewheel ride into St Andrews and down to the East Sands, the same stretch that had taxed me so considerably the previous evening. The weather looked promising with a hint of sunshine and patches of blue sky. I cycled past the ruined cathedral and the castle on a rocky promontory above the appropriately named Castle Sands.

I remember coming over to St Andrews by train with Edna, a friend in the Ranger Guides, and setting up a small borrowed tent in the campsite nearby. In the evening we attended an outdoor performance of *Macbeth* inside the castle walls. It was as memorable and dramatic a production of one of Shakespeare's plays as I have ever seen –soldiers standing on the battlements silhouetted against the night sky fought each other with swords and axes. The scenes with the three weird witches cackling about Macbeth and later the ghost of Banquo appearing between the crumbling walls made for a creepy and sinister evening and I was glad of Edna's company on our walk back to the tent in the dark.

I carried on past the *Old Course*, the famous, and considered to be one of the finest, golf courses in the world with the attractive and prestigious *Royal and Ancient Clubhouse* at one end. There was a stream of cars and coaches queuing to park beside the Links, home to several other courses too; golf has been played in St Andrews since the 15th century and attracts golfers from all over the world.

The view looking out across the extensive West Sands was quite magnificent. This was where I saw the only signpost on my whole journey relating directly to the North Sea Cycle Route, even though I had been following it more or less since Cambridgeshire. It showed a map of the route going through all the countries bordering the North Sea with the caption '6000 kilometres to explore'. That meant there was still a further 4500 km waiting for me at a future date.

I followed around the Eden estuary and over the fine-looking 16th century stone six-arch bridge at Guardbridge and into Leuchars. The RAF airfield was on one side of me and the railway station on the other. I remember trips to the Leuchars Air Show with my Dad by train to watch the air displays, always very noisy but highly exciting.

Other trips I made with my family by train were the annual Sunday School picnics to St Andrews by steam train. The day prior to the picnic would see my brothers and I go round to the park and practise running three-legged races by tying a scarf around two of our legs and attempting to run with our arms around each other's backs.

When it came to the actual race I'm not sure that our practice runs made any difference to the outcome. The sack races were the funniest though; I used to alternate between jumping and when that seemed too slow I would push my feet into the corners of the sack and try to run – usually ending up in a crumpled heap on the ground. Another one was the egg and spoon race, fortunately the eggs were hard-boiled or there would have been a very sticky mess everywhere. Once the races were all run, we lined up to receive our own white paper bag containing a couple of sandwiches, a packet of crisps with the salt in a screwed-up piece of blue paper, a Penguin or Golf biscuit and an apple. Then we walked back to the station to catch the train back to the Tay Bridge Station in Dundee – tired but happy little faces of children peering out of the windows.

From Guardbridge I could have taken a direct route to Newport and the Tay Bridge but I was keen to find out more about Tentsmuir Forest which lies in the far north-eastern corner of Fife. As a child I'd often looked across the mouth of the Tay Estuary and seen this forest on the other side but I'd never been to it. I think as a result of this I felt it was a strange and eerie place. Because it is a conifer plantation it takes on a dark and uniform shape and I imagined odd goings-on taking place there. My Dad took us everywhere else – why did he not take us to Tentsmuir Forest or ever talk about it? As far as I was concerned there had to be some sinister reason behind it.

It had taken me until my 60th year to enter Tentsmuir Forest but I was determined to find out what mysteries lay within. I found a marked cycle trail that went through housing for personnel serving at RAF Leuchars and after crossing a couple of fields I entered the forest. There was a sign informing me this was a National Nature Reserve and had been since 1952, when it was the second reserve to be declared in Britain. In 1954 there were already 1500 hectares of Scots and Corsican pines planted. Surely if it was an NNR then Dad could have brought us here? He loved exploring anywhere in the countryside whether it was hills, forest, or coast – it was all worthwhile to him.

I followed the track through the trees over to the eastern edge next to the sea and expected to see the sea but because of the extensive dune system surrounding the reserve the view was blocked by trees and sand. I turned north and stopped to read another sign about the pre-history of this area.

Evidence of hunter gatherers living here in the period after the last Ice Age, and artefacts including pottery, beads, whetstones (stones for sharpening), and needles have been found here from the Bronze Age. Then it was the turn of the Picts, followed by the Vikings who settled as farmers in this area.

A bit further on next to an old stone building I read about the importance of salmon fishing at the mouth of the estuary. Nets laid along the coastline trapped the salmon and they were stored in this icehouse, built in 1888. I was surprised to learn that this area, which I always thought of as a remote, desolate and unpopulated area, had so much history attached to it.

Its final purpose before becoming a NNR was as a military training ground, with the offshore waters being used as a target bombing range. During the Second World War Polish soldiers constructed a line of concrete anti-tank blocks and pillboxes along the shore and when the land was acquired as a reserve some of it was still within the danger zone.

That filled in some more sketchy memories for me because some of these wartime defences were visible across the Tay, and I would have looked at my Dad's map and seen *Danger Zone* typed in red across that area. This would all have added to my picture of a perilous place and perhaps I heard of some stories of unexploded shells being found.

As I approached the corner I could see from my map that the dunes extended quite a distance out, obviously an area of deposition, with sediment being brought either from the River Tay (Scotland's longest river) or from currents along the coast. Rounding the corner I was glad to notice more people out walking, cycling or jogging; their presence removed any remaining sense of unease I was feeling.

The real reason my Dad had never brought us here was much more likely to be that he didn't ever bring us over to Fife by car because, as I explained earlier, it cost too much on the 'Fifie'. I had built up a fantasy to go with the dark and mysterious forest I could see across the water. But now I could enjoy it for what it was. In fact, my next move was going to be to find a way through the trees on to the dunes beyond to get my first view of the city of Dundee.

I pushed my bike up a small dune and there in front of me was the Tay estuary and Dundee sitting proudly on its far side only a few miles away. I sat down on the sand – it was quite an emotional moment for me, to know that I would complete the journey I had set out on a month ago.

The view of Dundee on the north side of the Tay as I approached the end of my ride

I gazed out over the water, a picture of absolute tranquillity and loveliness, bathed in some of the best sunshine I had seen on the whole trip. There were eider duck on the flat-calm blue water, a seal bobbed its head up and a heron was standing quietly fishing in the shallows. It took my breath away and a few tears welled up in my eyes. My ride would soon be over and I wasn't sure when I looked out over this scene that I wanted it to be. Life on the road in so many ways is undemanding – few decisions or responsibilities need to be taken – there is freedom.

I was about to re-enter 'normal' life with all its demands and schedules. Perhaps during the few days I was staying in Dundee with my friend Mary I could ease myself slowly back into it – a sort of 'halfway house'? Mary is an easy-going gentle person and would make no demands upon my time or the lack of energy which would probably descend on me.

I thought about how different the cycling would have been over these last four weeks in dry, sunny and warm conditions such as I was experiencing now. Then I quickly realised that it would have made it a different journey, not the one I had just done.

Accepting the unusually-bad weather conditions had been the hardest part of the journey for me, not a lack of physical fitness which I thought might let me down. I had come through rain, storms, mud and floods – at times they had tested me to my limit, even exhausted me, but just like other times in my life I weathered the storms, reaffirmed my determination and kept on going. It was satisfying to know I had persevered and was completing something. That has not always been the case for me; there is a long list of things I have started and then ditched when they didn't suit me any longer.

The trip had given me time to reflect on the rich tapestry of my life that had gone before and even shifted my perception of some of it. Cycling to Dundee was perhaps my outer journey, but there had also been an equally important inner journey taking place simultaneously.

The support I received from so many people was crucial to my success and my lasting memories of the tour are of the thoughtfulness and generosity I received in abundance – from family, friends and total strangers, no matter whom. It had been a great excuse to connect personally with family and friends, old and new.

The time I spend close to nature is what restores my health, vigour and zest for life and allows me to give the best of myself to those around me. It gives me the energy to care, give my attention to and offer my support to others. There will always be time in my life to slow down and 'to stand meditatively and gaze over the fence.'

From Tentsmuir Forest it was a short ride along the coast to Tayport and then on to the Tay Road Bridge. The cycle and pedestrian lane runs between the two carriageways, and because the southern end of the bridge is higher I freewheeled the one and half miles all the way over to Dundee.

Straight in front of me rising above the skyline was the conical shape of *The Law* (572 feet), a volcanic plug, with its distinctive war memorial on top. It is Dundee's most idiosyncratic feature and is often the first landmark one sees when approaching the city. Many Dundonians won't know that there is a ten-foot diameter tunnel through its lower flanks which was built to take the railway to Newtyle – the trains were originally drawn by horses in 1833 – the line was closed just thirty years later.

Fortunately I didn't have to summit the Law, but to go anywhere north from the riverside involves a climb. First though, I pedalled through what remains of the dockyards and saw HMS Unicorn resting nobly by a quayside, but my final mile to Mary's house was a short and steep ascent of over 250 feet – I'll be honest and admit that I pushed the bike up that last hill, but with a complete sense of satisfaction.

Mary is a good friend from university days, also a geographer; she went on to have a long career with DC Thomson, the Dundee publisher. She was waiting for me and came out to greet me enthusiastically as I arrived, 'Hello, you've made it. Congratulations!'

We went inside and chatted pleasantly over a light lunch as I regaled her with some of my tales of the past few weeks. However, we were both aware that I hadn't yet reached the final objective of my trip and so made ourselves ready to leave the house – Mary was going to accompany me on my final mission.

Arriving at Mary's house after cycling 1560 km from my home in Dorset

227

Chapter Twenty-seven

THERE'S ONE BORN EVERY MINUTE

We got into Mary's car, drove for just under a mile and parked outside a white house, number 307. This number tripped of my tongue as familiar as any word in my vocabulary: 'Three, oh, seven'.

The owner was Richard and he lived here with his four and a half year old son and I was here to meet him at his invitation. This had come in response to a letter I had written six weeks ago:

> *Dear 307 Occupant,*
>
> > *This will come as quite a surprise to you I expect. I was born at your house, number 307...*
> >
> > *...I would love to drop by and say hello at the end of my ride...*
> >
> > *... you can contact me on...*
> >
> > *...I hope that we meet up in early July.*
>
> *Kind regards, etc.*

As Mary and I walked up to the doorstep it evoked a distant memory. I recollected it to her, 'The first thing I can ever remember is of being in my pram as my Mum pushed it up and over this step and into the porch

My siblings and I on the front door step of '307'

Donald, Jean, Di
Alan, Enid, Bryan
(Colin hadn't yet made his entrance)

– I could have only been about two or three years old.'

Richard answered the doorbell promptly, 'You must be Enid. Welcome back to your house.' I introduced Mary and as another man also entered the porch Richard introduced us, 'Meet my friend. Unfortunately you won't meet Magnus – he's at a sleepover with a friend.'

Richard's friend offered to make us tea and Richard led Mary and me into what *he* called the sitting room, 'Come on in. Does it feel quite strange being in this house again?'

Wow, it was more than strange. It was very obviously the same house where I grew up but I had changed and this belonged to a much earlier era in my life. One other couple had lived there after my mother moved out and before Richard moved in. Apart from a couple of internal walls knocked down to make bigger rooms the layout was the same; it was just the decoration and personal possessions that gave it a different look, and the time that had passed since I'd last been or more pertinently, lived, between those four walls.

I lowered myself into an armchair in the sitting room and a piano standing in the recess caught my eye. I said to Richard, 'We had a piano in exactly the same place. It just feels right for a piano, doesn't it?'

My mind went back to those cold piano-practice sessions in the front room – *our* name for this room. Next to our piano was a bookcase and as a young lass I would sit down in front of it and pull out some of the old books. There was a thick blue one with a torn linen spine, illustrated with black and white photographs – one photograph in particular fascinated and horrified me so much that I couldn't help being drawn back to it over and over again, and when the time came late on in her life for Mum to tell us to help ourselves to any books we wanted I kept that one.

Opposite page 148 is a photograph of a hand with dreadful blister swellings almost as big as the fingers themselves, with the caption 'DR ATKINSON'S FROST-BITTEN HAND.' I was full of wonder at what dreadful occurrence a person must have experienced to incur such an injury.

The book was Herbert Ponting's *The Great White South*, his account of Captain Scott's fated Antarctic journey. I also used to reread the last chapter where Ponting had copied in full Scott's poignant MESSAGE TO PUBLIC and his final diary entry, 'For God's sake look after our people.' A photograph of THE LAST REST showing the graves of Scott, Wilson and Bowers accompanied the entries. Totally engrossed in the content of that book, my mind would travel thousands of miles away to a distant land and to a past era trying to imagine what it was like.

The thrill of exploration, others or my own, has stayed with me ever since turning the pages of Ponting's book. I've lost count of the number of times when I've gazed in awe at something or someone on my travels. I am acutely aware of the extent to which my mind has been broadened by my travel experiences.

After finishing our tea and hearing about the importance of music in Richard's life he took us on a tour of the rest of the house.

The living room, also off the hall, was the hub of our house when I was growing up, especially in the winter as it was the only room with a fire, fuelled by coal and subsequently gas when we became a 'smokeless district' during my childhood. Stepping more than a few feet away from the fire meant entering the chill zone, but in any case the nine-inch television meant that we all had to huddle close around it to make out the indistinct and flickering images on the screen. One morning close to Christmas I remember coming into the room for breakfast and seeing my first-ever decorated tree balanced on top of a cupboard in the corner.

Years later in my own house, I used to keep my cat, Teuchy, out of the room while I decorated my Christmas tree. When I'd got it looking just right, I switched on the lights and would go and fetch her, carry her over to the tree and watch as she gazed wide-eyed at the lights and glitz. When I put her down she would play with the baubles, poking them with her paw and usually succeeding in pulling them off, on occasion knocking over the whole tree.

When my own two boys were small we would sit around our Christmas tree and sing carols together. Even while living in Botswana and house-sitting for a couple in Maun, we draped a string of tinsel over a tall pot plant and celebrated Christmas with roast turkey and all the trimmings. What a mistake when the temperature outside was hitting forty degrees! During the evening once it had cooled off a little we walked over to what we called 'The Swamp' – a pool or two of stagnant water, all that remained in the dried-up river bed – to see if the old hippo was still there – he was. He had been left behind by the rest of his pod when they went off in search of flowing water.

I've always celebrated Christmas around the world, the same festival but different, wherever I've happened to be.

I turned to Richard as my eyes took in the changes around the living room, 'It looks smaller than I remember it. You've got it looking very homely.'

We went through to the kitchen. I could almost see my Dad standing at the kitchen sink in his 'pinny'[1] washing the dishes as he did every evening after we'd eaten. My brothers were expected to take their turn, just as I was, in helping to clear the table or dry the dishes. Maybe because of this I've always expected household chores to be split evenly between the genders.

Looking up I noticed the pine-clad ceiling and said to Richard, 'It was my brother, Bryan's idea to cover the ceiling with pine. He had recently started work as a Quantity Surveyor and wanted to put into practice what he was seeing out and about in the building trade. Bryan and my Dad did that ceiling together.'

We walked out through the back door and into the garden, or maybe I should say jungle. Of all the features in the house this was the least recognisable. The lawn had disappeared under a mass of shrubs amongst which I could just see the top of a basketball net sticking out. 'Magnus loves it out here,' Richard commented, 'as do I too.' I was beginning to realise how much Richard and his son enjoyed this house and that pleased me.

I struggled to picture the fairly large open area of grass we used to play on as kids. Dundee wasn't known for long hot summers but we did get the odd 'heatwave' when out would come the paddling pool and from the shed some large cushions.

There were three of them and they had originally been seats on a bus which my Dad brought home one night – I have no idea how or from

---

[1] Apron – in his case a man's full-length version

where he acquired them. All I know is that the long one when turned over made a brilliant canoe, and by sitting astride one of the struts which held the sides together and using a spade or a branch we would 'paddle' to 'desert islands', i.e. the two-person cushions, upholstered in dark red leather, which were positioned on another area of the lawn. Bryan and Colin, my two brothers closest in age to me, and I could spend long days out in the garden in our make-believe world and it was only a heavy shower or bedtime that brought us in.

There was another game which involved all seven children and didn't require warm sunshine. I think it was my eldest sister's game and I was still quite young when we played this. It was called 'Three Things'; we each collected any three items, for example it might be a bat, a tin and a hat. We then spaced ourselves evenly around the garden and placed two of our items on the ground in front of us, the other one we held on to. At the signal from Jean we each ran to the next pair of items, dropped the one we were carrying and picked up a new one. We ran from bundle to bundle exchanging items until we ended up back with the three items that we had started with – or that was the idea – I seem to remember it often went awry and there would be a heated inquisition about who had picked up the 'wrong' item.

Sometimes as adults now, with our own children/grandchildren, we arrange to meet up for summer picnics in a country park midway between us and it wouldn't surprise me if 'Three Things' was suggested by one of my brothers or sisters in between Rounders or throwing a Frisbee, as a game to play. The younger family members would look at us in puzzlement, 'Three things – is that another of your ancient family games that's boring and pointless?'

I looked up at the back of the house, three storeys high, and mentioned to Richard: 'The attic extension was added by my parents, but unfortunately it was a bit late as my older brothers and sisters had already flown the nest by the time it was built.'

'It's a great space though for us,' Richard answered, 'it was one of the reasons we bought the house. Come back inside and we'll go upstairs.'

As we turned to go up the first flight of stairs an attractive stained glass window commanded my attention. I remarked to Richard, 'Much better than the stag's head that used to be above the window. It frightened the living daylights out of me as a young child and I couldn't go upstairs in the dark on my own.'

I was reliably informed by my older siblings that this was a special stag, 'a royal stag – one with at least twelve branches to its antlers.' So in broad daylight I would try to count the points but always found it hard to find as many as my big brother. Whatever the number, it was an early introduction to Scottish wildlife for me.

When out and out about in the countryside with my parents in the car, my Dad took pride in spotting eagles, stags and other species and pointing them out to us. He once arrived home with a pheasant: 'Road kill, freshly knocked down,' he told us. I watched transfixed with a mixture of wonder and repulsion as he laid it on a newspaper on the living room table and proceeded to pluck it. We had it roasted for Sunday lunch between us all – a morsel each, with each small mouthful the picture of the dead bird on the table as it was being plucked came back to me.

We mounted the stairs and past the bathroom which had doubled in size due to its incorporation with the 'box room' next door. An upper class household would have termed it the linen room I expect – a walk-in storage cupboard for the bedding, and in our case other paraphernalia. There was just space in amongst all the junk on the floor to squeeze in three little children, find a box to sit on and close the door.

Inside the box room with my two youngest brothers we held sessions of our 'Ladybird Club'. It was started in the month of May when I was ten years old; the meetings were held on Tuesdays and Thursdays in the early evening and entry was by password only – the first one was 'whitewash' (our house colour). Its objectives were based around the same ones as the Brownies – we worked towards badges (third, second and first class) and played games; the main difference being that in our club we had to learn about and be able to draw ladybirds. The secrets of the club, including tiny hand sewn notebooks and a coloured stand-up ladybird emblem were stored in a yellow cigarette tin labelled STATE EXPRESS CIGARETTES 555 which I still have.

This little club of ours only lasted for one summer but it helped to bond the three youngest in the family and our secret society gave us a certain status, at least among ourselves. I went on to join many other clubs in my time but that one was special because it was inaugurated by us.

The contents of my 'Ladybird Club' tin

Richard led the way up more stairs to the top floor where the two extra bedrooms had been added. 'This is Magnus's room,' he informed us as we went into the bigger of the two, and I could see what a great space it made for his son and all his toys. As a large family we could have had a ball in there if this room had been built fifteen years before it was. But I was more than happy to see the space being put to good use now.

Within a few years of Will and I moving to our house in Dorset we had major alterations made to our downstairs, merging the kitchen with two further small rooms to form a large family space. At the same time we had an extension added to give us a spacious utility room and storage area for coats, shoes and all our outdoor gear. The experience of my parents' house had encouraged me to enlarge our house while the children were still young and so all benefit from it. A grand lesson to have learnt as it's been a godsend.

I went over to Magnus's window and took in the view – I could see as far as the Sidlaws, a range of hills to the north of Dundee. In the winter we would often see snow on these hills even when there was none lying in our garden.

We followed Richard back down the stairs and into what used to be two bedrooms but was now one large lounge.

THERE'S ONE BORN EVERY MINUTE

'Gosh,' I gulped in amazement, 'I had heard from my brother that the previous owners had merged the bedrooms, but I couldn't have imagined what it would look like.' Richard was keen to hear my descriptions of the original bedrooms.

'This one we're standing in was the boys' bedroom. I remember a double bed shared by two of them and two single beds for the other two. Later on the double bed was replaced by two 'hospital-type' beds (again something that my Dad procured from some source) which were higher and could be slid over the two divans during the day to give them a bit of space in the middle of the room.'

I could recall sitting on Donald's bed which was situated behind the door and being shown his Meccano models or his printing set. It was here that on two separate occasions he handed over first his transistor radio to me saying, 'You can have this. I've got a new one now,' and at a later date his *Kodak* camera for the same reason. I looked up to and admired my oldest brother so it felt good to be the recipient of his gadgets and I took great care of them owning them for several years – the blue 'trannie' went with me to Edinburgh during my student years and the camera which took twelve small square photographs on one film wasn't replaced until I was in my twenties. It always felt like carrying a bit of Donald around with me. I smiled to myself at the fond memories.

I turned to look at the other end of the room and as I took it in I felt the emotion rising in me as I was reminded of the time I spent in this room – the girls' bedroom.

I saw myself sitting at my desk studying for my exams – during the winter I would position the desk underneath an electric fire attached on the wall, but in the summer I moved it over in front of the window so that I could see the hills in the distance. Having the room to myself was a luxury that was gained after my two older sisters had left home. Before that my bed was on the lower bunk with my eldest sister above, and Di had a single bed.

Jean, being the eldest, was the first to leave home. She took a modern job in technology in the 'New Town' of Glenrothes over in Fife and returned most Friday evenings for the weekend. I would lie in my bed

235

trying to stay awake until Jean and Di came to bed so that I could hear them whispering the week's events and gossip to each other. It was through one of these late night quiet utterings that I heard about Jean's intriguing 'finds' when she had 'come across' some items belonging to my mother associated with early methods of birth control and drawing her own conclusions, she commented to Di, 'Well, they obviously didn't work!'

I looked around me at what was once my old bedroom – there was a lump in my throat and for a few moments I did not say anything as various sentiments manifested themselves in me. It was a mixture of surprise, sadness, pride and love. I sighed softly and turned to the others, 'If it wasn't for the fireplaces it would be difficult to know these were the same rooms as I remember them.'

I stepped out of the doorway and out of the past which had just appeared so vividly to me – it had caught me by surprise. It was only a couple of steps into the remaining bedroom which had been my parents'. I knew this room would be the culmination of my journey.

It was as well that the bed was against the opposite wall from where my parents' bed had always been as just being in this room was a poignant enough memory for me. In my head I could clearly picture the furniture in the position it used to be and my parents' belongings placed around them. It was deeply moving. I stood quietly for a few moments, lost in my own thoughts.

Here was the place my mother gave birth to me; where I entered the world. Sixty years ago, at 4 o'clock one Sunday morning in August, my eldest sister woke up on hearing a baby's cries and recognising them as coming from a new born babe, said to herself, 'Another one,' and rolled over and went back to sleep.

I had followed my journey all the way back to its actual beginning.

🚲 🚲 🚲 🚲 🚲 🚲 🚲 🚲

Six days later I stood in Dryburgh Abbey with fifty three of my extended family as we celebrated the marriage of Stuart and Natalie. The soothing and mellow sounds of the harp vibrated around the century's old chapel. Stuart's father, Donald wasn't there, neither was his Uncle Alan, but we were there representing them and that is what families do. They pass the pride of many generations down the years and I was more than satisfied to take my place alongside my family to witness a new phase in this young couple's life. I was proud to have made it this far.

Stuart and Natalie's wedding at Dryburgh Abbey